GUERRI[LLA]
MARKETING
ON THE
FRONT LINES

35 WORLD-CLASS
STRATEGIES TO SEND
YOUR PROFITS SOARING

JAY CONRAD LEVINSON
FATHER OF GUERRILLA MARKETING WITH OVER 14 MILLION BOOKS SOLD

AND MITCH MEYERSON
FOUNDER OF GUERRILLA MARKETING COACHING

Foreword by MARK VICTOR HANSEN, Co-Author of *Chicken Soup For The Soul*

New York

GUERRILLA MARKETING
ON THE FRONT LINES

By Jay Conrad Levinson & Mitch Meyerson

ISBN: 978-1-60037-377-0   Paperback

Published by:

MORGAN · JAMES
THE ENTREPRENEURIAL PUBLISHER™

Morgan James Publishing, LLC
1225 Franklin Ave Ste 325
Garden City, NY 11530-1693
Toll Free 800-485-4943
www.MorganJamesPublishing.com

Cover and Interior Design by:
Heather Kirk
www.GraphicsByHeather.com
Heather@GraphicsByHeather.com

Habitat
for Humanity®
Peninsula
Building Partner

ACKNOWLEDGEMENTS

Special thanks to our editor, Dr. Patricia Ross, for your insightful additions and superb dedication to completing this book;

To Amy Belanger, for your excellent work on coordinating the authors, creating the book proposal, and helping to launch this project;

To David Hancock, for believing in this project from the beginning and for being such a pleasure to work with;

To all the authors in this edition for your Guerrilla energy and attitude—your contributions are brilliant;

And to all the Certified Guerrilla Marketing Coaches worldwide who are helping business owners everywhere increase their profits on tight budgets and in challenging times.

Thank you.

TABLE OF CONTENTS

PART TWO: Guerrilla Communication

PART THREE: Partnering for Profit

PART FOUR: Grassroots Guerrilla

PART FIVE: Innovative Guerrilla Tactics

PART SIX: The Guerrilla Organization

PART SEVEN: Guerrilla Marketing on the Internet

FOREWORD
The Power of Stories

Stories shape our lives; they feed us and keep us alive. *Chicken Soup for the Soul®* is the most successful publishing franchise in the world because of this power. And it doesn't matter what the subject matter of the story is. From business to Aunt Besse's recipe for bread, everyone wants to hear the real truth of people's lives. The reader wants to go through the process of engaging with the story so that they can feel the challenges and celebrate the successes alongside the author. This is why people learn best from stories. They connect your intellect to your imagination. In a well crafted story, you interact with its ideas so you are more willing to learn from it.

That is exactly what *Guerrilla Marketing on the Front Lines* can do for you. You get to interact with everyday small business people because, at heart, this book is a collection of stories about how the men and women in the trenches are out there making their way and being successful through hard effort and sheer intention. And because they are stories, you can intellectually engage with the strategies they present; in your imagination, you can play with the suggestions that are inherent in each to see what could work best for you in your own business.

Jay Conrad Levinson created the Guerrilla Marketing brand in the early 1980s to help small business succeed even on a limited marketing budget. Mitch Meyerson, in true Guerrilla form, developed the only Guerrilla Marketing Coaching program in 1999. There have been a number of Guerrilla Marketing books, done by some of the top Guerrilla marketers, but

Guerrilla Marketing on the Front Lines is the first book that truly documents real life case studies on how to use the principles of Guerrilla Marketing in your own small business. In these thirty-five chapters, you'll learn how to achieve your own marketing success by other small business owners who have made it to the top.

I work with entrepreneurs everyday; I help them to build a life of big dreams. It takes a good plan, hard work, and sound marketing strategies. This book will not only give you some of the essential strategies you need to build your business, it will inspire you to take a quantum leap forward.

Join my friends, Jay Conrad Levinson, Mitch Meyerson, Alex Mandossian, David Hancock, and thirty-two other world-class Guerrilla Marketing Coaches. Take delight in their stories and learn from what they do. And remember to celebrate your success as you take your business to the next level!

~Mark Victor Hansen, co-author of *Chicken Soup For The Soul*®

THE BIRTH OF GUERRILLA MARKETING

How Big Dreams and Tiny Budgets Spurred the Creation of an International Brand

Jay Conrad Levinson

In all my Guerrilla Marketing books and classes, I urge students to begin with a plan—a simple, short plan. I did not do that. I had no clue I was supposed to start that way. Instead, I knew I wanted to write a book and that writing a book was a lot more complicated and time-consuming than people imagined.

Still, it wasn't going to be complicated to just type a book on typewriter paper and get it into bookstores. So I spent the better part of a Saturday morning writing a book—an entire book. The name of the book was, "The Most Important $1.00 Book Ever Written." It was ten chapters of ten truths each. I didn't think it made sense to include my name in the book, so it was authored by "A communications professional who does what he loves, where he loves it, and does it fairly well." At the time, I was a freelance writer.

I took that book to the instant printer—this was in 1973—and he asked:

- What kind of paper stock will you be using?

- Who is going to typeset this book?

- Who is going to bind it?

- What kind of cover stock will you use?

- What color?

- How many do you want printed?

With help from the printer in answering those questions, I was able to have 240 copies of that book printed: thirty-two pages; red cover; 5-1/2 x 8-1/2; bound with staples; published by Positive Perception Press, Marin County, California and ready for bookstores. But was it really? Visiting the local bookstores in San Francisco, I saw thousands and thousands of books and titles and they all looked like a bigger deal than mine. How could I dare to imagine that people would buy my book over one of the thousands of other books?

So I looked in the Yellow Pages under "Display Racks" and after a few phone calls, I located one who had metal racks of exactly the size I needed for books, twenty-four of them in each rack. I bought ten racks for $1 each. Then, in an unconscious plunge into Guerrilla Marketing, I brought them to ten big and good bookstores, told each proprietor that I would give him the twenty-four books and the rack if he'd put the rack next to his cash register. At the end of a month, I'd come in and collect my $12 ($1 for each book purchased.) No risk to the bookseller. The book title did its own marketing, and we both knew it. One dollar for an impulse item was not outlandish in 1973.

At the end of the month, I went to the ten bookstores, collected $120 and realized that I was now in the publishing business, which I had not planned, and I was now the author of a book, which was my Saturday morning plan.

Of the entire process, I enjoyed writing the book but did not enjoy going to the instant printer, picking a paper stock, selecting a typeface, finding a typesetter (a service not offered by the printer), selecting a page design, finding a person to bind the book, taking the 240 books to the ten bookstores, or visiting the stores to collect my $12 each.

But the ten bookstores were the right bookstores for that book because one day I heard from a greeting card manufacturer who wanted to add my book to his line. He said he'd pay me twenty-five cents per sale. Hmmm....my baby for a quarter? But I said yes and received 300,000 quarters over three years.

For three years after this book hit the shelves, I worked three days a week from my home as a freelance writer. I was earning more than I did as a senior vice president and creative director of the largest advertising agency on Earth. I earn more than that now and work fewer than three days a week if you don't count e-mail.

I knew from the high school and college grades I had received that there was nothing special about me, so I wrote a book for freelancers like me, eliminating all the boring parts of publishing and focusing on the writing—the delicious, enticing, too-good-to-be true joy of writing.

Secrets of Successful Free-Lancing by Jay Conrad Levinson, published by Prosper Press, was a forty-three page, 5-1/2 x 8-1/2 booklet with an ivory cover. Using classified ads, it sold for $10 with an $11 guarantee, another unconscious foray into Guerrilla Marketing. My old friend, the printer, helped me with everything but the writing.

Soon I learned of a list of 10,000 freelancers. I purchased the list for $100, wrote a one-page letter with a no-reply envelope, did not take credit cards or cash, and sold 3,200 books at $10 each. That was fun! When I located a list of 1,000,000 free-lancers, I could earn $3,200,000 with each mailing. The only problem was that there were no more lists of freelancers.

So I wrote another book addressed to a broader audience than freelancers, *Earning Money without a Job*. This book was about individual enterprise, and it led to me teaching a weekly class at an extension division of The University of California at Berkeley. Feedback from the public was that I should make more suggestions as to how people could earn money without a job, so after a year of serious research (using a clipping service), I wrote *555 Ways to Earn Extra Money*, leading to even greater attendance at my class in Berkeley that was now called "Alternatives to the 9 to 5 Job."

One day, after about five years of delivering this class, one of my students asked if I could recommend a book for people with big dreams but small budgets. I said I'd be happy to and immediately made a trip to the library on the sprawling Berkeley campus. But I found no books on that specific topic. Oh, there were loads of books for companies that had $300,000 monthly to invest in marketing, but those companies were not my students. At least not yet they weren't. Many of my students did go on to form and lead Fortune 500 companies, but in those days of the early 1980s, they were penniless.

I visited the libraries at Stanford, in Sacramento, San Francisco, San Jose, and Oakland, but each time I came up empty. There were no books for companies or entrepreneurs with limited budgets. I had promised my students a book and here I had no book.

Plans are generally crafted at the beginning of an enterprise. Mine seems to have materialized consciously in the middle of the enterprise. As with all Guerrilla Marketing, it was created in response to a need. It seemed to me that in 1973, the universe needed some straightening out on the way things ought to be. If I didn't tell how to do it, who would? *The Most Important $1 Book Ever Written* took care of that.

I wrote *Secrets of Successful Free-Lancing* in 1974 in response to the problems of freelancers I had met who bemoaned the perils and uncertainties of freelancing. *Earning Money Without a Job* was in clear response to an ugly recession we were having in 1975. *555 Ways to Earn Extra Money* was in response to people who were asking for ways in which others picked up extra income.

Now here I was, owing a response to my students who were ready to graduate but were uninformed as to how to market their products and services. These were bright kids with bright hardware and software ideas for the new computer industry, as well as technical and economic ideas for the new solar energy industry. But they were powerless in marketing.

I had served some of the largest corporations on earth, using some of the most sophisticated marketing techniques and tactics along with advanced research and creative concepts. In addition, I had spent the previous five years helping small businesses and start-ups to compete in the marketing area. They couldn't use the big business, big money techniques I had used with the giants. They wanted the same results but without the same expenditures. I had been forced to come up with effective but low-cost tactics for these companies.

So I compiled a list: "527 Ways to Market Your Business Without Investing Much Money." This is what I was going to present to my class, but it was hardly a provocative and compelling title for a book. That same morning, I had read an article in the San Francisco Chronicle where Internet pioneer Blair Newman said, "What the economy needs now is Guerrilla Marketing."

Did a light turn on in my head? Did I accidentally discover the ideal title for a tome that promised conventional goals using unconventional means? You know these things happened, and so did I.

My students were overjoyed although neither they nor I knew that the book would then take on a life of its own. Houghton Mifflin, the publisher of books by Henry David Thoreau and Mark Twain, saw the vision and the promise in the book. Their ability to get it into bookstores worldwide, sell over fourteen million copies, and negotiate versions into forty-three languages, established a momentum for the book.

But nonetheless, it took on a life of its own for seven reasons:

1. There was an explosion of small businesses throughout the world. They needed advice about marketing, simply presented, and here it was. Guerrilla Marketing responded to that need.

2. I was teaching in the extension division of a major university, and this enabled word of the book to spread in the right places.

3. I was invited to speak before other groups throughout America at first and then throughout the world. Although not a trained speaker, I was quick to see that training myself would be responding to a need.

4. Other easy-to-target groups had a need to learn more about Guerrilla Marketing: trade-show exhibitors, attorneys, tele-marketers, home-based businesses, retailers, franchisees, entre-preneurs, and a host more businesses with absolutely no money to invest in marketing. (There are now fifty-six titles in the Guerrilla Marketing series, and more are coming, each one responding to a need.)

5. The Internet is the right marketing medium at the right time, and we at Guerrilla Marketing International embraced it in the early 1990's. We were able to enjoy an extremely high position in the search engines early on. Out of two billion marketing entries on Google, we're fourth.

6. We have a highly successful coaching program, developed and run by Mitch Meyerson. On a regular basis, Mitch trains, moti-vates, enlightens, and encourages Guerrilla Marketing disciples by training them to respond to needs, including their own.

7. Guerrilla Marketing works. It has been proven over these past twenty-three years to work for small and large businesses, new and established businesses, individuals, and companies on every conti-nent on earth. It doesn't matter if it's in rural or urban settings, during recessions and boom times, Guerrilla Marketing keeps on growing and filling more needs. By being organic and changing with the times, it is proving itself, as it has in the past, to be time-less now and in the future.

The birth of Guerrilla Marketing has been assisted by many midwives, and it has happened because of the burning passion of the original author, my enthusiasm at spreading the word throughout the world, my natural responsiveness to needs, and the simplicity of my books in a complex world.

By not doing battle with pretenders to the Guerrilla brand, and by encouraging them as much as possible, by leaning on evangelical Guerrilla Marketers who are certified coaches, the brand has grown due to inclusion rather than exclusion, accessibility rather than inaccessibility, and consistency through the decades and across international borders.

The book, which at first was a book only, is now lectures, seminars, an Academy, a series of CDs, a series of DVDs, workshops, workbooks, courses, a monthly newsletter, a weekly newsletter, and an association that serves as a support group for small business in response to their needs on a daily basis. See it all for yourself at:

www.GuerrillaMarketingAssociation.com

And see how Guerrilla Marketing works its magic by reading of the marketing wonders accomplished by the contributors to this book who are all Guerrilla Marketing masters.

About Jay Conrad Levinson

Jay Conrad Levinson is the father and founder of Guerrilla Marketing and has authored or co-authored forty-four books, published in forty-two languages worldwide. A former vice-president and creative director at J. Walter Thompson Advertising and Leo Burnett Advertising, he serves as Chairman of the Board of Guerrilla Marketing International, a successful marketing consulting organization serving large and small businesses around the world. Jay Conrad Levinson spent ten years as an instructor of marketing for the extension division of the University of California in Berkeley and has served on the Microsoft Small Business Council and the 3Com Small Business Advisory Board.

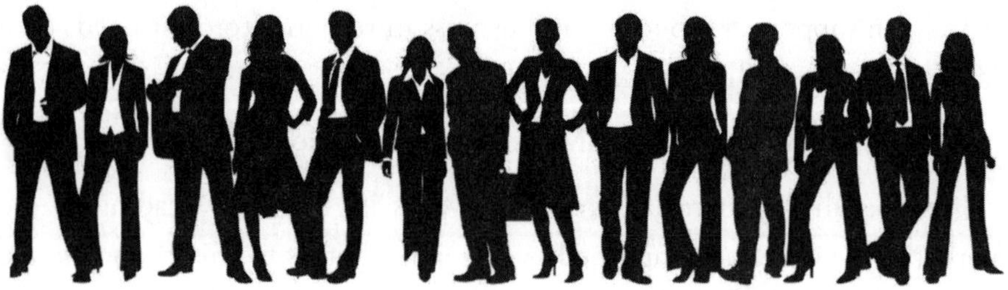

PART ONE
Guerrilla Essentials

Guerrilla Marketing is based on set of time-tested principles. As you just read, it was developed for small businesses in 1983 by Jay Conrad Levinson. It contains strategies that can help anyone grow their business and boost their profits on a shoe-string budget. These strategies are based on sound marketing principals that include taking consistent action, leading with intentionality, having a strategic plan, and more. Part One gives you an overview of the Guerrilla Marketing core competencies and gets you to assess whether or not you are indeed a Guerrilla Marketer. So get ready—you're going to learn from the best Guerrilla Marketing Coaches on the planet how you can launch your own Guerrilla Marketing attack today!

CHAPTER 1

GUERRILLA MARKETING COACHING
Taking It to the Streets

Mitch Meyerson

"The average person has four ideas a year which, if any one is acted on, would make them a millionaire."

~Brian Tracy

In 1984, Jay Conrad Levinson published his first book, *Guerrilla Marketing: Secrets for Making Big Profits from Your Small Business*. This book launched the Guerrilla Marketing brand as a trusted resource and set the stage for the best-selling marketing series in history.

Most people recognize that if their business lacks savvy marketing, it's usually dead in the water. Yet they often mistakenly confuse traditional advertising—which can be costly, complex and out of the reach for most companies—with Guerrilla Marketing.

While traditional marketing tools like expensive advertising are appropriate for mega-corporations, Guerrilla Marketing was created with small businesses and entrepreneurs in mind. Because it places highly effective, affordable marketing strategies and tactics within the reach of anyone who wants to start a business, it actually makes small size an asset instead of a liability.

And quite unlike what most people are used to, adherence to its tenets suggests that practitioners develop a novel attitude using unconventional strategies fueled by time, energy, imagination, and knowledge, instead of just marketing dollars. As a result, over the last twenty years, the Guerrilla Marketing movement has grown rapidly. *The reason?* It works. People all over the world have applied Guerrilla Marketing tenets to grow and sustain their businesses more profitably.

When I encountered the Guerrilla Marketing brand, I immediately recognized its power to make a difference in millions of people's lives. But as a business coach with a strong background in psychology, I knew that, although millions of people were buying the Guerrilla Marketing books, probably only a few were taking action on the brand's powerful ideas.

My experience in psychology told me that, despite their best intentions and strong beginnings, most people fail to act consistently and remain accountable to their own goals—that is, without the right kind of support. I believed Guerrilla Marketing needed something extra to reach its maximum effectiveness and profitability: a step-by-step action plan and coaching system.

Inspired by what such a system could do for the brand and for its adherents, I committed myself to creating the Guerrilla Marketing Coach Certification Program. My goal was to support business owners who wanted to launch their own marketing attack and needed additional guidance from coaches certified in Guerrilla Marketing principles and practice. To that end, I designed an intensive twelve-week program that trained coaches in Guerrilla Marketing concepts; ways to apply them in the "real world;" and advanced competencies and skills to keep their clients focused and accountable. I utilized Internet and teleconference technologies (very large conference calls) to expand the program's reach, creating an arsenal of Guerrilla Marketing Coaches around the world, many of whom you will meet in this book.

A Good Idea Is Not Enough—Guerrillas Take Action

"Most people have "one-way" brains—they acquire information and do nothing. Guerrillas have two way brains—they obtain relevant information and act on it."

~Jay Conrad Levinson

Following the sage advice in this quote, I decided to contact Jay Conrad Levinson and discuss my Guerrilla Marketing Coaching concept with him. One of the brand's fundamental precepts is "fusion marketing," a core principle which states that by partnering with others, a company can expand its product or service offerings to geometrically grow it profits. If Levinson and I each contributed our separate set of resources and worked together, we could dramatically expand the reach of the Guerrilla Marketing brand through my coaching program.

In a well-crafted fusion-marketing partnership, both parties win, as each one benefits from the expertise and influence of the other. So instead of developing a new brand and creating original content, I decided to take Levinson's rock-solid material and package it in an innovative way. Thus with a little time, energy, and imagination, I could increase sales of the Guerrilla Marketing books, extend the brand into the coaching industry, offer something new and useful to Levinson's customer base, increase his coverage into new markets, and earn more profits for both of our companies.

Approaching a Marketing Partner

We've all heard of *The Golden Rule* paraphrased as: "treat others as you'd like to be treated". However, in my opinion authors Tony Alessandra and Michael J. O'Conner go one better with their *Platinum Rule*: "treat others as *they'd* like to be treated." and what truly motivates them. I do my best to remember this rule in all my interactions with others; approaching Levinson was no exception. That's why, before I approached Jay, I was careful to.

- conduct research prior to our meeting. I took time to find out as much as I could about Guerrilla Marketing and the father of Guerrilla Marketing himself;

- clearly, concisely and specifically present my vision and expectations for our working relationship;

- propose a simple deal, one that didn't require either of us to look over the others' shoulders;

- highlight and lead with "what's in it for him," not what a great partner I'd make;

- give before I got. Since I was just starting out, I knew that this was a great way to build trust;

- avoid using a sales pitch. Instead, I viewed it as an opportunity to share a great idea.

When I met him, I explained to Jay that I wanted to spearhead a GM coaching certification program which would geometrically grow his brand. After discussing it for a while, he concurred that it made sense to combine his marketing model with my coaching expertise. Within a few short months, I developed a comprehensive coaching program based on a rigorous twelve-week intensive course teaching the essentials and applications of Guerrilla Marketing. It included downloadable classroom materials, group tele-training sessions, and a plan for marketing it. Since then, our program has certified more than 230 coaches, many of whom are also trainers and writers. (For the full story visit: **www.GmarketingCoach.com**.)

And like the marketing industry in general, our program has undergone necessary adjustments to accommodate rapidly improving technologies and ever-growing Internet use. As a matter of fact, my current e-commerce businesses were built by applying Guerrilla Marketing strategies and tactics. Notwithstanding these changes, we have remained faithful to fundamental, time-tested Guerrilla Marketing tenets. And we always will, because they are based on basic human nature, which hasn't changed in thousands of years and isn't likely to change anytime soon.

Are You A Guerrilla?

When working with a Certified Guerrilla Marketing Coach, business owners just like you are asked to rate themselves on sixteen Guerrilla Marketing core competencies, and then retake the test after they've completed the coaching process. They are usually astounded by the profoundly positive effect of this exercise as it defines and actively strengthens the weaker areas in the marketing.

Since this book is a way for you to learn and implement Guerrilla Marketing strategies into your business, it's your turn. Before you continue, spend a few minutes on the following self-assessment quiz and see how you measure up on the sixteen Guerrilla competencies. If you answer the questions honestly, and I sincerely hope you do, you will gain valuable insights into your current capabilities. Then, when you finish reading, create and implement a plan that makes the most of your strengths and "fixes" your weaknesses. When you have spent some time, preferably several weeks, working on your new Guerrilla inspired plan, retake the assessment quiz. See how far you've progress as a Guerrilla Marketer. You'll be glad you did.

HERE'S THE QUIZ

Directions: Read each statement and score each competency on a scale of "1" to "10" (1=poor, 10=excellent). Answer every question using your own perspective but also take into consideration how others, customers, clients, employees, etc., would answer them as well. Once completed, take a look at your answers and work on improving the skills that you rate six or less. This quiz is adapted from www.gmtoolkit.com. The sixteen competencies are shown below in parentheses.

_____ **1.** I see every contact with my customers and prospects as marketing. My words, attitudes and actions are all intentional and based on my marketing goals. *(Intentionality)*

_____ **2.** I look at all of my *marketing from the customer's point of view.* I consistently make time to ask my customers and prospects what is it they really want. *(Sensitivity)*

_____ **3.** I am *aggressive* in my marketing efforts. *(Aggressiveness)*

_____ **4.** My marketing attack includes an *assortment of strategies, tactics and communication vehicles.* I am familiar with Guerrilla Marketing's over 100 weapons and use many of them. *(Assortment)*

_____ **5.** If I surveyed my customers today they would agree *that I follow-up in a consistent and timely manner. (Follow-up)*

_____ **6.** I regularly *use a marketing calendar to track and measure* the effectiveness of my marketing efforts. *(Measurement)*

_____ 7. My friends, prospects, and customers would all say I am *enthusiastic and consistently positive in all my interactions.* *(Enthusiasm)*

_____ 8. I do not try to be all things to all people. Rather, I focus on having a *clearly defined marketing niche. (Niche)*

_____ 9. I have a clear and specific *strategic and tactical marketing plan* that guides my daily, weekly, monthly and yearly action steps. *(Marketing Plan)*

_____ 10. I use *online marketing as one of my major marketing weapons.* I utilize e-mail, a Web site, and the vast power of the Internet to reach new prospects and communicate with customers. *(Assortment)*

_____ 11. I build *strong one-to-one relationships* with my prospects and customers knowing that people buy from friends rather than strangers. *(Relationships)*

_____ 12. My business is *oriented to giving.* I often provide free consultations, tips, gifts and information. I make generosity a part of my overall marketing plan. *(Generosity)*

_____ 13. I look for ways to *amaze* my customers with exceptional service. *(Amazement)*

_____ **14.** I consistently use my *imagination* to develop marketing strategies that are unconventional and will capture the attention of my target market. *(Imagination)*

_____ **15.** I actively work on *developing marketing partnerships with other people and businesses. (Partnerships)*

_____ **16.** I *consistently act* on my marketing plan. *(Marketing Plan)*

(For a downloadable template of this assessment with tracking chart visit **www.GMarketingCoach.com**)

So how did you do? Are you pleased with your current Guerrilla Marketing skills? I hope so. If not, don't sweat it. Most of our coaching superstars will tell you that they, too, had their share of challenges in the beginning. The good news is help is only a few short pages away as the following chapters will focus on these sixteen competencies and real-world examples on how to become proficient in each of these areas.

In this book you'll learn from thirty-five world-class Guerrilla Marketing Coaches who are also accomplished authors, successful entrepreneurs, educators, degreed professionals and public speakers. They'll share invaluable insights into how Guerrilla Marketing works in "the real world." You'll find a treasure trove of true stories that illustrate how they've built their own and others' businesses using hundreds of diverse strategies, tactics, and tools based on Guerrilla Marketing. And most of these accomplishments were achieved on shoestring budgets.

Whether you are a small business owner, a marketing representative, a nonprofit staff member, an entrepreneur, a student, or an employee of a multinational corporation, you won't want to miss the powerful Guerrilla Marketing tools revealed in these pages.

If I could give only one piece of advice to someone who wants to achieve the kinds of successes the writers of this book have seen, it would be this: read each chapter in this book carefully and use every strategy and tactic that makes sense for you and your business.

After that, visit our authors' Web sites and familiarize yourself with their unique and collective styles, content, product and service offerings, professionalism and credibility; then cherry pick the very best strategies and tactics for you and your business while adding your own distinctive touch. (And if you're in need of a Guerrilla Marketing Coach to help you in a more personal way, you have the best-of-the-best to choose from!) So grab your favorite drink, sit down in a comfortable chair, and get ready to take a journey with our experts on the Guerrilla Marketing frontlines.

About Mitch Meyerson

Mitch Meyerson is a visionary, speaker, consultant and author of seven books including Mastering Online Marketing, Six Keys To Creating The Life You Desire *and* Success Secrets of The Online Marketing Superstars. *He has been featured on Oprah and has created three groundbreaking Internet based programs: The Guerrilla Marketing Coaching Program, The 90 Day Product Factory, and The Online Traffic School. He has trained business owners worldwide and is also a dynamic speaker and musician. Visit him on the Web at:* **www.MitchMeyerson.com**.

CHAPTER 2

GUERRILLA INTENTION
Dream It. Declare It. Achieve It!

David Wood, PCC

> *"True intention is demonstrated by attainment."*
> ~Dr. Victor Baronco

Whether you know it or not, you are marketing yourself every day to everyone. Whether you are standing in line at the grocery store or standing on a podium addressing a conference full of people, you're getting the word out about who you are and what you are passionate about.

As a Guerrilla Marketer, you always use time, energy, and imagination to market yourself and your business. However, no amount of time, energy, and imagination will amount to a hill of beans if you don't have the intention to succeed.

Intention—it's actually the first and most important weapon that any Guerrilla Marketer needs in his or her arsenal. Intention is you directly applying your mind to whatever it is that you want. You get a concept of what you want and then you put some force behind it.

Marketing is sending your message to the world. You want to get connected to your potential clients and customers so that you can give the world something they find valuable, and in return, you get something you deserve.

Guerrillas control the messages that they send because they set their intention. Non-guerrillas send unintentional messages all the time. They're not aware of what they are intending, so they can harm not only their marketing efforts but their overall goals in life. They want to close a sale for a consulting contract, for example, but their inability to make eye contact or the mumbled message they leave on an answering machine turns off the prospect. So let's start your journey off right. Let's get into the particulars of intention, how it works and what it can do for you and your marketing.

Have You Said It Out Loud?

Let me tell you a story about intention. I'm now considered by some to be one of the leading life coaches on the planet, and a very successful Internet marketer. However, if you could have seen me twelve short months ago, you wouldn't have been able to paint that picture.

I had just returned from India and I was in a severe state of anxiety. Lying in my bed, in blue flannel pajamas, I didn't feel very powerful. I could hear my virtual staff through my headset as we discussed our company vision for the New Year. But all I wanted to do was curl up under a blanket and pretend the world didn't exist.

It started when I was taken off a plane in a wheel chair in Mombay. Things had spiraled so out of control that I was scared of fear itself. My whole system freaked out; I had no idea what was happening, and I would often slowly count to ten, just hoping to make it through another day.

But something interesting happened. A week after an emergency exit back to my 'safe' nest in New York, I found myself saying to my virtual staff: "I see this as my year of public speaking. I know that I'm ready now to speak, to write a book, and do a radio and TV show. It's time to connect with the world!" These sounded like enormous words from a guy lying in bed, crying at random, and who hadn't spoken to groups in over six years. But I posted the goals on my wall and declared them to my staff. I didn't have a clue *how* this was going to happen, but that didn't matter. I had started the process because I put the intention out to make it happen.

A month later I got a call from T. Harv Eker's people (the Millionaire Mindset gang), asking if I would come and speak to twelve hundred people in Los Angeles about my success in building the largest e-zine of coaches in the world. I said "I'm not sure," because it wasn't the topic I wanted to speak on, and it wasn't paid. But with my goals staring at me from my cork board, I realized that saying no would be pretty silly for a guy who had just recently declared the intention to speak!

So I created a training program that teaches people how to build a massive newsletter list on a topic they truly care about and then leverage the list so they can choose whether or not they ever want to work again. I got me and my program to Los Angeles, and the talk was so successful that the audience bought six figures worth of the training program *in the first fifteen minutes following the speech.* (You can see the talk at www.SolutionBox.com/video if you're interested). I was astounded. All this from a guy experiencing enormous amounts of anxiety and fear who simply said, out loud, what was going to happen.

Business Follows Intention

We go about our days with a jumble of wishes and hopes and a long list of goals, sometimes not thoroughly considered. Intentionality is about getting clear and focused, so you can create what you *really* want. It's about being deliberate, imbuing each act with and decision with meaning. It's a tool for directing your life instead of "letting it happen."

Unintentional messages erect insurmountable barriers. Jay Conrad Levinson recognized that there are really two people within you—your accidental self and your intentional self. Which will you develop?

A true Guerrilla Marketer, a truly powerful human being, lives with intention, all the time. It isn't hard to do. The idea is for you to be who you are and not who you aren't—to be who you are by declaration, not by accident.

And something really remarkable happens when you live with 100 percent intention. If you're intentional about everything that you do, the business will follow. Marketing means expressing your values and your passion to the world; the business rewards will always come when you live that way. When you live with intention, you are being true to who you are. You become transparent; the world knows "this is what I want and this is who I am." When you market with intention, you market *you* to the world, and when you do this, everything that you've always dreamed of—a successful business, great relationships, you name it (literally)—is yours.

But What Intention Should I Set?

Intention is powerful stuff, and you actually set intentions all the time. You've been setting intentions all your life, whether you're conscious of it or not. Without realizing it you may have decided to be healthier, and you find yourself meeting people who do yoga. Or you think: I need more support in your business, and the perfect business partner appears.

You don't have to be conscious of any of your intentions. You can go with the flow, be intuitive, in the moment, with no consciously set goals. But this method doesn't work so well for everyone. If you're short on results, pick something you *really want to impact* and make it happen. Being intentional is really fun, it's attractive, and can produce amazing results.

From a marketing perspective you can set an intention on two levels. The basic level is for a simple business outcome: "I will increase revenue by 30 percent within six months," or "I will create a successful joint venture with Mark Victor Hansen during 2008."

However, a higher level would be to set an intention that includes your entire life: "Every person I interact with feels inspired," or "I am 100 percent honest with everyone I interact with, even if I lose something." This level of intention encompasses all aspects of your life, and actually begins to define *who you are*. You will find that that your "life" intention improves your business meetings or transactions. Think about it, if you live with intention, you will find that it impacts everyone you come in contact with: the grocery store assistant, your building janitor, the newspaper reporter—even your spouse!

When Business and Personal Merge

Remember, when you live and work with intention, you are automatically marketing you! By being the person you declare yourself to be, by setting intentions that define who you are, you can create success in every area of your life.

This is one example of how I applied this principle in my life. Realizing that my default position was often to look for what I can get out of a relationship, I set an intention to contribute to everyone I met. When I spotted John Gray (of "Mars and Venus" fame) in a hotel lobby last month, I struck up a conversation and found myself asking how I could support what he was up to. It was much more fun than asking for something, and two days later we had lunch, beginning a mutually promising relationship.

Have you seen someone be warm and friendly with you during a business meeting, but then rude to the waiter? Don't be one of those people who fakes it for business but lapses in your personal life. You never know who that person is in line behind you, or sitting next to you on the plane. They could be your future publisher, ghost writer, virtual assistant, husband, wife, or they could refer you to someone who will fill that role.

So now it's your turn. What's important to you? What would *really* make you smile in six months, or five years? I want you to write down five intentions. They can be *huge* or small, but I recommend being as specific as you can, and include a time frame. After all, you don't want it after you're dead. Here are some examples:

- *"I will have lunch with Richard Branson in 2008."*
- *"I will find the perfect publicist in the next three months."*
- *"I will be on Oprah by December 2009."*

- *"Every person I interact with will leave me better for the experience."*

- *"I will significantly improve three lives this year."*

- *"I will automate my business to the point that I have four days off each week, by December 2009."*

One thing you can be intentional about is networking and building relationships with people. You may invest in relationships because it feels right, and because you feel it may help you and/or them down the track. Instead of waiting or hoping for it to happen, why not set an intention, and make it happen? I'm currently developing relationships with several very cool and prominent people in the marketing, speaking and author industry. And I've set an intention of having lunch with Alan Alda, for the sole reason that he's awesome. Being intentional around relationships feels good, it's fun, and helps everyone.

And there's something also really wild about intention. Sometimes, you might focus, focus, focus on the intention, but in a quiet moment or a busy one, you forget about it and because you're doing whatever is next on your list. Then next thing you know, what you intended just dropped into your lap. Sometimes it's when you've let go of the conscious intention that you get what you were asking for.

Merging Action and Intention

Now, you need to realize something important about intention. Once you write it down or speak it out loud, you have two choices. You can sit and navel gaze, or you can act! The next chapter talks about taking Guerrilla Action, but it's important to address it here as well because I feel that action is so closely tied to intention. I realize that some people believe it's enough to declare your intention to yourself and the universe will do the rest. The folks in *The Secret* suggest that all you need to do is to feel and act like you have the things that you want. Once you have the feelings you would have if you had "it," you just let it go. But I'm a more practical fish. I say:

Action is how you make sure the universe gets the message.

And to make darn sure the universe knows what I want, I follow these five steps:

Step One: Create a Support Structure

Some people use a vision board to do this, say a cork board where you paste pictures cut out from magazines. You could frame an inspiring picture, or paste your face on the guest sitting next to Oprah. For me it's simply a piece of paper with my goals, stuck to the fridge. I've written a target list of the people I'd love to endorse my next book (which includes Richard Branson, if you're reading this Richard). One week after writing the list, I found myself on a networking call with one of the people who was on my list and he gave out his private e-mail address. The next week, I found out that the son of Steve Wynn (the Las Vegas hotel magnate, and another endorsement target that I had listed) just moved into my building complex. Coincidence? Maybe.

Did one create the other? I don't know, and I don't really care that much. What I do know is that as soon as I made my intention clear, things started to happen.

Step Two: Declare It

Once I have written down my intention, I tell my friends, family, and colleagues. Now, you can keep it quiet about what you want if you like. You can write it down in a hidden place and just have it be your little secret. But if you do it this way, you're limiting the internal shift that's possible. As soon as you consciously declare something, "things inside" start to line up with that. It's like you're saying, "Okay, I really do want it, I've said it. At the very least, I'll try not to *block* it now." But if you keep quiet about it, you're making it hard for the world to support you. After all, if your closest friends and colleagues don't know you're committed to more media publicity, how will they know to let you know of a publishing opportunity?

There's no woo-woo stuff here. First, you have to get even more internally aligned with your goal (i.e. be a *yes* in your subconscious), or you won't even be able to tell your friends without sweating. Second, the people you tell are now in a position to help you! And that's Guerrilla Marketing at its finest.

When I told a guy on the plane last week about my book and that I was looking for a publisher, it turned out he just landed a book deal and referred me to his editor. There's a very basic example of putting something out to the world, and the world sending support back. Simple.

"The universe rewards action."
~L. Ron Hubbard

Step Three: *Plan It*

Once you've declared your intention, the third step is to map out an action plan. It's actually fun to figure out how you are going to make your intentions real. You can also learn a lot. Drawing up an action plan adds a lot of fuel to your intention because it's also a declaration to your subconscious that you seriously want this.

If you can't see at this early stage *how* you could possibly make your intentions happen, don't worry. Set the intention, and the *how* will arrive. Last month at the Entrepreneurs Organization conference, I showed up early to the private KISS concert for members, where security had the whole area cordoned off. I had no idea how I was going to get in, but get in I was going to do! A guy showed up and headed for the entrance like he belonged there, so without even thinking I tagged along behind him like we were buddies. When he flashed his pass I nodded like I was part of the team and kept walking into the private interview with Gene Simmons. So even if you have no idea how it's going to happen, set the goal anyway!

Step Four: *Support It*

Great things are rarely accomplished alone. A Guerrilla Marketer knows that he or she must have a competent team around them to help them achieve his or her goals, even if it's just a cheering squad. A great support structure in place also gives your intention some extra punch.

If your tendency is to be scattered, to take on too much, to flit from project to project, or sometimes lose momentum, then reading this chapter or the whole book won't be enough, I promise you! And that's 98 percent of people.

So it's super smart to not only write down an action plan but create a support structure for your intention.

If you intend to make $1 million within twelve months, hang out with people who are playing at that level. If you want to be a sought after speaker, join a speaking organization, and build relationships with some of the top speakers. Buddy up with someone else who has the same goal, and schedule weekly or monthly mutual support calls. Or hire a coach who has experience in what you're shooting for.

And here's something very important to know: your actions may not directly lead to the desired result. But because you have the intention to do something, you may get off your butt and go to a meeting because of a goal you committed to. On the way to the meeting you meet someone in the elevator who has the perfect product for your business to promote. You may reach your goal in unexpected ways, or you may reach an entirely different goal, possibly one much better than the one you chose!

The key is to marry intention with action, deliberately and knowingly, and enjoy yourself along the way.

Step Five: *Seek Personal Development*

The smartest way to work on your business is really to work on yourself. A Guerrilla Marketer is always seeking ways to improve himself and herself. Everything, marketing, of course, included, is about relating and presence. And you can't get that in a book. We each need to do the hard work, find out what we're afraid of, and face it.

You can go to countless business seminars about accounting, hiring staff, marketing and distribution. But if you can't communicate well, it will be hard to maintain a loving partnership. If you are always self-focused, people won't be inspired to work with or for you. If you have underlying fears or anger, it will come through in every action, and potential clients and customers may shy away from it.

We all want to be (or at least be thought of as) charismatic, present, generous, centered, grounded, inspirational, motivational, adventurous and caring. So be that! Put aside at least one week out of the year for pure personal development; developing *who you are* as a human being. This will translate into every interaction you have, rippling out into great rewards.

I've invested tens of thousands of dollars, and months if not years of my life training in communication, listening, sharing my inner thoughts, touch, team work, energy, cleaning up the past, integrity, commitment, opening the heart—the list goes on. My life and thus my business have prospered exponentially because of this work I've done to improve myself.

Take the Risk and See What Happens

Sometimes, people get really scared of making a big goal or having a *huge* intention. Why? Because they don't want to fail. A part of me definitely thinks that perhaps it's better not to set goals and avoid disappointment.

Is it possible you could resist putting out the intention to make something happen because you would feel lousy if you didn't land it? You would you feel embarrassed in front of friends and colleagues if it didn't happen, and it confirm a quietly held belief that you're really not good enough to make it. But a Guerrilla Marketer faces his or her fears, and goes for it, regardless of what might happen along the way.

Yes, there is risk involved in setting goals. There is risk associated with declaring the goal publicly. You might not make it! So are you willing to take that risk? Are you willing to possibly look like a goose, in exchange for the great rewards that come from declaring your intent to the world?

Consider this powerful example from my friend and successful marketer Maria Andreu:

> Three years ago I made a decision to triple my income—which seemed impossible.
>
> I can honestly say that getting the courage up to create that intention was the hardest part—to actually believe that it could happen. It sounds like a small thing but it took a long time! I could imagine it "out there" happening to other people, and I

could yearn for it, but it took a lot of work to get to believe that not only could it happen to me, it *would*. Once that was done, it was about creating an intention that I lived with every day. Each morning, I repeated to myself that my intention was to grow my income to this desired amount.

Of course many days I slipped, wondering if I was just fooling myself, or if I was being a dreamer. But then, I got a project in a way that seemed quite magical, doubling my income overnight! This was the proof I needed that intention works!

How did Maria do it? Are there intention fairies? Of course not. In setting the intention Maria became a different person. She spoke like a person making three times more. She went after opportunities that her lower-income self would have been too shy to go after. She presented herself a different way. She believed different things. As Maria says: "It's not just about all of this 'manifesting' we hear so much about. Intentionality is manifesting's more pragmatic cousin. By creating an intention you open up your eyes to believing that something can happen, and then the work is half done already."

So What's Your Intention?

Now, you don't *have* to be consciously intentional. A valid way of living is to simply respond intuitively to what comes up in the moment. In this way you'll respond to an "inner guidance," which we could call "inner intentions."

However, not everyone wants to 'float around' in the moment, trusting in a divine force to guide their path. Setting conscious intentions can be enormously fun, attractive, and productive. So grab a blank sheet of paper, write yours down, place them on your fridge and watch what happens!

How do you know you really intended something?
Because it happens.

About David Wood, PCC

David Wood is a former Fortune 100 Consultant, actuary, pub singer in Australia, stand-up comedian, hang-glider pilot and snow-board instructor. Now a leading life coach and raving Internet entrepreneur, he maintains an e-zine of 70,000 coaches world wide, and is in the top number two sites on Google for life coaching. David shows professionals how to take what they already know and love, share it with the world, and actually get paid for it! He then shows them how to auto-mate it so they are impacting the world while asleep or on vacation, via his free video at www.SolutionBox.com/video. He also helps life and business coaches start and fill their coaching practices, and all people to take charge of their life, via his free download at www.SolutionBox.com/gift.

CHAPTER 3

GUERRILLAS TAKE ACTION

Managing your Actions to Make the Most of Your Marketing Time

Alex Mandossian

> *"Inaction breeds doubt and fear. Action breeds confidence and courage. If you want to conquer fear, do not sit home and think about it. Go out and get busy."*
> ~Dale Carnegie

Guerrilla Marketers know how important taking action is. This book, in a sense, gives you thirty-five different ways to take action, for we know that if we take action, things happen and our business grows. But there is a difference between taking action and taking smart action.

I'm no stranger to taking action. From 1993 to 2000, I worked on Madison Avenue. While I was there, I worked like an animal. There is no other way to look at it. I felt like I was in the galleys rowing, like in one of those old movies about the Vikings or the Romans. I was a chief marketing officer of a company on Madison Avenue, and I worked sixteen-hour days. Why? Not only did I want to keep my job, but I also wanted to make more money, and the only way I could do that was to get a promotion. I didn't get a pay raise every month like I do now, and I had very little time for freedom. In fact, if I had continued at that place, I would have most likely lost my marriage and would not have had the two beautiful kids I have now. That is definitely not taking smart action.

So how did I make the leap from working stiff to entrepreneur who takes time off to enjoy my family? I learned how to make the most effective use of my time. As a Guerrilla Marketer, I'm sure it would interest you to learn how to fit sixteen hours into eight hours, like I did, and turn your yearly income into an hourly income in less than five years.

Diagnosing the Problem

Let's say your day starts at 8:00 a.m. and ends at 5:00 p.m. Anyone who works for himself or herself knows that's a myth, but let's say this is the situation. Now, let's talk about all the different interruptions we face that we don't have control over. I'm going to list a few you're probably all too familiar with:

A phone call: do we have control over a phone call coming in? No. It is an interruption. How about e-mail? Do we have any control over solicited or unsolicited e-mail? We do not. How about regular mail, a letter, is that an interruption when you open that? Absolutely. How about when a co-worker or family member comes and taps you on the shoulder? Is that an interruption? If you didn't request it, sure it is. How about voicemail? No question.

It doesn't make sense for us, as Guerrilla Marketers, to allow e-mail, voice-mail, phone calls, physical letters, coworkers, or even family members to interrupt time during the day when we are generating revenue. All those things are time guzzlers. You've got to be honest with yourself. In order to take control of your actions, you need to figure out what your time-guzzlers are and write them down. Once you've done that, you need to say: "These are the problems that I have, and I need to structure my day so when I am attempting to produce revenue, I don't get interrupted." Then, make a pact with yourself that you're not going to allow these things to enter your life and seep into your revenue-generating activities. Even this small action step can get you focused because many times a problem is half-solved once you clearly define it.

The Solution

In order to put yourself in action as a Guerrilla Marketer, you need to get hardcore about the actions that you take every day to manage your day well. And know something here—this isn't about time management. Time management is a myth. Let me repeat that: time management is a myth. You cannot manage time. You can only manage actions, and when you are managing your actions well, you can appropriate those actions within the time span that you determine. If you give yourself eight hours a day, you are not managing your time. You are managing your actions within that time frame. Make sense?

What I'm about to give you are the seven secrets of action management, secrets that I use everyday in my business, and if you apply even one or two of them to your business, you will find that you are able to manage all your marketing and production actions much more effectively. And once I give these secrets to you, they will become strategies that will enable you to get sixteen hours worth of work done in an eight-hour day, triple your revenue, and quite possibly, double your time off. Ready to get started? Here's the first one.

Guerrilla Action Step One: Create Your Master To-Do List

We all know the importance of having a "to-do" list, and it is vital to any action-management plan. Now, I don't use a palm pilot or Outlook for this. I use a physical master to-do list. I physically write out the action items that I want to accomplish. I use a junior legal pad that's about five inches wide by seven inches tall, with fifty sheets on it. It's yellow and has about twenty lines on it. No matter what kind of pad you use, it's very important you physically write it out because this is the way that works. I've tried it other ways and it hasn't worked; it was too overwhelming.

I use this small pad because I like to fill it up. The twenty lines allow me to write down no more than twenty actions per day. I typically complete anywhere between fifteen and twenty; I have found that's all that's humanly possible. Furthermore, when I fill up my junior legal pad, I feel like I'm doing something, and that sense of accomplishment gives me a positive boost.

I have also found that it works better to write out your action management in advance— at least a day before. Sometimes I write mine a few days before. Whenever you do it, however, doesn't matter so much as you writing your master to-do list for the future. Why? Because it's easier to come to a desk that's clean and has a master to-do list that's already been written sitting on it. This way, you can start your first prime-time hour by attacking that list and crossing things out. Isn't that a lot easier than trying to invent things to do?

As I go through my day, I execute each action item, and cross out those suckers with a red felt-tip pen I bought specifically for that purpose. Do you know why I do that? I get to see all I've accomplished. I feel so good when I write those things down and then cross them out with a red pen because they're done.

At the end of the day, what happens? You often have items that weren't finished, and so the third element of creating your master to-do list is to take the items left over, flip the page, and put those items on a new list. Once I have started my new "to do" list for the next day, I cross those items I just moved off the previous days. If I didn't finish three items on, say, a Tuesday, I flip the page to Wednesday's list, write them down, and then cross them off Tuesday's list. I'm going to flip the page. Make sure you flip the page. Also, if you have twelve left over, you didn't have a very well-managed day, but you have twelve things to start out with tomorrow. So you resolve to do better and move on.

I can't tell you how satisfying it is to cross out every single one of those actions. Once I have everything crossed off, I rip out the sheet of paper from that day, scrunch it up and throw it in the wastebasket. That day is officially over, and even though I may have more for the next day, that next day hasn't started. I get to start my day fresh, every day, using this strategy.

Now, you may be wondering if and how I prioritize my list. When I'm creating my to-do list, I prioritize. I have to, but not in the way that you might think. Guerrilla Marketers, listen up. The fun first. Fun first. Sometimes, the fun is easy; sometimes, fun is hard. But I always do the things that are going to be the most fun for me because if I get to do something fun first, that puts me on a positive note for the rest of the day.

Action Step Two: *Block Out your Daily Prime-Time Hours*

This is very important, as important as creating the master plan for your day. What is a prime-time hour? A prime-time hour is anything you control 100 percent of and is going to generate revenue for you now or sometime in the future. Now, you can have just one prime-time hour a day or two a day, even four a day. I have four. I don't think you should have more than four, and if you're skeptical about that number, just know that most people don't have any.

Think about this. If you only have one prime-time hour a day and you work five days a week—many of us work many more than that—that's 225 work days per year. How many prime-time, revenue-generating hours are you giving yourself as a gift for the year? You are giving yourself 225 hours. As a Guerrilla Marketer, don't you think you can generate some revenue with that? I think so. In fact, aren't we robbing ourselves if we don't give ourselves prime-time hours? I would like all of you to block off one prime-time hour a day starting next week.

When you're considering which hour to block off, go for the most important hour of the day, the first one. Why? You are fresher in the morning than you are after having been beaten down by the events of the day. When you have your first, fresh hour of the morning in which to produce, you start with the positive. Think about it, what is the first thing that you typically do when you get in front of your computer? Check e-mail. Is that an interruption? Yes. And worse, it can start your whole day off badly. What if you wake up and see an e-mail from someone asking for a refund or telling you they're not happy with your services? Doesn't that put you into some type of emotional tail spin which you don't want to be a part of?

Now, rather than checking your e-mail, generate revenue for one full hour first and see how good you feel about yourself. You've already crossed out some things on your master action to-do list and so that makes handling any bad news a little easier. See what I am saying?   There's also another reason why I don't start with e-mails with their potentially bad news, and it has everything to do with intention. When people get bad news first, they concentrate on that bad news, not the good news. When you start with good news, it is not so bad afterwards.

So start with good news so that you have positive intentions to take you through the rest of the day. Start your day with a revenue-generating activity. And if you only have one prime-time hour, make sure that hour is in the very beginning. Eventually, you want no less than two hours a day that are prime time. Oh, and prime time is always during the day: nine to five, eight to five. Your choice, but it's not in the middle of the night.

Another element of prime time is to focus only on revenue-generating activities you can control. I think everyone knows what that means, and to do that, always avoid the daily interruptions you cannot control, like e-mail. Just turn e-mail off. Also, during your prime-time, don't listen to your voicemail, and don't take phone calls. That's why you have voice mail (but don't listen to your voice mail either during prime time). Don't open your letters. Tell your family it's prime time and get their support by agreeing that they cannot enter the office or call you (unless, heaven forbid, it's an emergency).

By setting prime time hours, and starting with a revenue-generating activity, you will feel great about yourself and you will be in a much more able to manage your actions throughout the rest of the day.

Action Step Three: During Prime Time, Put Pressure on Yourself —Use a Timer

In order for me to perform better, I put pressure on myself. I give myself deadlines, in a way, and I use this next technique to keep myself accountable. This technique is something different, and I really want you to at least try it. Since I can't manage time but I can manage actions, I put myself on a timer. I use a kitchen timer that cost $9 at Bed, Bath & Beyond. What do I do with this timer? I set it for forty-seven minutes (I'll tell you why that is in a minute) and I put it where I can see it, right next to my computer screen. As I work, I hear it ticking. Does that put pressure on me or what! It will do the same for you—put pressure on you to really put your head down and perform.

Now, when the beeper goes off, stop everything you're doing. It's incredibly important because you've got to give yourself a break. I give myself breaks. This is why I set my timer to forty-seven minutes because I like to have a thirteen-minute break. I am greedy with my time off. However, I recommend you set your timers to fifty or fifty-five minutes to start. I started with fifty-five minutes and gave myself a five-minute break and worked my way up to the thirteen minute break. This break is very, very important because it allows you to step back into a highly creative space, and that's where some pretty magical things happen. This is the essence of secret number four.

Action Step Four: Be Prepared—Capture your Big Ideas Digitally

Guerrilla Marketers are good girl scouts and boy scouts because we know how important it is to be prepared. You see, when you take a break from the task at hand, your mind will still be going on what you were doing. If you're brainstorming a new idea, if you are talking to a joint venture partner, it doesn't matter. Whatever you were doing your mind is going to keep going, and this is where the magic happens. So the bottom line is to be prepared to record that magic.

Here's what I do from 6:30 a.m. to 7:30 a.m. I'm in prime time—not for the whole hour, but for forty-seven minutes. When that beeper goes off, I go downstairs and either do some sit-ups, pushups or grab a glass of water or a cup of coffee. During that time, I have a digital recorder with me. It's one I got from Radio Shack, for about $60. You deserve to give this to yourself, so spend sixty bucks. Don't buy one that has two hours on it, or even sixty minutes. Buy one that only gives you fifteen minutes or at the most thirty minutes. I'll explain why in a moment. I keep that recorder next to me at all times because then I can record my big ideas the moment they pop into my head. And once they're recorded, you don't have to think about them anymore. You can purge them from your mind, freeing your mind to come up with more. I also keep my recorder handy during non prime time hours so that I can record everything that I think of as I think them.

Now, once you've digitally recorded five or six ideas, then I want you to write them down in an idea file; whether that is a notebook or a Word document, it doesn't matter. What does matter is that you've transcribed these ideas from the voice recorder. This is why I don't want you to have two hours worth of recording time. If you have two hours worth of ideas on your recorder, you're never going to transcribe them.

There's also another reason why I like to write things down. When you type or write, it's a different activity than speaking; it really is a different modality of learning. So as you speak into your recorder and then write down the ideas, you have engaged the tactile, the kinesthetic, and the auditory parts of learning. The more modalities you can use, the more the idea sticks. Heck, if there were a scratch and sniff part to this process, I would do that to!

Action Step Five: *Offer One Free Consultation Per Week or Per Day*

I don't care what you are good at or what you're selling. It could be coaching, mentoring, writing, publishing, or developing software. Whether you're an author or a service provider, you're going to have customers who have questions. These questions can turn into potential sales. Knowing this, I offer one thirty-minute free consultation per day for someone who wants information from me. People really like getting something for free, but the trick is to keep a tight lid on that thirty minutes.

So my free consultation has a twist. The clients know, up front, that at the end of that consultation, if they want to work with me, they are going to pay up at the end of the session. At the end of their thirty free minutes, I ask them if they'd like to proceed. If they say yes, they then owe me for my time—all of it. Let's say my hourly fee is $450 and our consultation lasted thirty minutes. They know before we set the appointment for the call if they want to continue with me at some point in the future, then they give me their credit card for $225 at the end of the call. Since my hourly fee is $450, the charge for thirty minutes is $225. Now if they want to continue for the full hour, great. If they want to go two hours, great, because that has become revenue generating for me, right? If they say no, then we hang up and the consultation is free—but with a caveat. While there are no obligations, no commitment, no further expectations on my part or theirs, they also don't get to talk to me again.

It really is a conditional free consultation, but it keeps everyone honest. Many coaches and service providers give free consultations, but they don't put their people on the hook. You have far fewer free consultations if you tell them they are going to pay for it if they are satisfied. Also, make sure you have your free consultations during non-prime time. Set aside a block of maybe forty minutes and call it gifting on your yellow pad. You are giving back to your clients, so you are giving them a gift, but believe me, if that "gift" becomes revenue-generating that is also a gift for you. It's a win-win because you gave them something valuable and they gave you a gift—their business.

Each week, I also have one hour every Tuesday at noon, 3:00 p.m. (EST), when I do a Guerrilla Marketing seven-step plan that Jay Conrad Levinson taught me. But I don't do it alone. For everyone who receives my MarketingWithPostcards.com autoresponder series, on day seven, they get to be part of this. You can be part of this, too. All you have to do is send a blank e-mail to Teleclinic@ThatOneWebGuy.com.

Now, what did I just do? I just pitched you a free tele-clinic, and I did it on purpose. This is one of my best spent hours because I get customers from these tele-clinics. I also get e-mail addresses that will go into a sub-list. That sub-list is a teleconference list and teleconferences are a huge source of revenue generation. So everyone who has given me their e-mail for the tele-clinic then gets e-mailed for the teleconference. The teleconference is also free, but I have built a list of very active subscribers by offering them free tele-conferences, and very active lists are huge revenue generators, believe me.

Just like the free consultations, I do that teleconference during non-prime time. I even plan for it in non-prime time, but that doesn't take much time because when you have a free teleconference class each week, you just use the exact same curriculum week after week. Don't worry about repeating yourself. Guerrilla Marketing is about building and maintaining relationships, and the more people listen to you, the higher level of intimacy they create with you. More intimacy equals better relationships and better relationships equal higher revenue.

So what I am doing here with free consultations and free tele-clinics and teleseminars is that I'm playing a trick on myself. I am finding ways to convert non-prime time into revenue generation. It is action oriented, and when you think about it as a gift that you're giving yourself—for all the reasons I just gave you—it keeps you motivated to stay in action the rest of the day.

Now, there is something that you need to know about this gifted time. With whatever amount of time you want to gift to yourself and your clients, or potential clients, figure out what you are going do and then do it religiously. It might be that you just do the one free consultation per day and not the tele-seminar, or vice-versa. Or, you may decide to model what I do and do them both. Whatever you do, however, think of it always as a gift—never, ever as a pitch. When you gift your time to help educate people, you will have access to more people wanting to listen to you. Don't promote yourself, just give them something they can use. But *do* tell them what your fees are and what your services are, especially when they are listening to you in context of what you're ultimately selling.

If you want to see what this all looks like just send a blank e-mail to Teleclinic@ThatOneWebGuy.com or opt-in to www.7StepActionPlan.com.

Action Step Six: *Find a Mutual Coaching Buddy*

It's great when you can give something to somebody, and they can give something back. What I like to do is find a mutual coaching buddy. Here's how you do this: hunt for an expert in the field you want to master. Make sure you have something of equal or greater value to share with them. Use one hour of non-prime time for the mutual coaching, and set a deadline for the number of coaching sessions you have. Agree on maybe four or six of these sessions and see how it works. Don't do it forever because you'll feel awful if you want to stop. Test it.

Understand, I am trying to get you Guerrilla Marketers to do work that generates revenue, and using one non-prime-time hour a week, every other week, or even once a month for a mutual coaching buddy is probably one of the best hours you'll ever use.

Action Step Seven: *Set your Revenue Quota Every Ninety Days*

Every good, productive action is attached to a plan, and my seven secret steps is no exception. While a ninety-day revenue quota might sound daunting, it isn't. This is how what you do. First, figure out what you can make in a year, then divide that into weekly goals. Make sure it's realistic, but at the same time make sure that you're not selling yourself short either.

Now, I like weekly goals because they're easy to measure. You can graph your progress or simply keep the numbers in a journal. However you keep track isn't as vital is actually doing it. The most important point is that once you have established what your weekly goals are, you write down *every week* if you made it or not. Then, every ninety days, review how you did and adjust it either up or down.

This is how I do it. I set my quota and then do the least amount of work possible to get there. When I reach my weekly quota, believe it or not, I stop working. I'll still take phone calls, but I will stop working. It doesn't always happen. I don't always meet it. But when it does happen, it sure is fun!

I remember making it on a Tuesday once, and I went on a little mini vacation. It took me about a day to plan, and from Thursday all the way through the following Sunday, I went on a vacation with call forwarding. I laughed the whole time, and I was laughing at time. I managed my actions, and I made it work to my favor that week.

Fortunately, I did get that revenue, but I did something most don't. I rewarded myself for it. Most people don't reward themselves; they just work more. But why do that? You are robbing yourself of the nectar of living. Isn't the whole purpose of work to play?

****

So there you have it. The seven secrets to action management. They will help you organize your enterprise on or offline. These tactics will help you complete sixteen hours of worth of work within an eight-hour day, as well as triple your income and double your time off. You don't even have to follow every step. You can start by following one or two of them, and I bet you'll be very surprised. And if you want to learn more of my secrets to success, make sure you check out my blog at www.AlexMandossian.com and sign up for the free audio e-book, "5 Secrets To Making Change Now."

One final note: When I tell you my secrets, I do it selfishly. Because if I am espousing it, I better follow it. I admit I don't always follow it. I do run amuck sometimes. So by me stating this in a major marketing publication, it will force my self and every cell in my body to remember to focus on this and get even better at it. I don't know if this is for the sake of embarrassment or because I am putting myself on the spot, but ultimately it doesn't matter. I am giving you my seven secrets selfishly because I want to be able to master action management. You know, the best way to master something you're learning is to teach it. That's what I'm doing right now.

And by the way, I'm going to take some time off now because I met my quota yesterday! I wish everyone good sales, and I hope our paths cross often.

About Alex Mandossian

Since 1991, Alex Mandossian has generated over $233 million in sales and profits for his clients and partners via "electronic marketing" media such as TV Infomercials, online catalogs, twenty-four-hour recorded messages, voice/fax broadcasting, Teleseminars, Webinars, Podcasts and Internet Marketing. He has personally consulted Dale Carnegie Training, New York University, Nightingale-Conant, Super Camp, Trim Spa, and many others. He has hosted teleseminars with many of the world's top Thought Leaders such as Mark Victor Hansen, Jack Canfield, Stephen Covey, Les Brown, Brian Tracy, Harvey Mackay, T. Harv Eker, Lisa Nichols, Loral Langemeier, Michael Gerber, Jay Abraham, Donald Trump and many others. He has trained over 13,300 teleseminar students since 2001 and knows that any entrepreneur can transform their annual income into a weekly income once they apply his principle-centered electronic marketing strategies. Visit www.AlexMandossian.com for more information.

CHAPTER 4

GUERRILLAS DON'T NEED SILVER BULLETS

Simplicity and Consistency will Turn Prospects to Profits

C.J. Hayden, MCC

"So often we dwell on the things that seem impossible rather than on the things that are possible."
~Marian Wright Edelman

Is there a hidden secret to successful marketing? It seems many entrepreneurs are on a never-ending quest for that one magic formula that will take all the effort out of marketing and attract an endless stream of customers forever. Searching for this secret key, they read dozens of books and articles, take countless seminars, and hire an army of consultants and coaches. And in the process, they uncover an amazing variety of seemingly brilliant marketing ideas.

One month, it appears that the answer to their prayers is attending networking events. They fill their calendar with dozens of different meetings, each of which they attend only once. They press their business cards into as many hands as possible, but no one ever calls them. So that can't be the solution.

The following month, they decide that meeting people in person is overrated, and the real future of marketing is on the web. They launch a beautifully-designed professional-looking Web site, filled with glowing descriptions of their products and services. But no one visits it. Maybe it's the web that's overrated.

They decide that perhaps both these approaches were off track. What they should have done all along was use direct mail. They write a four-page sales letter, buy some names from a list broker, send out a hundred-piece mailing, and wait for the phone to ring. The response rate is zero. And so it goes.

Searching for the marketing "silver bullet," too many entrepreneurs never recognize that the most powerful marketing weapon in existence is already in their arsenal. There really is a secret to successful marketing, and it's right under their noses. The magic formula for marketing a small business is choosing a set of simple, effective things to do, and doing them consistently.

If It Works, Keep Doing It

When I first started working with entrepreneurs as a business coach in 1992, I was inspired by an interview with Jay Conrad Levinson wherein he made this startling statement: "I hate to admit this, but mediocre marketing with commitment works better than brilliant marketing without commitment." I realized that the basic problem my clients were having with marketing was not that they didn't know what to do. In most cases, they already knew exactly what they should be doing to market their businesses. They just weren't doing enough of it.

That's when I decided to create a simple system that would help my clients narrow their marketing choices to just a few proven activities, then do those things over and over. I give them a tracking worksheet where they must list on one page every marketing activity they plan to engage in for the next month, and check each activity off every time they do it. It's not an idea list; it's a to-do list.

It was this system that helped Colin Campbell, a consultant in Newport, South Wales. Colin recalls, "Before I discovered C.J. and her system, my marketing was completely disjointed. I would be working on a newsletter, then I'd think I should be sending out mailers. I'd start creating a flyer, then decide I needed to work on a presentation. All these great ideas were on my list, but I could only get a little bit done on each one of them. It was never enough."

Colin had an added challenge in coming up with a realistic marketing plan, because he has two different businesses. He offers sales training and coaching to small business customers, and provides wellness management to companies in the service sector. With two businesses and dozens of marketing strategies to manage, "I was all over the place," Colin says.

What Colin learned from working with my system was that the answer to managing his complex marketing situation was to keep things really simple. Instead of trying to use a dozen different marketing strategies all at the same time, Colin streamlined his plan to make use of only two. And the key to his success is that he uses both these strategies consistently.

What I teach my small business clients is that there are hundreds of ways to market themselves, but each business owner is only one person. A corporation can afford to use many different marketing strategies at one time and hire enough staff to execute each one well. But a solo business owner doesn't have enough time or money to market like this. So the first thing I do is ask my clients to choose no more than three or four ways to market themselves at any one time.

Here's how Colin does it. The two consistent strategies he chose are networking and following up. "I go to three regular networking events now," he says. "Two of them are weekly, and one happens every month. I meet people there, and I tell them what I do. If I can't talk to them about my services on the spot, I call them on the phone later. My goal is to have personal conversations with people. I don't rely on marketing collateral to sell my business. I have some flyers, but I put them in people's hands, not in the mail."

Colin's results have been impressive. The first month he used my system, he doubled his net billing for his two businesses to £3,000 per month. "Let's make sure this works," he told himself. "I'll give it another go." The second month he tried it, he doubled his billing again, to £6,000 per month. "Now I've got more business than I can cope with," Colin declares. "My monthly billing is still going up."

If you're going to use only a handful of marketing strategies, you need to make sure you are choosing the right ones. So the second decision I help my clients make is which activities are likely to produce the best results. I ask them to rank all the strategies they are considering on three relative scales. Are they active or passive, personal or impersonal, and will they create credibility or just visibility?

The strategies they rank as the most active, personal, and credibility-boosting are the ones they should pick. Once they have chosen their two, three, or four strategies to use, I ask them to make a list of ten very specific activities they will do repeatedly for at least twenty-eight days.

If a client chooses "networking" as a strategy, for example, I'll have him decide how he will network. Will he attend networking mixers? Make lunch dates? Place phone calls to potential referral sources? Then I'll ask him to make a commitment to exactly how often he will do these things. Will he go to one event per week? Make three phone calls per day? Whatever he decides, he writes on his tracking worksheet. Then every day, he checks off what he has done.

Colin describes the simplicity of this approach as "frighteningly powerful." He explains: "You just pick out what's going to work for you, choose what you want to do this month, and commit to do it repeatedly. It's really straightforward. In the past, I'd have all these ideas, but each one took me in a different direction. This gives me a structure to put all the bits and pieces together."

Find Your Missing Ingredients

For most small business owners, I find that there's a specific place their marketing has gotten stuck. Perhaps they are struggling with filling their pipeline with qualified prospects, or maybe follow-up is a challenge, or they're having trouble closing sales. Once I've helped my clients choose what activities they want to use to market themselves, we examine what might be holding them back.

If a client is stuck on follow-up, for example, I'll ask "Why can't you follow up?" or "Why aren't you following up?" The answer to this simple question almost always uncovers a missing ingredient in my clients' marketing. Perhaps they aren't following up on leads because they don't know what to put in a sales letter. Or maybe their inconsistent follow-up is because they don't have an organized contact management system.

Once you can identify what your missing ingredients are, it's relatively easy to create them. All you need is a good recipe. So I provide my clients with a set of standard recipes for some of the most common marketing ingredients, tools like business cards, a thirty-second commercial, or a telemarketing script. With a step-by-step recipe like this, most of my clients are able to create these tools themselves with very little hands-on help from me.

Just as with choosing marketing strategies, we keep things really simple in the recipe. I ask my clients to choose no more than three missing ingredients to work on at any one time. Instead of being overwhelmed by all the possible marketing tools they *could* create, they narrow their focus to just the essential tools they *should* create to get their marketing "unstuck." By adding these tools to the marketing activities they already chose, they have a complete and powerful system.

Erin Ferree took my advice, literally, about using marketing recipes. Erin is a graphic and web designer in Belmont, California. "A missing piece in my marketing," Erin remembers, "was an easy, consistent way to fill my pipeline. When I first started marketing, I was pretty uncomfortable with it. But I've always been passionate about cooking. It was easier for me to talk to people about cooking than about design. So I decided to create recipe postcards to help me promote my business, Elf Design."

Here's what Erin did: "Four times a year, I wrote a fabulous new recipe like mango chicken stir-fry, artichoke and endame pasta, or apple cider bread pudding. I illustrated the ingredients, designed the postcards, thought up some clever copy for the back of the card to tie in my design services, and sent them out. Instead of me struggling to build a prospect list, people started asking to be on it! I ended up with one thousand people on my mailing list."

As brilliant as this idea was, Erin is quick to point out that it wasn't creating the postcards alone that got her marketing unstuck. "What I learned from C.J. was that the secret to successful marketing wasn't just about the tools I was using. It was the consistency and discipline to do a bit every day, even when I'm busy with a full book of clients."

Erin combined her postcard mailings with a few simple marketing activities that she could do consistently, such as writing articles, publishing a newsletter, and adding useful content to her Web site. As a result, she says: "I've raised my rates by 200 percent since I started using C.J.'s system, grown my revenue by 500 percent over the last four years, and I have all the clients I want coming in. I even get to turn away clients who aren't the best fit."

One Size Does Not Fit All

Notice how different Erin Ferree's approach is from Colin Campbell's. Colin spends most of his time networking and talking to people, while Erin focuses more on writing and publishing to attract prospects and stay in touch with them over time. And yet each of them has found success by choosing just a few simple things to do over and over.

The reason this approach works so well is that the activities they are doing are ones they themselves chose. Too many people sabotage their marketing by trying to use someone else's plan. But the kind of marketing that works for a real estate agent may be completely off target for a management consultant. And while an outgoing personality might thrive on a plan filled with networking mixers and speaking engagements, that could be a disaster for someone less extroverted.

Instead of trying to locate that one miraculous solution that works in every situation, it's much more effective to find a handful of ways to market that fit both your personality and the business you're in, then make a simple plan using what's right in front of you.

Terri Abraham, a licensed professional counselor in Marietta, Georgia, notes: "In my profession, I can't cold call. Since I don't market directly to clients, I have to focus my marketing plan on building referrals."

Terri used my system to design a plan that combines getting to know possible referral sources with building credibility in her community. She meets with other professionals to establish referral partnerships, writes articles, and volunteers for professional organizations and charitable groups. Terri adds, "I also send follow-up letters on a quarterly basis to therapists and psychiatrists who are working with my clients. It's both a 'best practices' effort and a marketing effort at the same time."

Having a simple list of activities that she chose herself, Terri says, "takes a load of pressure off me. I plan to do a few things consistently and I don't have to be the best at them. I'm not a great marketer and I detest the notion of selling myself. So now, I just go out and meet people, tell them about a service they may like to offer their clients and move on. I don't have to have the greatest pitch, the funniest story, the best-dress-for-success wardrobe, or any of that. I just have to be me, doing what I do and getting to know people."

For someone who believes she's not a great marketer, Terri has produced some substantial results: "When I began using C.J.'s system, I was averaging only six clients a week. At the end of the first twenty-eight days, I was seeing a minimum of thirteen clients per week. Now my client schedule is just about full."

To Get Started, You May Need to Stop

When I first start working with a new client, I always include the following quote from Winnie-the-Pooh author A.A. Milne in my welcome packet: "Here is Edward Bear coming downstairs now, bump, bump, bump on the back of his head behind Christopher Robin. It is as far as he knows, the only way of coming down stairs, but sometimes he feels that there really is another way, if only he could stop bumping for a moment and think of it."[1]

If you've been struggling to build your business by doing what feels like a million different things, maybe you need to stop bumping your head for a bit and reconsider. What might be a few simple activities that you could do over and over?

---

1 A.A. Milne. *The House at Pooh Corner (Pooh Original Edition)*. Illus. Ernest H. Shepard. New York: Puffin Books, 1992.

Here's the approach that has worked so well for my clients in four easy steps:

1. Choose just three or four marketing strategies to use at any one time. Make them active, personal, and credibility-boosting, instead of passive, impersonal, or aimed only at visibility.

2. Identify where your marketing may have gotten stuck, and what missing ingredients might make it start flowing again. Choose no more than three ingredients to work on creating over the next month.

3. Make a list of ten marketing activities, employing your chosen strategies, that you can do repeatedly for the next twenty-eight days. Be sure they fit the type of business you are in and your own personality.

4. List your three ingredients and ten activities on one page. Every day, look at your list and decide which items need your attention that day. Check off your progress as you go.

Guerrillas don't need silver bullets. All we really need is a simple, consistent action plan.

About C.J. Hayden

C.J. Hayden, MCC is a San Francisco business coach, and the author of Get Clients Now! A 28-Day Marketing Program for Professionals, Consultants, and Coaches. *Over 50,000 people have used her simple system to attract all the clients they'll ever need. C.J. works with clients one-on-one, and leads workshops and teleclasses internationally. Her favorite clients are people with business ideas that just might change the world. Find out more about C.J. at* **www.GetClientsNow.com**.

CHAPTER 5

KNOWLEDGE AND FOCUS

Guerrillas Don't Leave Home Without Them

Mary Eule Scarborough

"I couldn't wait for success, so I went ahead without it."
~Jonathan Winters

I'm a fortunate person indeed. In addition to being blessed with good health, great friends, supportive family members, and financial security, I have also enjoyed a well-rounded career in my chosen field, marketing. Over the past twenty-five-plus years, I have studied the subject copiously (in and out of the classroom); ran marketing departments for medium sized businesses; developed marketing strategies for Fortune 500 companies, and owned and operated two small businesses of my own. As you might expect, my experiences, observations, decisions, and results varied widely.

Along the way, I've made every marketing mistake at least twice, and as a result, endured more than my share of crushing disappointments. I have been handed my walking papers (both literally and figuratively) many times throughout my career and made decisions that turned out to be complete disasters for all concerned—except ironically for me.

You see, when I was a young woman I promised myself that I would become a "success," even though I had no idea how a successful person lived or how I would go about becoming one. But once it stirred inside of me, I couldn't shake the secret pact I made with myself and set about studying how other people achieved their dreams. That's when I discovered that "failure" was part-and-parcel of "achievement." In other words, I came to understand that I would never achieve anything noteworthy, unless I was willing to experience overwhelming disappointments. And while I accepted this at a rational level, I worried that I wouldn't have the wherewithal to transform one into the other when the time came.

But as they say, when the student is ready, the teacher appears. Then after spending years in the trenches and tens of thousands of dollars on a master's degree in marketing, I read my first Guerrilla Marketing book and was amazed by the impact that Jay Conrad Levinson's solid and well-thought-out tenets had on my awareness. I had finally been handed a road map—one that would allow me to face my inadequacies head on and exchange my "wing it" attitude and cluttered psyche for *knowledge and focus.*

Since then, I approach every situation, professionally and personally, confident that my belief and adherence to these two fundamental Guerrilla tenets means that I can compete (and win!) on a level playing field with anyone—even "the big guys."

I learned the hard way, but you don't have to. My story begins like millions of other entrepreneurs who turn their passions, also known as hobbies, into a business. I was a freelance editor working from home; I had recently received my bachelor's degree in English/Journalism from the University of Maryland. I was thankful for modest income I earned and, more importantly, that my job allowed me to work and stay at home with my two rowdy toddlers, Graham and Zach. However, I quickly learned that my entire family would starve to death if we had to live off my salary.

During that same time my boys and I decided to try our hand at making bread dough Christmas ornaments for our tree. I grew to love our whimsical creations and found myself spending more time at the kitchen table than at the editing desk. That year, I made so many ornaments that everyone on our Christmas list—and then some—had more than enough bread dough orna- ments to last their lifetime. Apparently, they were a big hit because before I knew it, I was getting requests from friends of friends, distant relatives and colleagues for more. They were even willing to pay me! Over time, I bolstered up the nerve to enter a local crafts fair to see if total strangers would hand over their hard-earned money to purchase one of my gems.

I'll never forget that first one! I took home $81 and thought I'd hit pay dirt. My huge success spurred me onward, and I continued to make and sell my decorations in the same manner over the next couple of years.

One day, unexpectedly, a lovely woman stopped by my display. After intro- ducing herself as a gift buyer from department store, Lord and Taylor's, in New York City, she asked me if I'd be interested in visiting her in "The Big Apple." She expressed a desire to purchase my ornaments for her stores and said she would also like to introduce me to one her colleagues, the president of a national giftware wholesaling company. I made that trip to New York and it turned out to be one of the most lucrative journeys of my life. Not only did I sell my ornaments to Lord and Taylor's (that year and many to follow) but I also signed a contract for representation with a Fifth-Avenue agent!

As a result of their stellar reputation and impressive showrooms in six major cities, my small ornament line was exposed to thousands of gift buyers across America. In less than two years, prestigious retailers like Spiegel Catalog, Macy's, I. Magnin's, and Abbey Press were carrying all or part of my ornament line. My little, accidental business was finally growing.

And imagine how excited I was when, in 1978, I received a request from The White House to create ornaments for the First Family's Christmas tree, not to mention a personal invitation from Rosalyn Carter for my whole family—rowdy boys and all—to attend DC's annual tree lighting ceremony from their balcony. "Yippee," I thought. "I've finally made it." Nothing could stop me now.

Over the next four years my sales continued to increase steadily. Despite my lack of planning I kept up with the orders. I still made and varnished every single ornament; packed and sent every box; wrote every invoice; and personally attended every trade show. I worked many days well into the wee hours of the morning and still managed to function. And at the end of the month, I paid my bills and had money left over in my checking account.

I was certain that I had figured out the business/marketing strategies secrets that meant I could have it all—a booming business and time with my kids! That's why I was not the least bit daunted when I could no longer keep up with the demand myself. "This is a good problem and simple enough to fix," I told myself. So without further thought, or planning, I snapped into action! I hired and trained five part-time employees, comfortable knowing that I'd make even more money with more business.

But things changed overnight. I had accurately predicted the increase in volume but my failure to consider, let alone develop, a growth plan made it impossible for me to perform at the next level. Yes, I was making more money than I ever had, but keeping far less. I was no longer the energized entrepreneur. Instead I was consumed with the day-to-day fires and working hard just to keep my head above water.

My checkbook was no longer my friend. I soon experienced constant back and shoulder pain from stress. It was aggravated by hiring even more personnel; moving the business to a larger location; experiencing the birth of my daughter; and slogging through the increased financial pressures associated with employee benefits. I'd wake up in the middle of the night worrying about how I was going to pay someone or why someone wasn't paying me. Additionally, it seemed like I could never get my work done because I was continually interrupted throughout the day with seemingly trivial employee issues! I rarely made it through a family get-together without getting called about the latest crisis; I was afraid to go anywhere and angry that I couldn't!

So what did I do? *I arrived earlier and stayed later.* Now as I look back through my rearview mirror, it's clear that my lifestyle was miserable and my business was spinning out of control! It was running me and no amount of extra hours could fix it. I kept doing and doing and doing, and like a captainless ship floating aimlessly in the ocean, I was not going to find a safe harbor.

I needed help and as I said earlier: "when the student is ready, the teacher appears." It's a wonderfully simple and kind assertion of a great truth. It recognizes that we continue to learn the hard way until we experience a significant event that serves as a catalyst for change. Often described as an epiphany, we suddenly open our minds to the possibility of change.

Mine was all too common. Returning to work after a much-needed family vacation I was greeted by the usual "you've-been-gone-and-we-didn't-know-what-to-do" chaos, three angry customers, and four late or no-show employees. I was in the midst of dealing with these when my mother called to tell me that my father was dying. An oncologist had just confirmed that he was suffering from liver cancer and probably had less than three months to live. My dad was a strong, vital, athletic man who was seldom sick, so in addition to feeling profoundly sad, I was also shocked.

Newly retired after a long and stressful career, he and my mom had already planned a two-month European vacation. They had both worked hard and saved so one day they could enjoy the fruits of their labor. But in what seemed like an instant, it was taken away. I have never been angrier or sadder before or since that day, even though that one terrifying phone call changed my life in many positive ways. That was the moment when it all became crystal clear. Life was so precious and way too short! And here I was twelve years into my business, up to my ears in debt and little time to enjoy my family.

I was pretty darn good at creating bread dough ornaments, but I was clueless about what it took to run a successful bread dough ornament business. My good instincts had served me well as a solopreneur, but my lack of marketing skills and knowledge were preventing me from growing my business profitably. I was operating by the seat of my pants and my dreams had turned into nightmares. Instead of spending time with my parents, I had worked harder and longer, and now time was running out.

Accepting that I did not have the emotional or physical wherewithal to make meaningful changes, I sold my business and walked away with barely enough cash to pay off my debts and take a couple of months off. I never looked back.

During the following months, I spent many bittersweet days with my dad and the rest of my family, and for the first time in twelve years, reflected on my life's journey so far. I was grateful for my many blessings; proud of my strong work ethic and hard earned accomplishments; and committed to redefining and achieving my goals.

I had two choices: continue doing things the same way and suffer the same results, or change. Gratefully, I chose the latter and applied to graduate school at The Johns Hopkins University, where four years later I earned my master's degree in marketing. As you might imagine, I learned a great deal about the world of business and marketing and was introduced to hundreds of theories and concepts, business philosophers, and marketing gurus—all of whom helped to expand my knowledge base. But I remained most impressed by Levinson's keen insights and unique perspectives and allowed Guerrilla Marketing tenets to guide me through the rest of my career.

I was particularly intrigued by his assertion that excellent marketing had less to do with a fat wallet and more to do with knowledge, attitude and drive. "Is this true," I wondered, "or just another altruistic notion?" I logically assumed that large corporations used their deep pockets to hire the best marketing and advertising minds in the world, and what made me think I could compete at that level?! I was about to find out.

In the early '90s I accepted a full-time, strategic marketing position with a well-known Fortune 500 telecommunications company. Sure that my learned colleagues would teach me a thing or two about marketing "the right way," I was understandably excited to be working for this business giant.

About an hour into my new job my boss, Mac, handed each of us (me and my four colleagues) a direct mail brochure and envelope. He told us that something was wrong with the mailer and challenged us to discover exactly what that was before 4:00 p.m. that afternoon.

As I began reading the material, I became increasingly nervous. I was staring at a magnificent four-color, bi-fold, high quality direct response sales letter—replete with original watercolor artwork. Additionally, it was extremely well written; the company's copywriters had done a masterful job of educating small business owners on the many benefits they, and their customers, would receive after purchasing a toll-free number. I had never seen a more compelling sales letter.

However, I soon breathed a sigh of relief because I found "the problem" in the very last sentence. It read: "If you'd like more information or would like to sign up for your own toll-free number, call our customer-service department at the telephone number located at the bottom of your monthly bill."

That's why I strode confidently into the conference room later that day. After a few preliminaries, Mac asked who had uncovered the error in the direct mail piece. In an effort to establish my foothold, I raised my hand like an overly eager nerd at a science fair and declared, "I do, I do, I do!" (At least that's the way I remember it.) Mac graciously called on me and I confidently replied,

> Well, it was really all too obvious, if you ask me. Here we have this really beautiful—and pricey—piece that goes on and on about the benefits of toll-free numbers and then, once we've convincingly persuaded our readers to purchase one, there's no 800 number for them to call! And that's just the half of it! Not only are we not acting like we preach, but we're forcing our customers to go digging around for their phone bill just so they can call us! And we're the phone company! How crazy is that?!

The phrase, "crawl-in-a-hole humiliation" is a weak description of what I felt as this scene progressed. My boss and four peers were stunned into embarrassed silence and instantly cast their staring gazes downward at their suddenly fascinating notebooks. Ultimately Mac screwed up his nerve and looked at me with what can only be described as a combination of pity and disgust. Then he quietly said, "Thanks for trying, but that's the wrong answer. Judy, can you help Mary out with this one?" She complied and offered the correct answer, "The problem with this piece is that the envelope is a bit too large for the brochure so it doesn't fit as snugly as it should."

My jaw dropped in disbelief and my red face vanished. And although I didn't have the guts to argue the point that day, I knew they had missed the mark. In spite of their advanced degrees and years of experience; they had lost their customer focus. This same scene (albeit different times, places and details) repeated itself over and over again during my corporate career and reinforced this key learning: The "big boys" are just as skilled at "talking the talk" without "walking the walk" as the rest of us! Deep pockets and unlimited resources have little to do with superior marketing.

I worked for this corporation for almost ten years and left to work with multiple companies as an independent marketing consultant (in addition to co-founding a new CLEC (Competitive Local Exchange Carrier) in Maryland). Fortunately, my reputation as an industrious marketing expert preceded me, and I found it relatively easy to stay busy. For the most part, I am asked to help companies solve a particular problem, one that is thwarting their efforts to increase sales, profits, market share, or revenues.

Most of the time, company executives feel that marketing problem's root cause is tactical such as poorly written ad copy, incompetent salespeople, or poorly trained customer care representatives. Regardless of the particulars, they always want it fixed right away. They count on me for "the secrets"— those enchanting tricks, slogans, gimmicks and words that will put an end to their dilemma. Little do they know that I am not a magician and unless they are willing to focus their efforts on improving their prospects' and customers' experiences, no amount of advertising is going to help them.

Not long ago, I was hired to help a medium-sized telecom reduce their tremendously high call center "abandon" rates (callers who hang up before they're connected to a sales representative). They were conducting a direct mail campaign that invited prospects to dial their toll-free number to learn more, or sign up for local and/or long distance phone service. And although they were pleased with the overall response rate (i.e. the total calls into the center) 12 percent of the callers hung up before speaking with anyone and another 5 percent hung up just after being connected to a consultant! Since this situation was seriously affecting their sales rates, they were desperate for a solution.

During our initial meeting, company executives said they were convinced of one thing... the sales letter copy was a key component of the root cause. They suggested that interested prospects called their center and, while on-hold waiting to speak to a representative, reread the letter and found it lacking, so hung up. They wanted me to rewrite the offending copy to alleviate the problem—either that or retrain their sales consultants.

However, after many years of experience and Guerrilla Marketing training, I knew it was rarely that simple. Additionally, I was curious because I hadn't heard anyone mention their customers' experiences. So I decided to start there and placed a call into their center, just as one of their prospects might.

My call was answered by a VRU (voice response unit) whose "robot man" instructed me to enter my personal information twenty-two times before I was given the option of being placed on-hold to wait for one of their human representatives! Even worse, after remaining on hold for more than five minutes the consultant who answered the phone asked me to repeat some of the information, such as my phone number and zip code, that I had already entered into their system. No wonder people were hanging up!

The fix was relatively simple. We altered the call flow and scripting so that callers were quickly directed to a live representative after two or three prompts. What's more, the "fix" was already contained within their system; they just weren't using it! This seemingly small solution resulted in a 35 percent decrease in abandoned calls, a 25 percent increase in sales, and hundreds of thousands of dollars in additional revenues in less than one week.

So why didn't these very intelligent people figure this out themselves? Once again, they lost focus on what marketing really means and chose instead to concentrate on tactics. They forgot that superior marketing requires a dogged commitment to delivering on the promised customer experience 100 percent of the time. No excuses. No fine print. No maybes. If you're going to tell people how wonderful you are, make sure you're wonderful.

Jay Conrad Levinson sums it up this way:

> Marketing is everything you do to promote your business, from the moment you conceive of it, to the point at which customers buy your product or service and begin to patronize your business on a regular basis. The key words to remember are everything and regular basis.

The meaning is clear: Marketing includes the name of your business, the determination of whether you will be selling a product or service, the method of manufacture or servicing, the colors, size, and shape of your product, the packaging, the location of your business, the advertising, the public relations, the sales training, the sales presentation, the telephone inquiries, the problem solving, the growth plan, the referral plan and the follow-up. If you gather from this that marketing is a complex process, you're right.

See marketing as a circle that starts with your idea for generating revenue and completes itself when you have the blessed patronage of repeat and referral business.

Oh, and by the way, the next time I founded a business—a competitive long distance company (CLEC) —my partners and I took $400,000 worth of seed money and transformed it into $24 million in revenues in less than three years. The difference? Knowledge and Focus.

About Mary Eule Scarborough

Mary Eule Scarborough is an award-winning speaker, writer, and certified Guerrilla marketing coach who weaves humor throughout her practical, plain-speaking advice. She draws upon her real-life experiences as a Fortune 500 marketing executive; founder of two successful small businesses; and independent strategic marketing consultant to aid companies, organizations, and non-profits both nationally and internationally. She and her husband, David, are the authors of "The Procrastinator's Guide to Marketing" (November, 2007, Entrepreneur Press, Irvine, CA). Additionally, Ms. Scarborough recently co-authored (along with Mitch Meyerson, the founder of the Guerrilla Marketing Coaching Certification Program) the soon-to-be-published book, "Mastering Online Marketing" (January, 2008) and is currently working on another book, "Guerrilla Marketing on the Internet" (September, 2008) with the founder of Guerrilla Marketing, Jay Conrad Levinson and Mitch Meyerson.

*She continues to write marketing articles for many online publications and the company's own Web sites: **www.StrategicMarketingAdvisors.com** and **www.TheProcrastinatorsGuideToMarketing.com**.*

CHAPTER 6

THE SMALL FISH SWALLOWS THE BIG FISH
Using your Guerrilla Weapons Wisely

William Reed

> *"Study strategy over the years and achieve the spirit of the warrior. Today is victory over yourself of yesterday; tomorrow is your victory over lesser men."*
> ~Miyamoto Musashi

We are all born into the world as small fish. The dream, the challenge, and the mission are to survive and thrive without ending up as a small fry. Guerrilla Marketing is a way of meeting that challenge as a *spirited* entrepreneur.

As a boy of eleven, I set out on a path to survive and thrive through the martial art of Aikido. This led to a career as a martial artist and entrepreneur living in Japan. Meeting Jay Conrad Levinson and his book *The Way of the Guerrilla* led me to discover how to apply the principles of the martial arts to business. This chapter will help you think like a martial artist when you plan your marketing strategy, select your marketing weapons, or train yourself to develop the attitudes and competencies of a Guerrilla Marketer.

Competitive Climate Change

Just as global warming took the world by surprise, there is a dawning recognition that there are also changes in our competitive climate that will have a sweeping impact on the way we do business.

Social, technical, and lifestyle changes have created so many options and demands on our attention that we live increasingly in an attention-deficit economy. It is as if we started with just a few stars in the sky, and now there are too many to name or count. This is a far cry from the eighteenth-century world of Ralph Waldo Emerson when you could build a better mousetrap and the world will beat a path to your door.

Consider some of the aspects of modern marketing and what impact this might have on your business or career. There's an old marketing joke that goes, "I know half of the money I spend on advertising is wasted—the trouble is I don't know which half!" The joke isn't as funny as it used to be because it rings more true today than ever before.

According to research commissioned by the Empire Research Group, the cost of selling has tripled over the past decade. It now takes 8.4 attempts for a sales representative to get in front of a prospect, whereas ten years ago it took only four tries. That means that salespeople have to work three times as hard to achieve half the results that they once did.

In 1992, a major motion picture company spent $5 million on average to promote a feature film. As of 2001, they were spending $15 million to get the same effect, triple the cost for the same results! Furthermore, the old ways of promotion are not only less effective but increasingly costly and time consuming.

One reason is the clutter factor. In 1996 the average consumer received three thousand messages a day. By 2007 the average consumer was being inundated by thirty thousand messages per day, a tenfold increase in eleven years! How many of these messages that flood your mind do you remember or act on?

The proliferation of media is one reason for the increase in messages. Network television used to dominate our screens with a few major TV stations. Cable boosted that number to the thousands, and the Internet made the number of stations uncountable. If you don't like the ad-filled radio stations in your area and the DJs who talk during the song to fill up more space, iTunes offers you over one thousand Internet radio stations with twenty-five genres to choose from. It is very easy today to change the channel and shut out a marketing message.

Moreoever, the attention-deficit economy has spawned products and services that both contribute to and have been created for shrinking attention spans. YouTube, one of the latest crazes on the Internet, is simply nothing more than a forum for short video clips—ten minutes or less—on any subject you care to post. It's what you want and when you want, from the comfort of your own chair. With Digital Video Recording, you no longer need to watch TV programs or commercials when they are broadcast. The iPhone is an example of a multiple communication device all in one place and completely mobile. Consumers are opting for anti-clutter technology, and that means that your message may not have a prayer of getting through. The captive audience may be a thing of the past.

Make no mistake, Internet surfing has gotten serious. Consumers are less willing to be spoon fed and increasingly more educated through their own product research. A study conducted by Pew Internet & American Life Project revealed that even by 2005, 78 percent of adult Internet users spent time online researching products and services, 72 percent read news online, 55 percent looked up do-it-yourself information, 24 percent bid in online auctions, and 17 percent shared information in chat rooms. Internet usage has a direct correlation to household income, but it is consistent across gender and racial segments. Can any advertisement compete with that?

At the same time, Direct Mail is alive and well. The U.S. Postal Service surveyed clients and found that 76 percent prefer contact by mail, 90 percent collect mail every day, 80 percent actively engage with their mail daily, and 73 percent actually read their direct mail. It is no wonder that, as MarketingSperpa reports, spending on direct postal mail advertising far exceeds any other offline advertising medium. Apparently, excessive e-mail and phone calls are driving consumers back to traditional tried-and-true advertising.

As a marketer, should you move toward online promotion or traditional print media like direct mail? When the data supports conflicting trends, it is hard to know what is fact and what is fiction.

According to Empire Research, the average professional ad, marketing, or sales campaign takes twelve to eighteen months to develop, and an additional twelve to eighteen months for a good program to show significant results. By traditional methods, that is three years or more to payoff on your marketing expenses, if at all!

If investments in marketing are less likely to produce returns, and if marketing messages are more likely to be lost in clutter or caught in one filter or another, and consumers are increasingly educated about products and services, then marketers have got to take a radically different approach.

A New Paradigm for Marketing Weapons?

Often getting noticed is simply a matter of offering something that a person wants or is interested in. An entomologist walking with a friend in a noisy section of New York repeatedly pointed out insects that he heard nearby. "How," asked the friend, "could he hear such a small sound in all that noise?" The entomologist took a coin out of his pocket and dropped it on the sidewalk. All of the passersby turned around to look. "People notice," he said, "what they are interested in."

In his book *Jump Start Your Business Brain*, Doug Hall cites research on nine hundred products over a five-year period, with participation from companies including Johnson & Johnson, Proctor & Gamble, Ford Motor Company, and American Express, which revealed that products with a clear Unique Selling Proposition had a success rate or 47 percent, while products without one had a success rate of only 23 percent, which is lower than the probability of winning at some gambling games! Combine that with U.S. Census data that reports that 75 percent of new businesses, products, or services fail within the first two to five years, and you have a scary picture of traditional marketing success.

However, if the implementation of just one marketing weapon can practically double a product's success rate as this study suggests, what might happen if you assembled a strategic combination of low-cost Guerrilla Marketing weapons?

Guerrilla Marketing offers a list of at least one hundred marketing weapons, over half of which are free, except for your investment in time, energy, imagination, and knowledge. That is a very good beginning. The problem is that knowing about marketing weapons is one thing, using them skillfully is another. However, it is not enough to simply add more weapons to your arsenal. You have to learn how to use them, and how to combine them in effective ways.

A marketing weapon is like a double-edged sword. It can cut both ways. A marketing campaign can backfire if you are not prepared to follow up with quality products and services. Bad news spreads faster than wildfire on the Internet. In February of 2007, a badly conceived effort by a New York Marketing company hired by the Turner Broadcasting System, Inc. ended disastrously. In an effort to draw attention to a Cartoon Network character, they posted electronic light boards around the city of Boston, featuring a moon man ominously thrusting his middle finger. These were mistaken for a bomb scare, and the fiasco led to arrests, $2 million in fines for the company, and resignation of the General Manager. Though the media reported this as an example of Guerrilla Marketing backfiring, it was not Guerrilla Marketing so much as bad judgment. It did illustrate that weapons in the wrong hands can be dangerous to the user.

Mistakes in information, quality defects, and failure to deliver on promises can earn a company more headaches than money. In what has been called the greatest marketing mistake ever, the soft drink giant, Pepsi, in 1992 conducted an ad campaign in the Philippines offering the one million pesos (about $40,000) to the holder of a bottle cap specially marked with the number 349. Unfortunately, by mistake 800,000 caps were printed with that number, causing more than 486,000 claimants to appear expecting their reward. Riots ensued when the company announced it was an error. The offer to compensate each "winner" with the equivalent of $20 in pesos did little to quell the anger, and the company was deluged with criminal and legal claims.

Good marketing can never make up for bad management or poor customer service. Publicity stunts do not build loyalty or trust, and they can carry enormous risks when damage is done. Marketing needs a new paradigm, for its greatest challenge now is to still be noticed and remembered by prospects, but for the right reasons.

Thinking Like a Martial Artist

In martial arts training, you learn how to use proper weapons. Such is the case with marketing. Not only must you handle marketing weapons with care, you must select the proper weapons for you, and use them skillfully.

In the martial arts, skill is developed through repeated practice of master patterns known as *kata*. In Guerrilla Marketing, this would be exercises that help you think and act like a Guerrilla. To use these exercises effectively, it is important to understand the learning process that takes place in the practice of *kata*.

In the martial arts, you learn in layers, and strengthen the layers through repetition of correct patterns of movement. Beginners start with superficial *knowledge*, where you might *recognize* a technique or know its name, but you cannot perform it well or consistently. If you have excellent models to learn from and a good teacher, then you progress gradually to the level of *wisdom*, whereby you *understand* the technique, perhaps well enough to teach it to others. If you continue to develop yourself and your technique, then you progress toward *universal mind*, whereby the technique *flows* naturally and appropriately to the circumstances. The deeper the level of learning, the more you are able to actually use it in your life.

An English translation of Miyamoto Musashi's *Book of Five Rings* was a national bestseller, selling over 1 million copies. It is a perennial bestseller in Japan, of course, and used as a reference for business strategy and personal development. It was touted at the time by the Overlook Press as Japan's answer to the Harvard MBA. What sort of lessons do business people draw today from this classic treatise of swordsmanship written in 1645 by one of Japan's greatest Masters of the art?

What lessons can we learn from Musashi? The key is to read metaphorically, and consider how its lessons might apply to you. The *Book of Five Rings*, contains books on Ground, Water, Fire, Wind, and Void, covering everything from strategy and psychology, to footwork and technique. Musashi's lessons have surprising durability. In the "Book of Fire," he offers practical lessons on how to use the sword—one of which is a reminder that holding a sword is no guarantee of victory—and that victory can also be won without a sword. Metaphorically, the sword can be compared to money, and its use to the employment of marketing weapons. We have already seen how throwing money into marketing is no guarantee of getting returns. In Guerrilla Marketing, before you spend money on marketing you invest time, energy, imagination, and knowledge.

In the first ring, Ground, Musashi says that it is difficult to realize the true Way just through the sword. He advises to study other ways and other weapons for the lessons they give, "to know the smallest things and the biggest things, the shallowest things and the deepest things." Though Musashi was a master swordsman, he was also a master painter, calligrapher, poet, and practiced the tea ceremony. He was a renaissance-style warrior, with depth and breadth which he said was a condition for mastery. In Guerrilla Marketing it is not enough to master web design or some other marketing technique. To understand people, to gain their trust and loyalty, you need to reach far and wide.

Musashi writes that if you master strategy, you will never lose even up against twenty or thirty opponents. In this, he was not speaking metaphorically, as he was undefeated in over sixty battles in a staggering variety of circumstances. He spoke of being able to freely control your body, winning with your eye, and conquering with your spirit. These are not the words of a man caught up in the technique of a particular weapon. Guerrillas must also master themselves, and the art of combining marketing weapons to maximum effect.

In the ring on Water, Musashi writes that in both fighting and everyday life the spirit should be determined but calm. Successful people do not move or speak in a hurried manner. There is a difference between being busy and appearing busy. A truly busy person accomplishes a great deal, but does not lose composure. A person who complains about being busy accomplishes surprisingly little for all of the fuss. Guerrillas are busy because they know how much can be done to improve themselves and their marketing. But they don't sacrifice themselves on the altar of success for the sake of their work. A balanced life with time for health, family, learning, and leisure is part of the Guerrilla's definition of success.

Sun Tzu's *The Art of War* is another classic in the martial arts literature. Though it was written in the sixth century BC, it has long been praised as a definitive work on strategy and tactics. It also contains many secrets for managing your mind and your marketing. It has been broadly applied by modern military and business strategists in many cultures.

Sun Tzu writes of the importance of clear and distinct instructions, saying that the worst calamities that befall an army arise from hesitation. How much clarity do you have in your own marketing instructions when you speak to your web designer or marketing manager? Guerrillas should be able to talk from a simple and clear marketing strategy, written in seven sentences on a single page, stating your purpose, target market, niche, competitive benefits, identity, weapons, and budget.

Sun Tzu tells us that the sovereign's function is to give broad instructions, but the decisions in battle should be up to the general. This means that the people at the front lines should be empowered to make decisions without having to clear everything first with the head office. Companies in service industries from airlines to hotels are realizing the wisdom of this by empowering front line employees to spend money and resources to solve customer problems without having to get permission for every request. This could be taken to a higher level still if front line employees were given basic training in Guerrilla Marketing, rather than leaving marketing issues to the marketing department. In customer service, Guerrilla Marketing really does happen at the front lines.

Sun Tzu finally makes us understand that to see the sun and moon is no sign of sharp sight, and to hear the noise of thunder is no sign of a quick ear. For real intelligence and sharp perception, you need to go beyond surface appearances and established practices. In Guerrilla Marketing this is done by developing your marketing intelligence.

The Small Fish Prevails

To survive and thrive in the face of superior strength. This is ultimately the lesson of the martial arts and the meaning behind the Zen proverb, "The small fish swallows the big fish."

Though it makes no logical sense, in the Zen spirit, it points to a meaning beyond itself. These simple words remind us that by shifting our thinking to a new dimension we can become spirited enough to win. It reminds us that we need to come back again and again until we find a way that works. Perseverance brings power.

Bring this spirit to your study and application of Guerrilla Marketing, and it will lift you to a new level.

About William Reed

William Reed is a Master Trainer in Guerrilla Marketing, based in Tokyo, Japan. He also has a seventh-degree black belt in Aikido, and a professional teacher's license in brush calligraphy. He first went to Japan in 1972, where his career for several decades has included work as a translator, journalist, and trade association represen-tative. He is fluent in Japanese, and a bestselling author in Japan on Guerrilla Marketing, business creativity, and Japanese culture. As an author, speaker, and a bilingual business artist, he combines the very best of East and West.

NOTE: *William Reed has produced a work of brush calligraphy the character for fish, which readers can access and download for free as a jpeg file, as a reminder to awaken the spirit of "The Small Fish Swallows the Big Fish." Visit the author's Web site at* **http://www.agili.jp** *for further information.*

CHAPTER 7

GUERRILLA RELATIONSHIPS

Laying the Foundation for Success

David L. Hancock

> *"The most important ingredient we put into any relationship is not what we say or what we do, but what we are."*
>
> ~Stephen R. Covey

As Guerrilla Marketers, we're well aware that the better relationship we have with our clients, the more successful we are. In fact, it's a proven statistic: it costs you six times more to sell something to a prospect than to sell that same thing to a customer.

Relationships are a cornerstone of Guerrilla Marketing because people like doing business with other people. The best way to capitalize on that is by aggressively pursuing and constantly maintaining relationships with every person who has anything to do with your business.

Marketing is absolutely every bit of contact any part of your business has with any segment of the public. Guerrillas view marketing as a circle. It begins with your ideas for generating revenue and continues on through to the goal of amassing, not large sums of money in profits, but a large number of repeat and referral customers. I know. That's not the conventional way of thinking, but remember, Guerrilla Marketing is all about unconventional strategies, secrets, and tactics for earning conventional goals—those big profits you want to make from your small business.

If you build good, strong relationships, profits will flow into your bank account. I promise. It's what happened in my company, Morgan James Publishing, because it is built in part on this principle: instead of trying to make sales, Guerrillas are dedicated to making relationships because long-term relationships are paramount to a Guerrilla's success. It is the relationships that you make and keep that ensure you'll have customers coming back again and again wanting to buy what you have to offer.

The Anatomy of a Relationship

One of the biggest mistakes business people make when they think about business relationships is that it is one sided. You give your customers everything they need and they'll be happy. It's based on the old adage, "the customer is always right." But would you continue a friendship where you kept giving and giving but never received anything back?

Guerilla relationships are based on a very old idea, the idea of quid pro quo. It's Latin for "something for something." You give your customers something that they need—a great product with stellar customer service or the willingness to go that extra mile for them. The customers in turn need to give something back—their patronage and their recommendations.

This is a true relationship, and to get that kind of response from your customers and clients, Guerrillas understand that *involvement* is key to any relationship. You don't just sell them something once and then let it go at that. You follow up. You make an effort to know what they want and provide it to them. You also show your gratitude for their patronage. People also like to be acknowledged. One antiquarian bookshop I know every once in a while gives a free book to a good customer, one that fits the customer's interest. The book is given with a smile and a big thank you. This makes the customer feel appreciated.

Every good business knows it's not so much the new customers that you rely on. You want to make sure that your existing customers will come back and use you again and again. The benefits of that are obvious.

Throughout this book, you're going to find nuggets of useful information that will help you build lasting relationships with your clients. What I'm going to tell you in the rest of this chapter is a few of the ways in which I used Guerrilla-style relationships to help build Morgan James from a start-up to a $15 million enterprise in four years.

I'm going to delve into some of the ways that Morgan James has built relationships both with its authors and with some key players in the book industry. Books are my business, and I've spent years developing many of the important business relationships that allow us to get our books in bookstores as well as enjoy the widespread Web coverage we've been able to achieve.

From Banking to Books

I'm actually in an interesting position. I'm both the publisher and a contributor to this book. I understand fully what a book can do for your business. I call books "universal passports"; Rick Frishman calls them "ruby slippers" because a book is the thing that gets you through the door at Oz (you'll be reading his chapter shortly). Either way, a book is something magical. It is a way to get your message out to the world and, for us Guerrilla entrepreneurs, it is a way for us to gain instant credibility and build our businesses. With a book, you're automatically perceived as an expert in your field.

Now, I'm not a writer, and I actually got into the publishing business not to help me but to help others like me. I'm a mortgage banker by training, and the story of how I got into the publishing business is instructive. As a broker, I had achieved moderate success, but it was nowhere close to what I knew I could attain. Sound familiar? I had reached a point in my career where I felt I had earned as much money as I could, reached as many people as I could, but I wanted more. I wanted to become a celebrity in my market.

I tried everything. If there was a seminar on sales or marketing I went to it. If there was a home-study course I took it; if there was a book, I bought it. I was taught by Tom Hopkins, Todd Duncan, Stephen R. Covey, Bill Bacharach, Tony Robbins, Zig Zigler. You name them, I studied them. Everything worked, but nothing worked. I was able to streamline a few things. I hired a couple of assistants, manage my time a little better, earned a little more money, worked a few less hours. I definitely got the right mindset, but I found myself still working harder and harder, putting in long hours at the office away from my bride.

Nothing made a real difference until I discovered *Guerrilla Marketing, 3rd edition.* I was blown away by the concepts. I immersed myself in Guerrilla Marketing. Jay Levinson said if I want to become a celebrity in my market, to charge more and negaotiate less with my clients, I need to have credibility. And the fastest way to get credibility is to write a book on your subject of expertise. Ah ha! The reason I was unable to make substantial progress was because I lacked the credibility and posture I needed to "leapfrog" my competition.

I thought, I could do that. After all, I've studied some of the best material available. So that's what I did. I wrote a book on sales and marketing as it related to the mortgage business. I figured the worst thing that could happen is my clients would learn something that could help them earn a little more money, and if they earned more, I'd earn more. (I was on the wholesale side at the time; my clients were the loan officers who helped you get the money to buy your house.)

So I wrote the book and got it published. I didn't realize at the time that it would be such a hard thing to do. It was with a small traditional publisher, and from this experience I learned the traditional publishing process is horrible. It was definitely one of the worst experiences I ever went through. They took my rights; they took control. I didn't even like the way the book looked when it came out, but you know what? It worked! It literally doubled my income in less than eight months! I became that expert. I was able to charge more, negotiate less, and reach more people. It also started magically opening doors for me. I was able to start building strong relationships with the right people. People would call me back that before wouldn't give me the time of day. I got the respect I never had but always wanted. I even got on local media when they needed an expert on the mortgage market. After all, I wrote the book.

You might think I did a ton of PR and marketing to get all that attention and respect. But I didn't do squat. I didn't do tours; I didn't take out ads. I did a press release, and I put my business card in the book and gave it away to everyone I met. The book started selling so well that the publisher wanted me to basically quit my day job to support the book, but I wasn't about to trade in a $200,000-plus-a-year job for a $15,000 royalty check. It just didn't make sense.

What did happen is I realized, "Wow! Jay is right. This Guerrilla Marketing stuff works, especially the part of leveraging a book to grow your day job." I immediately began telling everyone that if you wanted grow your business you needed to have a book. I focused primarily on my clients because after all, if they earned more money, I'd earn more money. Some took my advice and wrote books based on their expertise. They actually got picked up, and beat up, by publishers, yet they exploded their business anyway. Some got self-published with good results, but not at the same level as the others. Most were trying to get their books out, but just got more and more discouraged because they couldn't get published or didn't know exactly how to start. I ended up creating monster.

I had to do something. So my bride and I sat down and decided I should start my own publishing company to help facilatate what I'd been teaching. We named it after our two children so it would have a great sounding name. When I first conceived of a publishing company, I didn't have the aspiration of selling a lot of books. I really was more interested in how a book could help its author. I still am, for that matter. It all came together when I enrolled in Mitch Meyerson's Guerrilla Certified Coaching program. As I learned how to leverage my relationships so that everyone can win, I started to form a plan. What if I really could help others like me in the same way that I was helped? By this point I had published two other books and self-published one all the while asking questions, learning the ins and outs, and most importantly discovering what I didn't like about either route. So I created Morgan

James Publishing—the business plan for the company was my Guerrilla Marketing final as a matter of fact! My first intention was simply to allow authors a vehicle to publish their book so they would have the credibility without all the hassle.

But something interesting happened, something that almost always happens with good relationships. The more we taught our authors to leverage their book and the less we tried to sell them, the more the books sold. The authors who were really using their books to leverage their business sold a lot of books. In terms of a relationship, Morgan James authors were, and still are, holding up their end of the bargain.

In exchange for all that they do for Morgan James, I take care of my authors. I always have and always will. I make them a part of the whole process of publication—from the title and cover design to deciding when the book is going to be released. I give them a ton of resources and tools to help them learn how to market their books effectively. I pay them higher royalties, and they maintain control of the rights to their books. That means that the author can publish the material in the book through other channels or lift it entirely from the company and turn it over to another publisher. I even heartily encourage my authors to take their material and offer it in other media—audio books or video programs for example—and they can either publish it with us or elsewhere. For I know that the more an author is able to use the material in the book, the more books will be sold. It also has the added benefit of that all-important customer loyalty. My authors come back to me when they want their next book published.

So no matter how successful we are, we always rely on Guerrilla Marketing principles and tactics, and we never, ever forget the relationships on which we built this company. In fact Morgan James has trademarked its tag "the Entrepreneurial Publisher" because of its unique collaborative approach with authors and other publishers. What it really comes down to is this: I treat my authors as partners, not as "intellectual property suppliers," and they in turn help me by selling more books.

Relationships Build Alliances

But relationships don't just begin and end with your clients—while they are important, they aren't the only ones with whom you do business. In fact, a major reason for my success is that I built a strong relationship with one of the largest book distribution companies on the planet, the Ingram Book Group.

Because at first we weren't big enough to work with Ingram directly, I started by working with an Ingram-owned printer. I figured that if we were as successful as I knew we could be, Ingram couldn't help but notice us. So I developed a great relationship with the printer and eventually leveraged that relationship to get a meeting with Ingram.

As the whole story unfolded, I realized what a great sense of humor—and timing—God has! By this time Morgan James had only been in existence for three years. We were selling huge amounts of books to the bookstores and on Amazon. It was a nightmare to manage. So out of desparation, and the still evident realization that we didn't yet have what it takes to work directly with Ingram, I started to investigate other distribution options. I identified the top four companies I would be willing to work with, and the very week I began reaching out and leaving messages for numbers four, three, and two distribu- tors, I got a phone call. In fact, I remember it literally being like this—I hang up from leaving a message for the number two distributor, and the phone rings. It is a Senior Vice President of Ingram. He wants to know who I am, what we are doing, and how are selling so many books!

It was a great phone call. We got to know each other a little. I shared my passion and he shared his. We know there had to be a way to work together. So we arranged for me to fly down to Tennessee to meet. He picked me up at the airport, and I couldn't help but notice his car. Now on a side note, I'm a real car guy. I love cars. I love the statement they can make about you and how they can be part of your personality, how they can show your economic status and such. My new VP-friend at Ingram was driving a car I wasn't expecting. Sure it was a nice car, fully loaded, a few years old, a Nissan Maxima. I expected a Senior Vice President of the largest distributor in the nation to be driving something better. But hey, that's just me. I just noted it, and went on chatting.

Throughout the day we did the usual business-meeting things. We toured the printing facilty, the warehouse and distribution facility. We talked about books, markets, and marketing books. We had lunch at a great barbeque restaurant that only locals could find. During the afternoon meetings, we even met with John and David Ingram and had a round-table meeting with several of the other Senior VP's where we talked about Morgan James's unique approach. In fact it was at that meeting that we got our tag. One Senior VP leaned back in his chair and said "Wow, you guys are really 'Entrepreneurial Publishers', aren't you?" Needless to say we ran with that!

My VP friend and I got along well. We knew we were going to work together; all we needed to do was figure out how. When the VP offered to drive me back to the airport, I accepted, knowing that this would be a great opportunity to get to know him even better on a more personal level. Remember, no matter how many dollars you're talking about, they mean nothing in comparison to the ability to really getting to know a person. As we got into his car, he started to apologize for not having a nicer car to drive me around in. He knew I was probably expecting him to have a more upscale car and that he would have rather been driving me around in a luxury sedan or something like it. Now, since I'm a car guy, I pursued this conversation to learn more.

He explained that Ingram has an unwritten company policy about the executives showing their money. In fact one exec was fired a few weeks prior and the only thing that anybody could pin it to was the fact that he recenetly started to arrive to work in a nice Porsche!

We had a great time talking about that and what kind of cars we liked. When I asked him what his dream car was, he said, "a BMW 7 Series." My heart started pounding. I love BMWs. I'm a BMW freak. I know that the best way to really build a solid relationship is to find something in common with the other person. The best friendships are built on common interests, ideas, likes, and dislikes. I actually owned the exact car he wished he had. This was my in, and I knew it. We talked about BMWs all the way to the airport, and I knew exactly how I was going to solidify this relationship.

When I got home, I immediately went to my local BMW dealership and bought him a BMW 745iL exactly the way he described it, silver with gray leather and all. I shipped it to him with a hand-written note saying how much I enjoyed our time together and how I looked forward to working together. I also wrote, "by the way, now you can have a nice car at work!"

Now before you get ahead of yourself here, know I'm not an idiot. I didn't want him to get fired. After all, we just spent all this time building this great relationship, so what I sent him was an actual BMW 1:18 Scale model, precision finished to a showroom-quality look. It was an exact scale-size replica of the BMW 7 Series he wanted, complete with real leather interior!

When he got it, he was blown away! It is still sitting proudly on his desk today. Needless to say, Morgan James formed a partnership with Ingram that is very profitable and gets stronger by the day.

Relationships are about people relating to other people. We help each other, laugh with each other, commiserate over hardships, and celebrate successes. Business relationships are no different. No matter who walks through your door, who calls you on the telephone, remember that and you'll soon have a network of very valuable friends who will help you grow your business and keep your profits soaring.

Building Relationships Everyday

Morgan James was ranked forty-forth on *Fast Company's* 2006 "Fast 50" reader's choice list for our leading creative thinking, significant accomplishments, and because they see us as having a "significant impact over the next ten years." We got there by never forgetting that our business was built on the principle of people helping people. From the way we answer the phones to creating lasting and lucrative partnerships, Guerrilla Marketing works at building good, strong relationships. And, how could it be otherwise? Once you find the thing that works, you do it over and over and over again.

I fully intend to stay constant in my pursuit of positive relationships with people in all facets of the publishing business. I see it as a strategic advantage—

and I hope that you will start building your own mutually beneficial relationships so you, too, can start reaping the profits that will inevitably follow.

About David Hancock

David L. Hancock, founder of Morgan James Publishing company (established, 2003) was named a Finalist in the Best Chairman category in the 2006 American Business Awards. Hailed as "the business world's own Oscars" by the New York Post, The American Business Awards are the only national, all-encompassing business-awards program honoring great performances in the workplace. David has worked hard to revolutionize book publishing from the author's standpoint. His Entrepreneurial Publishing model enriches authors as well as his company.

David is the also the founder of The Entrepreneurial Author University and founder of The Ethan Awards, the only international, all-encompassing entrepreneurial-author awards for business authors. David sits on the advisory board of The Mark Victor Hansen Foundation and on the Executive Board of Habitat for Humanity Peninsula. David has also authored too many books to list here but they include The Entrepreneurial Author, Guerrilla Marketing for Mortgage Brokers, *and* The Secrets of Master Marketing. *David and his wife Susan live in Hampton Roads, Virginia with their two children, Morgan Renee and Ethan James. For more information or to contact David, visit* ***www.MorganJamesPublishing.com.***

PART TWO
Guerrilla Communication

Now that you have a solid understanding of the Guerrilla mindset, it's time to laser focus your message and start getting it out. Every Guerrilla Marketer knows that communication is key to their marketing efforts. This section leads you through the process of crafting your marketing message so that you know how to engage your target market on an emotional level. You want to let your potential customers and clients know that you unquestioningly understand their problem and that you have a clear solution. Be prepared! This section will give your message fire, and the people that you're communicating with will be motivated to take action!

CHAPTER 8

GUERRILLA COPYWRITING TACTICS

How to Master the Greatest Money-Making Skill of All Time—Quickly and Easily

Lorrie Morgan-Ferrero

> *"I have always believed that writing advertisements is the second most profitable form of writing. The first, of course, is ransom notes..."*
>
> ~Philip Dusenberry

Imagine pulling up a Web site on the Internet only to find it completely devoid of words. When was the last time you were inspired to do business with someone after receiving a blank e-mail? How about from a blank post-card in the mail? *No one is motivated to do anything by blank space.* It's the words, or the copy, you read that make all the difference in the reaction you get from your prospects.

Copy is widely known as "salesmanship in print," a phrase coined by John E. Kennedy in the early 1900s. Looking to expand your sales team? Well, look no further. Copy is your twenty-four-hour salesman. It works for you tirelessly while you go about your day. *Copy never complains it's working too hard, never asks for a raise, and it never sleeps.* You write it once and use it over and over again. With the advent of the Internet, prospects can learn about you regardless of geography. Copy doesn't spoil. The words drive the sales. But be forewarned…just as good copy can skyrocket your sales, bad copy can slaughter them.

When you can identify powerful copy, you get your message *noticed, read,* and *responded to.* Whether you write the check for a copywriter, pass it off to someone on your staff, or do it yourself, you need to be able to look at your copy from an expert angle and evaluate it to see if it's doing the job, which is bring more dollars into your business.

For example: Is it in the right voice? Does it represent your company? Your product? Your branding? Most of all, *will it get read?* If it won't, the rest of your marketing doesn't matter. They won't get beyond the headline.

The good news is writing copy isn't rocket science. In fact, it's a pretty simple process. Copywriting gives smart business people like you an edge over every person in your industry who undervalues this skill. I promise. Here's why you really do need to know at least the basics of how to write your own copy:

Reason Number One: *Copy is the only known "magic bullet" for making more money*

One of my colleagues wrote some copy for the Learning Annex. It must have been underwhelming because there was a very low turnout for the training. Then she revamped it, using more specifics, benefits, and titillating language. Registrations jumped 25 percent more than the previous copy pulled. There is no skill more directly responsible for pulling money into your business than copy.

Reason Number Two: *You know your business better than anyone*

Your business is the direct result of a dream. *Your* dream. And no one understands why your business exists or who it is meant to serve better than you. That means there is nobody better to write your marketing message than the creator—*you!* Sure, you could educate someone else about your business. But the truth is he or she will *never* know as many details as you, the owner.

Reason Number Three: *Not knowing how to write copy sacrifices speed to market*

Face it. Whenever you get a good marketing idea, you need copy by default. So if you need to wait for someone else to craft copy for your every brainstorm, you can look forward to your competition jumping on the business.

Reason Number Four: *To be more successful, your business must evolve over time*

You don't think the way your business looks today is going to resemble what it ends up looking like five years down the road do you? Of course not. You'll grow and expand over time, so you'll constantly need new copy.

Reason Number Five: *Copywriting is the most expensive skill to outsource*

Copywriters get paid the equivalent of the down payment to a house or a new car for every project. That's right. You can expect to pay anywhere from $3,000 – $25,000 for something as commonplace as a sales letter. And it will be worth it because of the return on investment. But can't you think of other ways to invest that money? Sure you can.

Inside Tricks from the Oldest Profession—*Selling!*

So you're ready to raise your hand and have a try at honing your own copy? Great! Let me take some of the guesswork out of it for you and pull back the curtain to reveal some time-tested copywriting tricks—the *Guerrilla way!*

Guerrilla Tactic Number One: *If Writers Write, Do Copywriters Copy? Yes!*

Believe it or not in the copywriting industry one of the fastest and most reliable ways to write copy is to start your own swipe file. A swipe file is a collection of copy that has been previously field-tested. I want to be clear— *the purpose isn't to plagiarize other people's copy.* Swipe files are kept to not only inspire you, but they are helpful templates for your own copy. Study them and you'll soon begin to see formulaic word patterns emerging.

What Qualifies As a "Swipe?"

Just as copy is everywhere there are words, *swipes are everywhere there is copy*. To be sure your swipe file is brimming with *good* copy here are some places to collect it from:

- **Junk mail**: There's gold in that 'thar mail; don't just toss it in the trash anymore! Millions of dollars are spent by mega-corporations on field-testing that copy. See what you can learn from it, especially the more prolific conglomerates like the credit card, airline, and phone companies. You should also sign up for mailing lists in your own industry.

- **Print ads**: Go through the back pages of some of your favorite magazines and look for the word-dense ads. Those are the ones for your target. Again, big bucks go into paying for those ads. If you see them reappear month after month, you know they are earning their keep.

- **Infomercials and radio spots**: Even though these are verbal versions of copy, be sure to pay attention to them. An infomercial is like a long copy sales letter read aloud. It is designed to grab attention and work the listener into a frothy state of excitement. Radio spots are shorter and pithier. They also are written with excitement-driven language to get the prospect to take some sort of action.

- **Historical copy**: There are classic examples of proven copy you should definitely have in a swipe file to model. For starters, look for ads by P.T. Barnum, Eugene Schwartz, David Ogilvy, Leo Burnett, Claude Hopkins, Joseph Sugarman, Gary Halbert, John Carlton, and Dan Kennedy. This site has a pretty comprehensive collection (www.hardtofindads.com). What worked one hundred years ago continues to work today because as human beings we are still wired the same, regardless of our high tech world.

- **Copy that made you buy**: Something pushed your hot buttons to get you pull out your credit card and buy. Trace it back to the exact page, phrase, or sentence that got your juices flowing. If it's good enough for you, it's good enough for your audience.

Start collecting your own swipe arsenal and watch your copy improve tenfold!

Guerrilla Tactic Number Two: *Start a New Habit*

Have you ever seen brilliant copy you later forgot about? (Well, let's be honest—we *all* have.) So to prevent snappy copy you see in the field evaporating from your brain like last night's dreams, start this habit: begin carrying around a spiral-bound notebook of index cards and a pen (get them at any office supply store). As you're walking around in the world or driving from place to place (careful with this one) jot down notable copy on the radio, billboards, benches, in the supermarket—*wherever*! The more you raise your own awareness to how other marketers are trying to reach you, the stronger your own copy will become.

Guerrilla Tactic Number Three: *Swipe File Shuffle*

If I told you there was one sure-fire technique that would drastically improve your copy every time, would you actually do it? I ask because even professional copywriters often skip this crucial tactic. Here it is: Grab a piece of copy from your swipe file that really resonates with you. Copy it out *by hand* a minimum of three times (the more times the better) on a legal pad. Forget the computer. There is something mysterious that somehow switches on your copywriting brain when you do it manually. The more times you copy the same piece, the better your own copy will be—and you'll also be able to write it faster. *Don't be afraid of the long copy either. That's when you're really going to see the formula expose itself.*

Guerrilla Tactic Number Four: *Trick Your Writer's Block into Submission*

One of the barriers many guerrillas have to writing copy is just getting started. They freeze (happens to the best of us, frankly). Here's how to stealthily get around your own psychology. Start off your "writing" through speaking. In other words, record yourself talking about your business. (There are free conference numbers you can use with recording built right in like www.nocostconference.com or www.freeconference.com.) Then get it tran-scribed (www.idictate.com or www.internettranscribers.com are both reli-able). We don't tend to get "speakers block" when we're talking about some-thing we're passionate about. Plus, some of the word order and phrases you speak about your business can make for some compelling copy. Since you aren't in front of every prospect 24/7, using your own words in your copy can almost make it seem like you are.

Guerrilla Tactic Number Five: *Turn On Your Prospect*

Mark Twain once said, "There are two reasons why a man buys anything. The reason he tells his wife. And the *real* reason." What he meant was although we like to believe we buy based on logic, what actually spurs us into action is *emotion* (yes, even *you*!) So in order to write copy that sells, you have to separate the features out from the benefits. The "features" are the adjectives or descriptive parts of your product or service. The "benefits" are the emotional component. Take a regular ballpoint pen with a red shell for example. The fact that it's red is a feature. Finding it quickly in the middle of the night when you get a million dollar idea is a benefit. When you can show a prospect how buying what you're selling will vastly improve his life, you can count on getting more sales than just by describing how cool what you have is.

Guerrilla Tactic Number Six: *Focused Discipline*

Copywriting legend Eugene Schwartz got a heck of a lot done because of one simple rule. He used a timer to laser focus on his writing for thirty-three minutes. During that chunk of time, he allowed himself to do nothing but write. When the timer went off, he stopped whatever he was doing—even if it was mid-sentence—and took a five minute stretch break. It's that simple. Focusing on a task in a measurable chunk of time propels you toward reaching your goals. Let's break it down:

1.   Get a plain, old kitchen timer.

2.   Set it for thirty-three minutes (or in the ballpark).

3. Get rid of *all distractions* (yes, especially e-mail).

4. Write like a maniac *without editing*.

5. When the timer goes off, *stop*, no matter where you're at.

Guerrilla Tactic Number Seven: *Mind Mapping for Dollars*

Mind maps are an innovative tool to organize your thoughts. (And face it, in copywriting there are *a lot* of thoughts). Mind maps really keep you focused and are the secret key to my ability to write quickly. Because copywriting is *not* a linear process, but a more creative one, mind mapping is perhaps the most useful tool a copywriter could ever use in his/her arsenal. (There is software to make the process look prettier at www.mindjet.com but you can easily do it by hand.) It works basically like this:

1. Write down a central idea (in this case your product or service) on a large piece of unlined paper.

2. Brainstorm your ideas in branches off the central topic. Put down *everything* without editing or judging.

3. Look for relationships among ideas and group them together.

4. Even if you have never mind mapped before, you'll quickly see how easy it is to organize your thoughts.

Let's Get This Party Started

Remember, your copy doesn't only sell for you, it represents the essence of your business. The words you choose to describe what you do have an impact on how you are perceived in the marketplace. *People do business with those they know, like, and trust.* Copy can be used to build and solidify those relationships. Any place you put words is an opportunity to strengthen loyalty with your target market. When you harness the power of copywriting, you naturally pull your target market closer to you. Now that you have an enviable supply of copywriting ammo in your cache, you should be winning the war on bad content.

About Lorrie Morgan-Ferrero

*Lorrie Morgan-Ferrero of Red Hot Copy has helped entrepreneurs generate millions of dollars in sales using powerful words and solid marketing. Her clients come from all over the globe to master quickly her rapport-building style of copywriting with her proprietary, step-by-step system. Learn more at **www.RedHotCopy.com**.*

CHAPTER 9

GUERRILLA WORDS THAT SELL

Ten Easy Ways to Get Bigger Results from Your Sales Copy— Even If You Hate to Write

Jenny Hamby

> *"Advertising is fundamentally persuasion and persuasion happens to be not a science, but an art."*
> ~William Bernbach

As a small-business owner, you know that your company's success hinges largely on your ability to promote your business and persuade prospects to sign on the dotted line. Yet many entrepreneurs overlook the single most important member of their sales team: their marketing copy.

In the early 1900's, copywriter John E. Kennedy defined advertising as "salesmanship in print," explaining that promotional materials should say exactly what a good salesman would say when meeting face-to-face with a customer. When your copy is weak, ho-hum, or boring, prospects ignore your marketing and even become annoyed that you're bothering them, just as prospects slam the door or hang up the phone when contacted by poor sales-people. Powerful copy, on the other hand, allows you to attract and qualify prospects, make more (and larger) sales, and ultimately boost your sales and profits, just as a good sales team does.

Now, if you're like many small-business owners and entrepreneurs, you're not crazy about copywriting. Perhaps you don't believe that you're a good writer. Perhaps you don't like how long it can take to write promotional materials. Maybe you've tried it but produced lackluster results.

You may even be tempted, or have resorted, to hiring a professional copywriter rather than master the art of writing persuasive copy yourself. But learning how to write effective copy is one of the most precious and profitable talents you can possess. Not only does learning how to write effective copy give you a greater understanding of your customers and improve your ability to close sales, you also become much more adept at evaluating, hiring and managing professional copywriters when you do have the budget to make that type of investment.

In the next few pages, you'll learn ten powerful yet commonly overlooked copywriting strategies that you can use to attract qualified prospects, win more customers, and boost profits. Best of all, these are copywriting strategies that are easy to use—even if you hate to write.

1. Enter the Conversation in your Prospects' Heads

To easily break through the clutter of promotions competing for your prospects' attention, figure out where they are in their search for the solution you provide. The more actively they are searching for a solution, the more receptive they will be to your message—and the more likely they will be to say yes to your offer.

For example, let's say you own a carpet-cleaning business and you want to send an offer to your mailing list to boost pre-holiday business. You could simply send a flyer or letter to your customers announcing your offer of "get three rooms cleaned and get the 4th for free." No doubt you would sell some carpet-cleaning packages.

But you can strengthen your marketing copy and improve your response rates by identifying where your ideal customers—the people who are most likely to say yes to your offer —are, and then address their pain, frustration and desire in your pitch. You might know from experience, as well as from common sense, that people who will be hosting their families' holiday dinners get stressed out about how their homes look. You can address this source of pain by pointing out that you can help their carpets look as beautiful as the dinner table they're setting. You could even add that cleaning the carpet can eliminate a source of snide comments from that one ever-critical relative who, without fail, is able to find something to complain about at every event they attend.

Mirroring the conversation in your prospects' heads not only makes them more likely to notice your promotions, it also makes them more receptive to what you have to offer when you contact them. When your copywriting mirrors the conversations in your prospects' heads, your message is able to fly below their marketing radar. It's almost like knowing the secret password for getting into an exclusive clubhouse.

To make your sales copy resonate with your prospects, research their problems, pains, and frustrations. Also research what it is that they really want as a solution and how they think they will benefit from using your product or service.

When rewriting the marketing materials to promote the eighteen-day NLP (Neuro-Linguistic Programming) Practitioner Training offered by Tim and Kristine Hallbom of the NLP & Coaching Institute of California in Burlingame, we interviewed past attendees of the program, asking four simple questions:

1. What were you looking for when you found the NLPCA program?

2. What problems or frustrations were you trying to solve?

3. What about the program appealed to you and why did you decide to sign up?

4. What were the top three benefits you gained by participating?

Interviews yielded dozens of unique answers to the questions, which were transcribed and incorporated into the sales copy. The list of sixteen general lessons you'd learn by participating in the event, such as "replace limiting beliefs with empowering ones," was expanded to include fifty-eight more specific examples that were shared from past attendees, such as "understand

and fix your communication mistakes ... so you can react properly when people 'blow things out of proportion' or take your comments in the 'wrong way,'" and "practically eliminate the day-to-day stress that leaves you frazzled, frustrated, and grumpy."

The revised marketing brochure won rave reviews. The Hallboms received dozens of comments from readers saying, "That sounded just like me," as well as significantly higher registrations. In fact, five years later, the sales copy from the brochure is still filling seminars, having been repurposed into Web site copy as well as still being used as a direct-mail brochure.

2. Develop an Irresistible Offer

To increase the response you get from your sales copy, you need to structure an offer that is virtually impossible to resist—and then only by accepting the fact that not jumping on the generous opportunity you've provided may well turn out to be a significant loss.

To develop an irresistible offer, think about these three components:

1. **Value**: Making clear the value of what you're offering in relation to the price that you're asking is huge. Everyone loves a good deal. Everyone. It doesn't matter if you're marketing to the housewife who has $3.09 left in her wallet for the week or the executive who is shopping for a new yacht; humans are wired with the desire to get more for their money. To increase the attractiveness of your offer, spell out the value of what you're offering whether it's a free resource, such as a report that normally sells for $29.95, or special pricing on a product or service, such as $5 off an oil change. Help prospects understand exactly the dollar value of what you're offering to them.

2. **Bonuses**: Along with getting a good deal, people like to get a little extra for their money. To increase the attractiveness of your offer, incorporate items and services that won't cost you much to provide, but that have a significant perceived value. Whenever

possible, incorporate bonuses that further prove your expertise, keep your business front and center in prospects' minds, and keep them coming back to you. For example, you could offer a free audio program with the purchase of your home-study course, a free stadium seat cushion with the purchase of a new bicycle, or a buy-one-get-one-free dinner coupon the next time patrons visit your restaurant.

3. **Scarcity**: A great bargain and loads of free goodies won't be enough incentive to make many prospects act. To get people to act immediately, incorporate an element of scarcity into your offer. For example, limit the availability of your free gifts to the first thirty-seven people who respond or offer special pricing only to people who act by a certain deadline.

3. Ask For and Specify Action

Many business owners—and even professional salespeople—make a critical mistake when selling. They refuse to ask for the sale or they ask for it in a roundabout, wishy-washy way that makes it easy for prospects to say no. This usually happens because you don't want to seem too pushy. Just as in face-to-face selling scenarios, many business owners make the same mistake when writing their marketing materials.

However, just as in face-to-face situations, better results are produced when you're direct and ask for the offer. Asking for a specific action is especially critical when writing copy because you don't have a human directly involved. Where you'd normally have a salesperson asking for pertinent sales information, such as name, address, and credit card information, your copy needs to specify exactly what you want prospects to do. Do you want them to request a free report, place an order, or call for a free consultation? Tell them.

Then, think about what exactly they need to do to comply with your request and, again, tell them what to do. For example, "Fill in your name and primary e-mail address in the form below, and then click the button that says

'Send My Report'" or "Pick up the phone, dial 815-254-4939, and use Priority Reservation Code GMFL07 to claim your free consultation valued at $149."

Kathi Dunn is founder of Hayward, Wisconsin-based DUNN+ ASSOCIATES, one of the country's top book cover design and branding firms for authors, speakers and experts. When she, along with her husband and partner Ron "Hobie" Hobart, decided to participate in the trade show offered as part of Mark Victor Hansen's Mega Book Marketing University, they began to look at ways they could generate more booth traffic and capture more qualified leads.

In past years, they had followed the lead of other exhibitors and sent out a standard-sized, four-by six-inch postcard to promote their trade-show booth, as well as the breakout session they teach one morning before the start of the regularly scheduled program. In a typical year, they generate "about" thirty leads. (Like most small-business owners, they're so focused on serving their clients that they never got around to worrying about the finer points of marketing, such as creating a tracking system and analyzing results, so they didn't know with certainty exactly how many leads were produced at each show they attended previously.)

In 2006, they decided to shake things up a bit by sending out an oversized, full-color postcard that promoted a drawing for a $3,995 deluxe cover design and coaching package, a free resource kit, and a 50 percent discount offer on their audio program. They also invested considerable time honing their unique selling proposition, carrying their USP (Universal Selling Proposition) and message to all of the marketing pieces used to promote their participation in the trade show.

But they didn't stop there. In previous years, the duo would wait for authors to visit their trade-show booth, spend a few minutes chatting with visitors, and then ask for a business card if prospects seemed interested in considering DUNN+ASSOCIATES for their book cover design and branding services. At the 2006 Mega Book Marketing University, Kathi and Hobie included a response form on their oversized postcard, instructing prospects to drop off the completed form at their trade-show booth to claim a free resource kit and enter the drawing. They also committed to asking every visitor to their booth for a business card. The end result? The pair generated 125 qualified leads—approximately 25 percent of the event's attendees and more than quadruple the number of leads they generated in past years.

4. Give Yourself Room to Do the Job the Right Way

There's a persistent myth floating around that prospects won't read sales letters if they are more than one page long. In fact, prospects will read long copy—as long as it's pertinent and interesting.

The proper length for your marketing piece depends on what you want prospects to do. You must give yourself enough room to persuade prospects to take the next step. If your goal is simply to get them to visit your Web site to claim a free report, a simple postcard could easily do the trick. However, if your goal is to convince prospects to register for a $3,000 weekend bootcamp, you're going to need enough room to present a compelling argument why attending your event will be worth their time and money.

To ensure that prospects don't get bogged down and lost in long sales copy, use the following formatting tips to make it easy to scan and digest your copy:

- Use easy-to-read fonts and limit the number of fonts you use. One font for body copy and another for headlines and subheads is plenty.

- Incorporate subheads throughout your copy. Make the subheads slightly larger than your body copy and even a different font.

- Make paragraphs short, no more than three or four lines each. And don't be afraid of using one-sentence—and even one-word—paragraphs.

- Use bulleted lists to present benefits, problems you can overcome, and other types of lists.

- Use **bold**, *italics* and/or <u>underlining</u> to emphasize key words.

5. Develop a Copywriting Alter Ego

Consumers are overwhelmed with information and marketing offers. To capture their attention, your marketing message must not only pertinent and well timed, it must be interesting to read. To capture attention and interest, your copy must be vibrant, edgy and confident.

Many business owners struggle to write sizzling copy because they don't want to brag, they don't recognize themselves as being as successful and unique as their customers do, and/or they don't feel comfortable in the spotlight. As a result, their copy is safe, grey, and frankly, boring.

Remember, using copy to market your business puts you at a slight disadvantage. Unlike face to face communication, there is no human voice, facial expressions, or body language to grab and hold your prospects' attention. There are only words. To stand a chance of holding a prospects attention and persuading them to take action, your copy needs to jump off the page. Prospects need to hear your voice in their head and feel you sitting beside them.

The best way to create a powerful voice is to create a copywriting persona, someone who is like you—only more vivid. Someone who is bold but not arrogant. Someone who is full of facts, logic, and interesting, relevant stories. Someone who is assured that what you're offering is the perfect solution for your prospects' problem and confident that prospects will say yes to your offer. Before you sit down to write a lick of copy, get yourself in character. Become the Technicolor version of yourself —and then fire up your computer.

6. Develop Consistency and Continuity Throughout your Marketing Program

You've no doubt heard about the importance of branding to the success of your marketing program. While many small business owners dismiss branding as something only large organizations need to worry about, branding at its most basic level is quite simple and cost-effective. Because branding can mean simply that you use the same look and "feel" when designing your marketing materials. For example, your business cards should look like your letterhead, and the look should be carried over into your Web site design.

The same sense of consistency and continuity should be present in your copy, as well. Just as prospects shouldn't be left wondering where on earth they ended up when they visit your Web site because there is such a disconnect between the look of the print ad that hooked their interest and the look of your Web site, there should also be no chance of losing or confusing your prospects because of what your copy says.

Continue the conversation you're having with prospects from marketing piece to marketing piece. Let's say you have mailed a postcard that sends your prospects to a web page (a landing page) that offers a free report revealing the 7 things to look for when hiring a catering company. When the prospect goes to the landing page to claim their free report, they should instantly know, through the headline, introductory copy, and graphics, that they've landed on the right page. The page's headline could read "Claim Your Free Copy of '7 Questions to Ask When Hiring a Catering Company.'" After prospects provide their contact information to order the report, they could be redirected to a thank-you page that says "Thank you for requesting your free copy of '7 Questions to Ask When Hiring a Catering Company.'"

7. Test, Track, and Analyze

The fun—and sometimes frustrating—part of marketing is that there are a myriad of factors that can influence the success of a promotion. The headline, the offer, the timing of your promotions, the number of pieces in your marketing sequence, the type of marketing media used, and delivery method are just a handful of the elements that can make or break your marketing success. To figure out which combination of elements works best to promote your business to your ideal audience, you need to test the effect of each element.

The simplest way to test promotions is to run an A/B split test. Here's how it works: divide your list in half, with every other person receiving version "A" of your marketing piece and the rest of your list receiving version "B," while holding all other variables constant. Send the promotions out and track which piece produces the best results (more on that below). Whichever package wins becomes the "control" or package to beat.

For example, to determine which headline will work best at promoting your offer, you could send a direct mail letter to your list; the only difference between letter A and letter B would be the headline. Because there would be no difference between the two letters other than the headline, you'll know that the letter that produces the most responses has the winning headline. You could then continue to test different headlines until you were satisfied that you have found the very best headline for your letter. At that point, you could move on to test other elements of your promotions.

To accurately measure the success of each marketing piece—and of each test you run—you need to track your results. To do so, you first need to assign a unique promotional code to each version of your marketing piece that you test. For example, one direct mail package might be coded DM21 and the second package might be coded DM22. Here are five ways to incorporate your tracking codes in your promotions and capture them when prospects respond:

1. Type the unique promotional code in the lower right hand corner of your response form.

2. Present the tracking code as a department number; for example, "Mail or fax your response to Hamby Communications, Inc., Department DM21"

3. Use different telephone extensions to track the responses, such as extension 21 vs. 22.

4. Create different versions of the same landing page if you want to drive prospects to your Web site; for example, www.mycompany.com/dm21.

5. Generate a tracking link for each promotion when marketing online. (If your ad- tracking software produces long links seemingly filled with gibberish, use a service like www.TinyURL.com to produce a shorter, easier-on-the-eyes link.)

Once you've tallied up the number of responses attributed to each promotion, you can then determine the effectiveness of each promotion by dividing the number of responses by the number of prospects contacted. For example, if you mailed one thousand postcards and received thirty-four replies, you would know that the postcard produced a 3.4 percent response rate (34/1000 = 0.034 x 100 = 3.4 percent). If you had tested a postcard against a short sales letter that made the same offer, you would then know which piece was more effective. For example, you may have found that the sales letter was slightly more effective, producing a 3.7 percent response rate.

Determining which combination of elements produces the greatest response to your offer is not the only reason to track and analyze your promotions. Doing so can also spotlight ways to market your business more cost-effectively. In the example we just used, you could carry your analysis one step further by comparing the revenue produced by each form of promotion with the cost of producing each promotion. For example, although you found that the sales letter produced a better response, you may have also found that the sales letter cost more to reproduce and mail. In terms of return on investment, then, the postcard produced the better results.

8. Customize your Marketing Message for Each Audience

Your customers and prospects want to feel unique. They want to know that you view them as individuals, not merely as part of a faceless mass of people with money. One popular way to let prospects know that you view them as unique individuals, as well as to increase their interest in and response to your promotions, is to customize your message.

Common ways of customizing your materials include addressing envelopes to the individuals on your mailing list by name vs. sending mail to "CURRENT HOMEOWNER" and incorporating the prospect's name in the salutation and in the body of your marketing piece. However, most consumers are savvy enough to realize that you're using nothing more than a database and mail merge to customize your marketing materials.

A much more effective way to customize your marketing message is to tweak your message, and even your offer, to reflect what you know about each segment of your database. When promoting a series of seven certification preparation courses offered by APICS, the Association for Operations Management, in partnership with a Chicago-area junior college, I customized the promotions for classes two through seven to reflect the attendance records of prospects. For example, when promoting class number three, we contacted everyone in the database who had taken classes one and two. The two-page sales letter acknowledged that class number three was the next recommended course in the sequence that they needed to take to achieve their certification. Prospects who did not respond to the sales letter were contacted via phone during the last week before the seminar started. These simple telemarketing efforts dramatically increased enrollment, in some cases, close to doubling the class size. By customizing the promotions, we achieved response rates as high as 84 percent for some of the classes, even though expenses were less than $125 per course.

Here are a few tips to keep in mind when customizing your message to various segments of your database:

- When promoting an offer that people logically could and should purchase multiple times, acknowledge their past purchase of the product. For example, offer past customers the chance to sign up for your complete lawn care services at last year's prices as a reward for their continued patronage.

- When promoting something past customers probably would not want to purchase again, send them the same letter or promotional piece you're sending to prospects. Also include a cover letter that acknowledges their past purchase and asks them to share the enclosed promotion with a friend or colleague who could benefit from the offer.

- When responding to a request for information, start your reply by letting prospects know that you're contacting them in response to their request. For example, if you're mailing a direct mail package of free information about your business, write something like "The information you requested is enclosed" on the envelope.

- When using a multi-step marketing sequence to promote your business, reference earlier attempts to contact prospects. If the sequence was launched when they opted-in to your mailing list or otherwise requested information from you, again, remind them that their request is why you started contacting them.

- To make it easier to customize your marketing messages, segment your database as much as possible. For example, make sure that you're able to track exactly who   has—and who   hasn't—purchased every single product or service that you offer. In addition, you can segment your list using criteria such as when they last purchased from you, how they contacted you, and the most pressing problem that they're trying to solve.

9. Identify and Address Objections

Prospects will always have reasons why they don't want to respond to your offer, whether you're simply offering free information or you're trying to persuade prospects to buy something from you. To write effective copy, you need to identify the objections that your prospects have and then overcome them in your copy.

- To identify which objections keep prospects from responding positively to your offer, start by brainstorming. You know your customers well, so start by writing down the objections that you know off the top of your head. Be sure to include common objections such as, "I can't afford it" or "I don't have the time."

- Take notes each day about the objections you hear when talking to prospects and customers.

- Ask prospects why they've decided not to buy from you. People like to share their opinions and help others, so explain that you would value their input on how you can improve your service.

- Spy on competitors. Read the promotional materials used by your competition and take note of the objections they raise and overcome.

- Put yourself in your prospects' shoes. Sometimes, all you need to do is take a step back and look at your marketing process with a critical eye to spot reasons why prospects won't response to your offer. If this is difficult for you, ask a friend (ideally someone who could be customer) to critique your marketing for you.

Once you've created a list of objections, identify ways to overcome them. When you successfully overcome objections when selling directly to customers, take notes about what you said and how the customers reacted. You can also ask prospective customers for their input via surveys, focus groups, or one-on-one interviews. Finally, examine how other businesses overcome the same types of objections, and don't be afraid to look outside your industry for inspiration.

David Oliver, founder of BipolarCentral.com, discovered firsthand how important it is to not only overcome objections, but to identify which objections are most important to your audience.

Creator of "The Bipolar Supporter's Course," a program filled with practical strategies for supporting a loved one with bipolar disorder, David had created a version of his course specifically for parents whose children had been diagnosed with bipolar disorder. After months of driving thousands of leads to his Web site and testing components of the sales letter in the effort to boost response, he was ready to completely overhaul the piece.

He called us to help him and this is what we did. We created a new version of the sales letter that contained three major changes. First, we changed the focus of the headline from addressing the parents' desire to cope with their child's bipolar disorder to a headline block that addressed the parents' desire to help their child cope with the illness. This simple change put the emphasis on parents' overwhelming and primary desire to help their children overcome the challenge and pain presented by mental illness. We found that the parents who are most likely to buy this particular product are much more concerned about their children's ability to cope; their own ability to cope is far less important.

Second, the introduction of the sales letter quickly zeroed in on parents' fears that their child would not be able to lead a "normal" life because of bipolar disorder. Their fears are certainly justified; unless it's managed properly, the disease can have a devastating effect on an individual's relationships, education, finances, health, safety, and career.

The third and most important change incorporated into the new sales letter was raising and overcoming objections. As an experienced, successful Internet marketer, David's sales letters easily overcame common objections such as "I can't afford this" and "I don't know if this product is worth what you're asking." However, this particular sales letter had overlooked one major objection, "What makes you qualified to give me advice about my child?"

The revised letter provided a detailed look at how David became an expert on successfully managing bipolar disorder, which he did after taking almost a full year off of work to focus exclusively on helping his mother recover from a major bipolar episode that left her virtually unable to function normally. Not only did he conduct exhaustive research into all sources of printed information available on bipolar disorder, he consulted with dozens of leading bipolar experts, from doctors and therapists to pharmacists and attorneys. He also met and talked with hundreds of supporters around the country, including parents of children with bipolar disorder. Finally, he worked with his own mother to design a customized support plan based on the proven, effective strategies he learned through his research to help her manage the disorder. The plan has worked so well that she leads what most people would consider a "normal," successful life, and unless she shares the information, new people she meets have no idea that she suffers from a mental illness.

Overcoming the main objection that was holding parents back from investing in his course and refocusing the sales letter on his prospects' primary concern paid off. In the first week after launching the new letter, David sold more courses than he had sold in the previous five months.

10. Reuse and Recycle

Once you land on copy that works, keep using it over and over and over. While behemoth companies may have the budgets and resources to come out with new ad campaigns every few years, smart Guerrilla Marketers recognize that they'll get the biggest return on their investment of time and, if they hired someone, money by repurposing their copy in multiple ways. For example, if you create a hefty direct mail package or free "report" to sell your main product or service, you can borrow chunks of copy to use in postcards, advertisements, telemarketing, e-mail autoresponder messages, follow-up sales letters, brochures, articles, press releases, etc. While you can and should continue to conduct tests to improve elements of your control, rarely should you consider tossing out an entire marketing piece, especially if you're doing so because you think your audience is bored.

Repurposing copy is a great way to keep your copywriting expenses under control if you decide that you'd rather hire a professional copywriter so that you can focus on other aspects of your business. Good copywriters are pricey. You can limit your investment by hiring a copywriter to create your foundational sales piece, such as a sales letter. You can then use the professionally written copy as a launching point for other promotional pieces.

Large companies use teams of sales professionals to qualify prospects and close sales. As a Guerrilla Marketer, you may not have the budget to employ dozens of sales professionals, but you can develop an arsenal of powerful promotional materials that work around the clock to attract, qualify, and convert prospects into paying customers. The key is creating powerful copy that mesmerizes, reassures, and resonates with your ideal prospects.

About Jenny Hamby

Jenny Hamby is a Certified Guerrilla Marketing Coach and direct-response copywriter who specializes in promoting seminars and information products. To claim a free copy of her report, "37 Ways to Improve Copywriting Response Rates," go to www.SeminarMarketingPro.com/GMFL.

CHAPTER 10

THE FIVE-TOUCH MARKETING SYSTEM

How to Attract the World to Your Business

Grant Hicks

> *"Trust is the single most important prerequisite for creating client relationships that produce big results with little time and effort...Without trust, people will not believe that you are acting in their best interests."*
>
> ~Bill Bachrach

If you have ever tried to learn something new, you know it can be a frustrating process. For example, if you have ever learned to play golf, you know it can be challenging to learn how to drive a golf ball off the tee.

There you are on the driving range hitting ball after ball. Along comes Mr. Golf Pro who gives you a few pointers and you try them. You decide that no matter what, you are going to learn how to hit a tee shot—remembering that you have that company golf tournament next week and you don't want to be embarrassed.

Ball after ball, you change your grip, change your stance, change your swing. You test; you try; it starts to slowly take shape. Then, to your amazement, you drive one effortlessly like never before. Wow, you say to yourself, wasn't that easy?! You try it again. You lean over and reach for another ball and put it on a tee. Stance ready, grip ready, head down, and then *whack*. Wow, another beautiful shot. Now you can feel your excitement run through you, and you grin from ear to ear. You've discovered the secret. You hit another, then another, smashing them straight down the driving range. You look around to see who is watching. You notice a young man struggling to hit the ball as he turns to watch you whack yet another ball straight down the fairway. You decide to go over and offer a few simple tips, and then you resume your booming drives. You have mastered it. The moral of this story: learning how to hit the ball like a master is learned by doing.

Marketing Involves Action

You cannot pick up a how-to book on golfing then hit a golf ball like a golf pro. You cannot go to a golf seminar then join the pro golf tour. You learn by doing. So it is true in marketing. I learned how to market by trying this, trying that, testing this, implementing that. Then all of a sudden, I discovered my booming drive in marketing. It is called the Five-Touch Philosophy.

I want you to learn by doing. I will explain the philosophy first, and then show you step by step how to implement it. Once you see yourself actually implementing and *doing* your own Five-Touch Philosophy, you will discover the secret of marketing and why the Five-Touch Philosophy works so well compared to most marketing methods you and I have learned and tested from reading hundreds of books on marketing.

I discovered the Five-Touch Philosophy while testing and implementing different marketing ideas into my business in 2002 and co-writing and researching information for my first Guerrilla Marketing book, *Guerrilla Marketing For Financial Advisor*, with Jay Conrad Levinson (Trafford Publishing September 2003). It took me trying over 40 different marketing ideas to actually develop the Five-Touch System.

I also did this research because I was frustrated. I own and manage a small business. I was trying to figure out how to attract more people to my business, but I was irritated because all the marketing ideas that I tried worked to some degree, but I knew there must be a better and simpler way to attract the right people to my business. That better and simpler way is the five-touch system.

With the Five-Touch Philosophy, I learned how to attract people to our financial advising business (total strangers who called us), who told us everything about themselves and then invested their life savings with our firm.

The Five-Touch Marketing System

If I asked you the name of a great marketing idea, you could probably name a few. However, if I asked you the name of a great marketing system for small business, could you name any? The Five-Touch System is exactly what the name implies, a system to develop five touches or contacts with new customers or prospects.

What it does for your potential client or customer is it makes them familiar with you and your business. Imagine you are driving along a highway and your spouse turns to you and says, "We need to eat, but we don't have much time." At the next stop there are two restaurants, one is a common food chain, and the other is a local diner. Which one do you choose? Like most people who are in a rush, you choose the recognizable name brand or food-chain restaurant. You go to where you are going to be most comfortable. Now I did not say the cheapest, the best service, or best value.

Did I mention quality? No, none of these entered the equation, yet so many businesses try to market themselves as good value, good price, excellent service or great quality. The diner across the street from the chain restaurant offers great service, selection, price, value and quality ingredients, yet day after day people pass by this restaurant and they wonder why. Is it only for people who are not in a rush? Guess what. The whole world is in a rush. The owners thought they put the proper ingredients together to make a great restaurant, yet the doors are open and the parking lot across the street is full every day and theirs is empty. They don't have the name recognition because they have not learned the five touch philosophy of marketing.

If I asked you the name of a great financial advisor and you said a name I had never heard of, I might not feel comfortable going to see them. But If I had heard of them before, saw their ads or marketing and possibly received a mailing, seminar invitation or phone call, I would feel more comfortable in seeing them.

How Do People Get to Know Your Business?

Successful marketers know that people want to know about your business before they will do business with you. How do they get to know your business? Use the law of familiarity to your favor!

During my research, I discovered that I was 80 percent more successful after the fifth contact. Why? People knew us and were comfortable in choosing us. Here's some interesting statistics:

- 5 – 10 percent chance of having a person become a customer or client after one contact;

- 10 – 20 percent chance of having a person become a customer or client after two contacts;

- 20 – 30 percent chance of having a person become a customer or client after three contacts. I also discovered that most marketing programs stop or marketers give up after three tries;

- 30 – 40 percent chance of having a person become a customer or client after four contacts;

- 50 – 70 percent chance of having a person become a customer or client after five touches or contacts.

It amazingly jumps up after five touches:

- 70 – 80 percent chance of having a person become a customer or client after six and seven contacts;

- 50 – 80 percent of all new business developed after the fifth, sixth and seventh touch or contact.

I also spoke to several financial advisors who were doing different marketing strategies and discovered some interesting information:

- 40 – 50 percent of advisors will call once and never call again;

- 25 – 40 percent will contact a prospect the second time and follow up;

- 10 – 20 percent will contact them three times;

- 5 – 10 percent will contact or touch people five times or more before doing business with them and become very successful opening new accounts 70 – 80 percent of the time and earning in the top 5 – 10 percent of advisors.

Why stop marketing after two, three, or four times when you are halfway there? Your chances of success can be greatly increased if you continued or developed a strategy to do five touches or contacts.

Are You Losing Business?

When was the last time a prospect or customer gave you a big account or bought a big-ticket item on the first meeting? If this happens to you all the time—good! You're doing your marketing right. If not, you need to face the facts. There are several important reasons why people do not do business with you, but mainly, a customer or a client does not choose you because they didn't have enough contact—touches—with you before they decided to not do business with you.

You need to allow your potential customers to get to know you. Do it this way:

1. Get to know you (or your staff and business etc.)—familiarity.

2. Get to know what you do (what your business does) and see what the solutions are that you offer—solutions.

3. Get to trust you and or your business—trust.

4. See the benefits to them (not to you)—benefits.

5. See why you are different from competitor—differentiation.

1. Familiarity

If a customer doesn't know you, has never heard of you, then you don't exist in their mind. You need to find ways to allow people to get familiar with you and your business.

2. Solutions

Even if they have heard of you or know you slightly, they really don't know you, your company or what you or your company really does. Whenever you meet someone new in business, you usually ask them, "What do you do?" People want to know what you do and *what solutions you offer*. You need to get the word out to your potential clients or customers that you have a great solution to their problem.

3. Trust

Most important, even if a potential customer or client knows you, they are not familiar enough with you or do not feel comfortable doing business with you. In other words they don't trust you or your people or your business enough to engage in any transaction. You need to build trust with them.

4. Benefits

Now they know you, possibly they are even comfortable enough to do business with you, but they do not see the perceived value or benefit of doing business with you (meaning you, your staff, or your business). Benefits sell. Period. You must get your customers familiar with the benefits of your business so that they can move to number five.

5. Differentiation

You have to differentiate yourself from the competition. And often, the competition is a business they already know and trust. Once they know you, and are familiar with you, trust you and see the benefits to what you do, you now have a greater chance of doing business with them. In short, you need to get them to understand why they should choose you versus the competition.

When you follow this system of developing familiarity, solutions, trust, benefits, and differentiation, the customer will respond to your marketing and you have a 50 percent or greater chance of attracting that new customer through your marketing than you did before you read this chapter. You will also develop stronger loyalties with your existing customers, and that is a major plus point because your existing customers are your best resource!

How Do You Attract People to Your Business Everyday?

I discovered, after talking to marketers of small businesses, that they some-times give up after the fourth contact and wonder why they are not successful. They are 80 percent of the way there and all they have to realize is that people will not do business with you until they are familiar with you and comfortable. They fail to realize that you need to constantly market to your prospects and customers in different ways to make them familiar with you.

During one seminar I gave, a financial advisor asked when he should give up on a prospect. The answer is simple: when they are no longer qualified. If you believe that you have answers to their problems and you can solve their problems better than anybody else on the planet, then why wouldn't you want to continue to try to help them? Believe in yourself through your marketing. You have the power to help them.

Here is an example of the Five-Touch System. First you need to get the customer's attention. Whether you do a targeted mail drop, e-mail or ad to your target audience, you are trying to generate a response to have them take another step towards getting to know you or your business.

This is the system that I have set-up in my financial advising business. It starts with a simple advertisement in a local paper targeted to retirees (my target market for this campaign) that had a strong call to action in it (which I will explain in more detail later) The call to action is to give *free* informa-tion that solves a problem for my prospects. In this case it was how to avoid costly money mistakes such as paying too much tax, taking too much risk in retirement, or not properly protecting your assets. In the ad there is my Web site address and my business address. I ask them to call for their free, problem solving information. I tell them they can call at any time and leave a message on the answering machine. They could also drop by my business since the address is on the ad. If someone read the ad and was interested, then they could also learn more at my Web site. The same ad is on the Web site.

Now, there is one more step that I take in the local paper. It's the differ-ence between a traditional ad and a guerrilla ad and it's what makes my ads get noticed. In the same paper where I have my ad, I always back it up with an article or advertorial—a paid article. The article talks about all of the financial errors retirees make with their finances and the problems it can cause. These articles aren't hard to write. You write them from your experiences with your clients. For me, I see people making simple but costly errors with their retirement plans every day, so I developed a few articles to address and identify problems I have seen with my experience, making it realistic and illustrating true life examples that people may relate to.

So my potential client has read my ad, my article, and I've now gotten them to my Web site. This is exactly where I want them, because online they can learn more about me. The natural tendency of people doing business with you is that they want to learn more about you and your business. Give them that opportunity. In fact, this is the main reason why every business on the planet should have a Web site. It allows people to connect with you and your business in a comfortable way. It also gives a potential client or customer a way to find out interesting things about you.

Have you ever been to a restaurant and there is a story about the history of the restaurant on the menu. Do you read it? Absolutely. It helps you connect with the restaurant. Make sure you and your staff have good biographies on your communications materials as well as on your Web site. Most important, tell people something interesting about yourself. Tell them a mini story about you or your company. People remember two things, pictures and stories. Make sure you have both. For example, I played professional hockey in Europe. I now live in Canada and since most Canadians love to talk about hockey, this usually generates questions or a discussion about hockey at some point. But my client had to find this out first before they met me. Stories allow the reader to connect with you; they build familiarity and allow people the opportunity to build a relationship with you, your company or someone on your team.

At this point in the process, they have seen one of my ads (one touch), which I run every few weeks, see articles (two touches) which are also run every few weeks, and go to the Web site (three touches) to learn more. Then they possibly may ask a few people (four touches) if they have heard of our firm or us. At this point they have not contacted us, and I do not know who they are. However, they know who we are, and what we do, and how we specialize in our business with retirees. They have had three or four touches: an ad, an article, possibly the Web site and possibly asking a friend or colleague about us. It is only then that they know enough about us to request "free problem solving information" designed specifically for them.

I repeat this cycle of ad, advertorials, or articles, every few weeks. I do this for a specific reason. In the financial business I know that people have a major money or tax issue at least two times a year. I know that they may have a money issue coming up in a few months. They may choose to ignore the ads for now, but I have planted a seed. Eventually, when the money issue comes up, they have a financial problem and my booklets of information (that they can get for free) can help solve their problem. They decide to pick up the phone or e-mail us for the free information. We gather their contact information and mail out the free booklets. They are looking for solutions to their problems. They want to avoid making errors with their money in retirement or they are looking for a second opinion.

Once we have sent them a brochure, we now have permission to contact them. We know they are interested, motivated and somewhat qualified, because the information is targeted to people who are retired on Vancouver Island in British Columbia. Once we receive their contact information, they are sent the information along with a free book (which I buy, by the way). Why do I send a free book to them that I've purchased with my own money? *When was the last time you threw away a brochure?* How about a book? People never throw away books, especially retirees. They will throw out your marketing materials, CDs, or brochures, but never a book.

The package I send also has articles, which I wrote, about solving their financial problems; we want our potential clients to know that we are the ones who know about their problems. We also put in another call to action about protecting their assets and offer strategies to guarantee their investments in retirement. They have the option of calling or e-mailing again for more problem-solving packages. They will also receive information about us in the package and the benefits of dealing with us along with a free one-hour consultation, no-obligation information session on how to avoid costly financial errors in retirement. A week or so after they have received the information package, they will receive a follow-up letter and an e-mail to see if they want to come in and talk to us for free.

All in all, they have had at least five touches with our office and know who we are and what we do. If they don't call us for a free consultation a few weeks after we sent them the initial packet of information, then they are sent an invitation to attend one of our information sessions or seminars on the exact topic that is discussed in the problem solving information kit: planning a secure retirement and costly financial errors in retirement. We send the seminar invitation for one reason only. It gives people a chance to come and meet us without committing themselves to a one-hour consultation where they will be sold something. Most people are afraid of the high-pressure sales pitch. This gives them an informal way to meet us and get comfortable with our firm. At the seminar the focus is about addressing problems seniors and retirees have with their finances. They can sign up at the seminar for the free one-hour session or request the additional information kits on protecting their money and guaranteeing their retirement.

Give People the Opportunity to Connect with Your Business

At this point we have had five touches with them, and we only have their name and contact information in a database. Now, what I have found is that all we have to do is sit back and wait. And what happens next, happens time and time again. After a few weeks pass, we will get a call for an appointment. This always amazes me. Some strange person or couple has called in for an appointment. They know everything about us, possibly met us at the seminar or workshop. They are prepared to tell us everything about themselves and their financial problem.

Because they are comfortable with us and know who we are, they are usually prepared to invest their retirement savings with us. Now think about it for a minute. A stranger calls us, tells us everything about himself or herself in the first meeting and is prepared to give up most, if not all, of their money to us! I've never seen this happen before, but that is how the Five-Touch System works.

So to review, here is my system for "touching" a potential client. He or she:

- reads a targeted advertisement or mail drop;
- reads an article or advertorial;
- checks our business out on the Web site;
- phones a friend or colleague to find out more about us, sometimes their lawyer or accountant or other business professional;
- calls in or drops in to request one of our information kits.

Once our kit is mailed out, the potential client receives a follow-up call to see if they received the kit. (We are also making sure we have the right address and phone number.) Sometimes, at this point, this potential client will request additional kits or a free one hour consultation.

If we don't get a phone call, a seminar invitation is mailed. If this is the case then:

1. A follow-up call is made to see if they would like to attend the seminar.

2. They attend a seminar.

3. They receive additional follow-up requests (what I call the "drip" method, which I will discuss next).

4. They e-mail us with a question to see how we respond to them.

5. They receive an e-mail from us.

6. They call our office to book an appointment.

At this point you can see that the system is designed for more than five touches, but it takes a combination of five touches to get the system going. Remember, it is not five mail drops, but consecutive marketing activities along with a combination of other actions that make up the five touches. In other words, it is five different touches, not five of the same marketing contacts or touches.

The Prospect Follow-Up System—A Must Have

Once you have people call, e-mail or drop in on your company with their contact information, you can develop a drip system—a prospect follow-up system—to capture these people over time. What I do is send them a monthly e-mail if they have e-mail to keep in touch. We also sent monthly one page mailers about different financial errors we see retirees making. They also receive future seminar invitations that are designed to be exclusive invitations, not just a mass seminar mailing, since we want a more personal contact at the workshops, not just a big seminar. We try to restrict attendance to twenty people. We then put the potential customer on a bi-monthly marketing campaign to continue to attract them.

Obviously there are several drip-marketing programs that we could have developed to keep in touch with these prospects or new customers. We used the above, but there are others. You need to decide which kind of drip system works best for you. But with a drip system in place, we have found that, over time, some of our contacts would call in months after having received the information package. We also found that the follow-up phone call to make sure the potential client received their information kit was critical to the program. It put a very human touch into the system.

Once we get our new clients in, we deliver! We help them solve their financial problems. But they came to us because we were persistent. They called us for the appointment because they wanted to come in and discuss their financial problem or challenges. They responded, not because we advertised about our products or services, but because we advertised solutions to their problems.

The success we have had with the system will help you follow-up, establish trust, develop your customer relationships, and receive more referrals and new customers. The Five-Touch System is all about developing a customer's trust in you and your company so you develop long-term relationships with them.

Other Key Elements

It is important to note that this system did not work overnight. It was created and refined over time. As I developed it, I found that there are also a few key elements to the system that are peripheral to the five touches.

First it is measurable. We know how many people call each week off of each advertisement. We can measure the cost of the ad and the people who came in and measure the profitability of each ad. While we cannot measure the impact of the article or advertorial, each time the ad runs with an article, the response rate usually doubles. We also know that while the seminars and workshops cost money, they too are measurable. We gained some really nice people as clients doing the workshops, so I would highly recommend them as part of your five touches.

Second, a guerrilla marketer knows that persistency is key. We did not abandon the system once we were really busy; we just kept on marketing. If we did stop, it would be like stopping a five-hundred-car train—it takes a ton of energy to get it going again.

Third, it focuses on certain people that I am trying to attract. I identified my niche market and concentrated on them. If you think your audience is everyone, I would recommend that you define a target market or target markets to get started and then market to each market individually. Just know that each market that you work in needs to have its own Five-Touch System designed for it.

Fourth. The information kit I send is also part of the Guerrilla Marketing philosophy—invest time energy and imagination, not necessarily money, into your marketing. Sure the ads and kits cost money, but I was giving away something for free. In an information age, every business can give away free information that solves a problem for your consumer. If you sell windows, you can give free information on how to avoid spending a fortune on buying windows and making mistakes when purchasing windows. That would be a valuable kit to builders and consumers of windows. You can give away free samples if you have them, but giving away something for free, especially information that solves a problem, is invaluable. Whatever you give away for free, it starts your relationship off right with your potential clients because they see that you are willing to help them without necessarily asking something in return.

Fifth and final key to the system is that it is a system. Each component is thought out and delivered as a touch or communication. It gives people you don't know an opportunity to build a relationship with you, your associates and your company. It is the touches that give familiarity, comfort and trust to your business. Once you develop your system, you will find as I did they will call you, tell them everything about themselves and give you their money.

Stay Focused

Jay Conrad Levinson said it best:

> Guerrillas know that the single most important element of superb marketing is commitment to a focused plan. Do you think commitment is easy to maintain after an ad has run nineteen times and nobody is buying? It's not easy. But marketing guerrillas have the coolness to hang in there because they know how to get into a prospect's unconsciousness, where most purchase decisions are made. They know it takes repetition. This knowledge fuels their commitment. Anyhow, they never thought it was going to be easy. As real estate is location, location, location, marketing is frequency, frequency, frequency.

Don't give up on your prospects. And don't be afraid to try new strategies. Today's Guerrilla Marketer knows they need to combine high tech with high touch. If my strategy above doesn't quite fit your business, then broaden it. Don't be afraid to use all the tools the Internet makes available to us as marketers. If you need to tweak my system, I won't be offended. In fact, each business needs to personalize its own five-touch system. To help you do that, here is a list of potential touches or contacts that you can use to develop your own five touch system:

1. Ad
2. Email
3. Website
4. Mail drop
5. Direct mailing
6. Targeted mailing
7. Inserts
8. Website link
9. Web ring
10. Articles
11. Advertorials
12. FREE samples
13. Contests
14. Free giveaways
15. Referrals
16. Word of Mouth

Also, see the "Guerrilla Marketing 100 list," (www. GMarketing.com) for more ideas.

The five touch system is a process that keeps working day in and day out. It is about finding people that will want to do business with you, qualifying people and having them call you. Imagine what it could mean to your business if a system was in place to generate new customers on a regular basis? My Five-Touch Marketing System is the key to my success and it can be yours as well.

About Grant W. Hicks, CIM, FCSI

Grant Hicks, fellow of the Canadian Securities Institute, is a professional speaker, writer, co-author and a Retirement Planning Specialist. He is the owner of Hicks Financial, which focuses on providing Retirement Planning Solutions and ideas. He manages **www.FinancialAdvisorMarketing.com**, *a Web site for financial professionals around the world from his offices in Parksville, British Columbia on beautiful Vancouver Island, Canada. He is co-author of* Guerrilla Marketing for Financial Advisors *with Jay Conrad Levinson, Trafford Publishing, September 2003. His new books include* Guerrilla Marketing For Financial Advisors 2 *with Jay Conrad Levinson (Entrepreneur Press 2007), and* Retirement Simplicity for Canadians, *(Trafford Publishing 2007).*

CHAPTER 11

GUERRILLA POSITIONING

Benefits in Action

Al Lautenslager

> *"I knew a man who grabbed a cat by the tail and learned 40 percent more about cats than the man who didn't."*
>
> ~Mark Twain

The primary investments of a guerrilla marketer are clearly, time, energy, imagination, information, and knowledge. So many times when marketers market, they think they have to run out and buy an advertisement in the newspaper, the yellow pages, the radio or television. This couldn't be further from the truth and those involved with the application of that time, energy, imagination, knowledge and information have proven it doesn't take a blank check book to market.

Marketing is made up of many, many, many things all working together and if those things are low and no cost then your bottom line gets fatter. Some of the often overlooked marketing concepts that can be implemented for a company or organization are the concepts of positioning and talking to customers and prospects from the perspective of benefits. These two basic Guerrilla Marketing concepts have been proven to work significantly in the marketing of a company or organization. Let's look at these in action.

Benefits in Action

> *"I'm great, our employees are great and our company is great. Isn't that enough for people to buy from us?"*

How many times have you looked at an ad and saw tons of information about a company? How many times have you listened to a sales rep's presentation telling you all about the company history, how big their equipment is, how many certifications their people have and on and on and on....all about them? Who cares?

How many times have you visited a Web site only to be hit with the glaring, "about us" section or the "take a virtual tour of our company," button? Who cares?

My guess is that the answers to the above questions are: "a lot, several and too many times." Now how many times are you really interested in the information related to the questions above? My guess is not many, few or none.

For, you see, you as a prospect are not interested in "them." Your customers and prospects don't care about you. Who do they care about? Who are they interested in? Who do they care about? *They care about themselves.* They are interested *in their own situation.*

Prospects and customers want to know what you have that will benefit them. What are you offering that will help them, regardless of your history, origin, size or stature.

Knowing this one thing can "transform" your marketing and the ensuing communication of your marketing message to your target market. Yes, I said transform. I know that's a heavy word but that is what people have told me after realizing and applying this one concept.

It's All About the Benefits

We are talking about perspective here. If your marketing is not talking to customers and prospects from the perspective of, "What's in it for me, the prospect or customer," then *change it.* Change it now. Undergo that transformation. Yes it will happen. Try it. Rewrite it all. Re-do it all. Don't highlight the "about us" section on your Web site. Sure people want to check you out but there are lots of other things that will show and prove your credibility.

One of Webster's definitions of benefit is something that promotes well-being. That's exactly what we are talking about here. A benefit is something that makes your prospect or customer feel better, smarter; makes things more convenient; hassle free; saves the prospect money, or avoids pain. These are all things that answer the question, "What's in it for me, the prospect/customer?"

How many times have you driven past a business where they are proudly displaying a plaque stating, "Founded in 1910?" Do you really care when the business was founded that you are about to do business with (if they have what you want or need)? No. You don't care. Who cares? No one. However for all you dissenters, wait one minute. There *is* a corresponding benefit. The benefit related is if you have been in business that long, there is a good chance you'll be around when your prospect or customer needs you or wants to buy from you. Reliability is the benefit and that answers the question, "What's in it for me, the prospect/customer?"

Got it? Understand what a benefit is now? Who do your prospects care about? Not you—them!

First class seating on an airplane is not a benefit. First class seating is a feature. The benefit that corresponds to this feature is comfort (wider seats, free drinks, nice meals). The benefit related to the feature of first class seating truly makes a customer feel better with more convenience and less hassle.

I suggest that you make a list of all the benefits you offer to your clients and prospects. Go ahead list them all and remember I said benefits, not features. What do you offer that makes people feel better, do their job better, save them money, take the hassle out of things or make more convenient? List every one of them.

Example list of Benefits:

- **Convenient payment options**—we accept credit cards.
- **Convenient location**—close to home and the mall.
- **Save money**—Special discount member rewards program.

- **Save time**—Express checkout for gold members.

- **Make smarter**—Daily e-mail alert with news headlines.

- **No hassle**—Unlimited return and exchange policy, no questions asked.

Yeah this company is great, the proprietor is great and all the employees are great but that's not enough for people to buy. These benefits are plenty of incentive and reason to buy. These are all about the prospect and not about the company. These are things prospects do care about. Who cares? The prospect does.

Okay, there was some bad news there but it wasn't that bad was it? I hope not, because you have to have benefits. If you don't you better come up with some or stop reading now.

What Are You Really Selling?

If you're still having trouble nailing those benefits, think about what you are really selling. People don't go to the eye doctor to buy eye glasses. They go to buy vision! You don't go to the movies to buy tickets. You go for entertainment. When I go to Home Depot or Loews to buy a drill bit, I don't care how hard the steel is in the drill bit. I don't care what kind of package that drill bit comes in. I don't even care what it costs. What am I really after…? *Holes*. I am buying a drill bit to get good holes for my home projects or repairs. *Holes* are what I'm really buying.

A pet store doesn't sell dog toys to dogs. They sell them to dog owners. Dogs could care less that a squeak toy looks like a hot dog. The owner will buy it because it's cute and thinks the dog will like it because it resembles something to eat. Wrong. It's cute. That's it. I just recently saw a couple of entrepreneurs introducing "Doggie Dessert." Have you ever seen a dog with a sweet tooth? Have you ever seen a dog turn down food of any kind? Dogs just eat what's in front of them whether its dessert or the main course. Doggie Dessert isn't selling dessert for dogs. They are selling dessert for dog owners who like dessert after their meals who think their dogs will too. What a country!

Think about what you are really selling and this will help you come up with your benefits more easily.

Your Competitive Advantage

Now that you have benefits, what's next? Let's put the list you make to work (the list of all your benefits). Before we do that I want you to make one more list. Yes, this is the interactive part of this book. Work with me here. Make a list of all the benefits your competitor offers. You can do this collectively for all your competitors or for individual competitors. Put as much thought into this as you did for your own list of benefits. You'll see why shortly.

So you now have two lists (or more if you looked at each competitor separately). Now compare your list with the competitors' list of benefits. Do thinks look similar? They probably do. That is typically the case with companies in the same business, but (here comes the famous but statement...) that is not necessarily a good thing. Do you want to be just like your competition? Forget that. Here is the better question: Do your customers and prospects want you to be like your competition? If you are, why would they buy from you?

Ah, now there's a great question all businesses need to consider, study, and *answer*. I'll repeat the question.

Why would Someone Buy From You?

There is an answer to this question, even if your benefit list is the same as your competitor. You need to then ask your customer why they buy from you. It may be a reason you haven't thought of or haven't put on your benefit list. What is the reason they bought from you? Why didn't they buy from your competition? If it's because your competition doesn't offer the same benefit to your customer that you did, then you're on to something. That something is a *competitive advantage*.

You're competitive advantage is the benefit you offer that your competition doesn't. It is the reason why your customer buys from you and not your competition. Hopefully that reason is unique. Many people have head that you need a unique selling proposition commonly referred to as an USP, but hey this is a marketing book so I call it a Unique Marketing Proposition or an UMP, (not to be confused with an umpire at a baseball game).

Why should I buy from you if I am one of your prospects? You better be able to answer this quickly, succinctly, and with a great deal of confidence and enthusiasm or I'm off to another vendor/supplier.

If you can say that you are the "only one," that offers something. You not only have a unique offer, you ought to tell the world! If you are the only one that offers a certain product or service (exclusivity) or has a certain set of knowledge, or inside secrets (expertise), then you truly have a unique proposition to offer. That's a competitive advantage. If you have something that is the best, you have a competitive advantage.

A Tasty Case with Real Meat on the Bone

When I go to Cincinnati, Ohio, I go to the Montgomery Inn Restaurant. Why? Do they have a competitive advantage? Is there a compelling reason for me to buy from them? You bet there is. I buy from them because they have "the best" spare ribs that I have ever eaten. They are the "only one" that has a "unique" sauce for their "specially" prepared ribs. They are the only ones that know the secret for that flavorful sauce. Look at all those reasons to buy.

I'm not the only one that realized those competitive advantages. World-famous clientele have done wonders spreading the word about Montgomery Inn's wonderful ribs and sauce. Among distinguished guests who have savored the great taste of Montgomery Inn are Presidents Ford, Reagan, Bush and Clinton, Elizabeth Taylor, Tom Selleck, Elton John, Pete Rose, Sparky Anderson, Johnny Bench, Andre Agassi, Arnold Palmer, Mark McGwire, John Glenn, Neil Armstrong, Bill Cosby, Britney Spears, Al Lautenslager, and Bob Hope.

FOR THE BEST RIBS IN THE WORLD:
Montgomery Inn
The Rib King
9440 Montgomery Rd.
Montgomery, OH 45242
513.791.3482
www.MontgomeryInn.com

(Who would have ever thought you'd get a rib restaurant recommendation from a marketing book? Hey that's a competitive advantage. This is the only marketing book in the world that recommends the best ribs restaurant in the world!)

Okay. Get it now? Let's do a quick mid-chapter recap:

■ What's in it for me;
Communicating prospect benefit not just features;
competitive advantages are why people buy.

■ Unique marketing proposition;
Why should I buy from you?
What are you the best and only?
What are you really selling?
Eat ribs at Montgomery Inn, Montgomery, Ohio.

You do all of the above and it will put you in a position where you will be known in your marketplace for the things you want to be known for. That will make people buy from you.

Positioning In Action

One of Webster's definitions for position is a point of view adopted and held to. That certainly is the case as you use positioning as part of your marketing. You adopt a point of view and share it with others so they eventually adopt the same point of view.

In terms of marketing, that point of view adopted and held to is a perception. Positioning is a perception in the minds of your prospects and customers, and that perception is reality.

Positioning = Perception

Perception = Reality

Therefore

Positioning = Reality

(Our algebra teachers would all be proud.)

If I mention brown delivery truck to you, you immediately think UPS and maybe make reference to their recent commercials that have ingrained in your head, "What can Brown do for you?"

If I mention less filling, great taste, the reality you perceive is Miller Lite beer. Back several years ago the commercial starring Clara Peller shouting, "where's the beef?" positioned Wendy's in the minds of their prospects.

All of these are examples of positioning and in the world of marketing, placing these perceptions in the mind of a prospect increases the likelihood that those prospects will become paying customers. Not only does position equal perception equal reality, it also leads to sales.

Positioning at Work

Here is the best positioning advice I can give you that you can put to use right now! (This is worth way more than what you paid for this book.) *You are an expert!*

When I recently was following up with someone that I had met at a networking event, I asked her what her job was. She told me she was a consultant. I said that's great, consultants are a dime a dozen. (Except me. I cost more than a dime.) I then asked what she consulted about. She told me that she helps companies put leadership programs into place.

I stopped, thought about, "expert positioning," and told her that she was no longer to refer to herself as a consultant. I told her she was now a "Leadership Expert."

She nodded like she kind of got it but I could tell she wasn't quite sure about this positioning concept I was telling her about.

She called me the very next day and joyously told me about a prospect who she had been calling on for months, signed a contract with her for her services, all because she said she was an *expert*! She didn't use the world consultant. She positioned herself in the mind of her prospect.

People like to buy from experts. People trust experts. People have confidence in experts. It's okay to call yourself an expert. Try it. Position yourself in the mind of your prospect as an expert. You will be perceived as an expert and that perception will be reality which could lead to a sale.

Other "Expert" Examples:

- Lawyer = Legal Expert

- Florist = Celebration/Special Occasion Expert

- IT Worker = Computer Technology Expert

- Collections agency = Cash Flow Expert

- Manicurist = Beautification Expert

- Bus Driver = Transportation Expert

Tagline = Positioning = Increased Revenue

A tagline can also position a business. A recent business owner approached me for consultation about creating a tagline to position his business. After inquiring about the nature of his business, I learned that he owned an appliance retail store. I then learned that his store sold refrigerators, dishwashers, washers, dryers, grills, microwave ovens, water softeners, and related appliances. I knew right away that his company's name, Henderson's Appliances, wouldn't properly position him. After more meetings and more brainstorming and more attempts to create a perception in the minds of his prospects (and that's positioning) we came up with his new tagline:

Henderson's Appliances—We cook it, We clean it, We chill it!

You can drive by Henderson's Appliances today and see a big sign on his storefront that reads:

Henderson's Appliances—We cook it, We clean it, We chill it!

All of his delivery drivers wear uniforms with logo's embroidered on the shirts that read:

Henderson's Appliances—We cook it, We clean it, We chill it!

If you ask anyone in his target market that he markets to, where they go to buy new appliances when old ones break down, they typically reply, "I'm not real sure about the name of the business but it's that place that cooks it, cleans it and chills it." This business owner has positioned his company in the minds of his prospects with a simple tagline.

Other tagline examples:

- Dentist—*Just Relax. We know the Drill.*

- Bakery—*A Fresh Approach To Your Morning.*

- Plumber—*We Are Your Security Plumber. No Leaks Anywhere.*

- Financial Planner—*Your Peace of Mind is a Piece of our Mind.*

- Caterer—*We'll Make You the Guest, Not The Host, at Your Own Party.*

- Body Shop—*We're the One For You When You Run Into Old Friends or Strangers.*

- Appliance Store—*We Cook It, We Clean It, We Chill It.*

- Car Wash/Detailer—*Leave The Details To Us.*

- Orthodontist—*We'll Give You The Straight Talk.*

- Cleaning Service—*We Do The Dirty Work.*

- Sub Sandwich Shop—*Made With Nice Warm Buns.*

Source: "Guerrilla Marketing in 30 Days" (www.gm30.com)

Add positioning to the communication of benefits and an ensuing competitive advantage and you give your prospects the reasons they should buy from you. These are very powerful marketing concepts that take some thought. Don't skim over them lightly. Benefits, competitive advantages and positioning are not always as obvious as you might think.

Montgomery Inn in Cincinnati didn't realize that they had the best ribs until more and more people started telling them and telling others. Their competitive advantage developed over time as they realized this. It wasn't obvious on day one.

Use these concepts and tactics in your planning, development and execution and you will see how powerful they can be. Oh, and to invite me to your dinner at Montgomery Inn, just send me an e-mail at Al@AlLautenslager.com.

About Al Lautenslager

Al Lautenslager is an award winning marketing/PR consultant, direct mail promotion specialist, author, speaker and entrepreneur. He is the principal owner of Market For Profits, a Chicago-based marketing consulting firm and also the president and owner of The Ink Well, a commercial printing and mailing company in Wheaton, IL. His articles can be seen on over twenty online sites in addition to being a featured business coach for the online site of Entrepreneur Magazine, entrepreneur.com. A member of USA Today's small business panel, and a certified Guerrilla Marketing Coach, Lautenslager is also a much-in-demand speaker on the subject of marketing. Al's latest book, Guerrilla Marketing in 30 Days *is co-authored with Jay Conrad Levinson. His Web site is* **www.Market-For-Profits.com***.*

CHAPTER 12

GUERRILLA SPEAKING

How to Generate Leads, Customers, and Huge Profits from your Presentations!

Craig Valentine

> *"Talk to people about themselves and they
> will listen for hours."*
> ~Benjamin Disraeli

Most small businesses and entrepreneurs would be absolutely shocked if they knew just how much money they are leaving on the table by either not using or misusing the art of public speaking to market their business. After this chapter, you will have an unfair advantage in using presentations to quickly generate leads, customers, and huge profits. You will learn how to accomplish more with a one-hour speech than most will accomplish with a month of frustrating marketing efforts. If you want to rapidly raise immediate and long-term profits, I am convinced that public speaking is your most essential tool. Come with me to uncover its power. In the next few pages, you will learn how to use public speaking to:

- sell loads of your products/services even before you finish your speech!

- generate more qualified leads in one hour than most entrepreneurs get in one month;

■ get heavily compensated even from your "free" speeches;

■ make your audiences TALL (Think, Act, Laugh, and Learn).

How to Sell Loads of your Products/Services Even Before You Finish Your Speech!

Guerrilla Speaking Case Study Number One: The Power of One Story

If you had picked up my telephone in the year 2000, you would have heard a lady from a company in Michigan say, "Mr. Valentine, we want you to be a speaker for our upcoming event. We need you to do about forty-five minutes and we are willing to pay you $3,500." Back in 2000, I was still a fairly new speaker (even though I had won the Toastmasters World Championship) so I was thrilled to have my first high-paying keynote speech. On the other hand, I was also extremely nervous.

To make things worse, they flew me out first-class. Then they picked me up in a black limousine, took me to an expensive restaurant, wined and dined me, and finally dropped me off at a five-star hotel. The next morning they scooped me up in the same limousine and drove me to the event. Just as I was about to take the stage, the lady who brought me in tucked into my jacket a check for $3,500! I jumped up on that stage, grabbed the microphone, looked out on that audience and guess what I did? I gave them a $150 speech.

That's right I failed miserably. It was so bad that the lady who convinced all the higher -ups to hire me could not even look me in the eyes when I finished. Needless to say I felt devastated. Even the limo driver was looking at me as if to say, "You mean I still have to take *you* back?" I have never heard from them again.

Fast-forward seven years to today and you may be shocked to know the following truth about my speaking business. Here it is: My rehire rate is a startling 92 percent! That's 92 percent! Do you know what that means? It means that if you hire me to speak once, chances are very good you are going to hire me again. Not only that, but I get spin-off business, sell thousands of dollars in products per event, and get amazing opportunities I never even knew existed. So that begs the following question: What made the difference between that dreadful Michigan event and my engagements today?

The answer to the question above continues to earn me thousands upon thousands of dollars each and every time I tell that story in my speech. Why? Imagine telling that story to a group of up-and-coming speakers. No matter what the *process* is that took me from the Michigan failure to today's successes will sell to that audience. This is because of the following fact: When your audience buys into your story, you can consider your product or service as sold.

When people buy into your story, they will buy into your message. When they buy into your message, they will grab whatever products and services you make available to them. Speaking is all about telling a *story* and selling a *process.* Your audience members want access to the process that took you from where you were to where you are so they can use it to do likewise. When you position your product or service as that bridge, you will put profits into your pockets. Here is what I tell my audiences (usually up-and-coming speakers) at the end of the Michigan story:

> What made the difference between 2000 and today? A process made all the difference. After that disastrous event, I re-dedicated myself to the art of public speaking and, over these last seven years, I have uncovered a process that has propelled my speaking career. I firmly believe this process will take you from wherever you are as a speaker to wherever you want to go. And I am so excited because, after all these hard-fought years, I have finally been able to bottle-up this process and put it into a system you can use immediately. This system is called "The-Edge-Of-Their-Seats Storytelling Home-Study Course for Speakers."

Imagine having your audience members sprint to the back of the room to purchase your products or services even before you have finished your speech. This will happen for you as long as you accomplish three things:

1. You make them TALL (Think, Act, Laugh, and Learn) throughout your presentation.

2.   You sell them with your powerful, relatable story.

3.   You position your products/services as the bridge.

What story are you telling in your speeches? What bridge are you creating? The best thing you can do for yourself as a speaker is to become a masterful storyteller. Tell a story, sell your process, and reap your profits.

How to Use Presentations to Systematically Generate More Leads in One Hour than Most Entrepreneurs Get in One Month

Guerrilla Speaking Case Study Number Two: Speak TALL and Carry a Big List

In *Mastering Guerrilla Marketing*, Jay Conrad Levinson said: "No matter how successful your attack, never lose contact with your customers. If you do, you lose your competitive advantage…"

A few years back my business partner, Darren La Croix (Founder of The Humor Institute), kept telling me, "Craig, you have to start collecting names when you speak. You need to begin building your list."

I always replied, "List shmist, who needs it? I am doing fine with my product sales at my events." Little did I know how much money and recurring income I was leaving on the table each time I spoke.

Then one day it happened. Darren called and said, "Craig, I just sent out a marketing sales letter to my list promoting my new course and guess how much I sold?" Not really paying much attention, I said, "Okay Darren, how much?" He said, "A little over $23,000 today." Stunned, I perked up and asked, "In one day? Okay Darren, what was that you've been saying about a list?"

Suddenly I was sold on building my list. Building a qualified list of prospects and customers will propel you far beyond most marketers who attempt to turn their presentations into profits. Using the storytelling formula to sell your products will be profitable. However, you are still leaving tons on the table if you do not follow-up on those who have not purchased from you. Here is a phrase that Darren and I came up with that you should burn into your memory: "Speak TALL and carry a big List." Doing both will lead to a remarkable connection and recurring profits. As Levinson reminds us: "The Guerrilla is always aware of the extraordinary power of follow-up. What's the Guerrilla's middle name? Follow-up." (*Mastering Guerrilla Marketing*).

The key to Darren's profits, and now to mine as well, is the list because it allows us to do follow-up marketing to qualified prospects and actual customers. The question is how do you build this list from the speaking platform? There are several methods we use, but none will work if you are not making them TALL (Think, Act, Laugh, and Learn) during your presentations.

After all, speaking is the perfect opportunity to quickly build confidence and familiarity with your audience. Guerrilla Marketing teaches us that these two factors will determine from whom your prospects will buy. We will get to the speaking skills later. For now, let's look into some of these list-building strategies:

1. The clipboard: Towards the end of your presentation, you can have volunteers pass around several clipboards to your audience members. Each clipboard should have sheets with about twenty-five spots for names and e-mail addresses. The key is to make sure you have built up one of your *processes* so that the audience is dying to get access to that bridge. Then you offer part of that bridge *for free* when they place their name and e-mail address on the clipboard. In other words, they see the clear and compelling benefit for signing up.

2. Name that Newsletter: Nobody wakes up in the morning saying, "I just can't wait to get on someone else's newsletter today!" However, people do wake up thinking, "I really would like to know how to become a better speaker"; or "I would love to have some tools to build my business"; or "I have got to get my finances together, I wonder if anyone can help me." That's why it always floors me to see presenters say things like, "Sign up for my newsletter today. It's *free!*"

    So what? I can sign up for a million newsletters for free. The question is what will I get out of it? What's in it for me? I used to have a hard time getting people to sign up on the spot for mine until I changed the name from "Craig Valentine's Free E-Newsletter" to "*Free* Public Speaking Mastery Toolkit!" Now that the benefit of mastering the art of public speaking is in the name of the newsletter, people line up in droves to sign up. Name your newsletter with a benefit and you will start seeing lines of people anxiously waiting to become your next prospects.

3. Offer a drawing to collect business cards at your event. The key here is to offer one of your products free and promote the benefits of it by selling it with a story while you do the drawing. This kills two birds with one stone, because now you are building a lust for that product and a list for your profits. Later you can use online tools and content to entice them to opt-in to your newsletter. There are some people who cannot stand when the speaker sells from the platform. The great thing about using a drawing is that nobody gets offended when you talk about a product that you are about to give away. People love freebies so they get wrapped up in wanting your product and they yearn to hear all about it!

These are just a few of the ways to build your list while you are speaking. Again, none of these ways will work unless you make your audience TALL (Think, Act, Laugh, and Learn). You will find that the more you connect with them, the faster your list will grow. Let us turn to where you can get these opportunities to speak in the first place.

Get Heavily Compensated Even from your "Free" Speeches

Leverage is a key Guerrilla Marketing strategy and effective public speaking can create an explosion of unique and profitable opportunities for you. Mitch Meyerson and Jay Conrad Levinson, in their Guerrilla Marketing Coach Certification Program, teach that "leverage is the act of applying a small force in order to obtain a big impact."

You may be asking, "Okay Valentine, I see how speaking can be profitable, but where can I get speaking opportunities in the first place?" Of course this depends on your target market. However, you will be surprised at how speaking to certain mixed groups can be your best tool for getting in front of your specific market. By mixed groups I am referring to audiences containing people from separate companies and associations. One example of these, which is almost always looking for speakers, is the Rotary Club.

Guerrilla Speaking Case Study Number Three: The Speech that Never Ended

A few years back a friend asked me to speak to his Rotary Club in Baltimore City at 8:00 a.m. on a Saturday morning. Honestly, I could think of nothing I would have rather done less than spend my guarded Saturday morning speaking for free to a tiny group that has never heard of me.

Whoa, was I wrong! What I did not realize at the time was that my opportunities were about to explode. I agreed to speak as a favor to my friend and wound up in front of twenty-four people that Saturday. To my surprise there were young professionals, seasoned executives, and everyone in-between. I gave a short twenty-minute presentation on the art of public speaking, mixed in some relevant stories, and drove home some universal points. Afterwards I shook a few hands and figured that was it.

As a result of that twenty-minute free speech to twenty-four Rotary Club members, I got four new clients. It gets better. One of those clients is a Federal Government Agency that has hired me to speak at their National Public Affairs Conference in Washington DC as well as several other engagements around the country. Another State Government Agency has hired me multiple times too. Thousands upon thousands of dollars in speaking fees have come from that free speech. That is how easy it is to move from free to fee. The best part about it is you could be next. Look up your local Rotary Clubs, Kiwanis Clubs, Chambers of Commerce organizations and other mixed groups and volunteer to speak at one of their meetings. You will be extremely glad you did.

Why did this work so well for me and will work wonders for you too? It is simply because of this undeniable fact about the business of speaking: "The best and easiest way to get speaking opportunities is for people to see you speak."

This goes back to having your audience members gain confidence and familiarity with you so that they walk away saying, "We should use her for something in the future." No demo tape, Web site, or press kit will do as much for you as twenty minutes in front of the right audience.

This is, of course, assuming you can make your audiences TALL (Think, Act, Laugh, and Learn). Once you do start building a solid list, it will be easy for you to start creating your own events and inviting your prospects and customers to attend. These can be fee-based workshops and seminars that they will gladly attend because of your constant valuable contact with them.

You can also hold free workshops, fill them up, and leverage them profitably with additional back-end products and services. Visit worldchampionsspeakers.com to get a feel for the types of profitable events you can produce.

Six Ways to be Heavily Compensated from Every Free Speech you Give

When you first start giving speeches, you will most likely do several of them for free. However, that definitely does not mean you should not be compensated. In fact, you should be heavily compensated for every free speech you give. The key to profiting from your free speeches is leverage. Here you will find how to make the biggest splash with one free speech. When you get your speaking opportunities, use these six strategies to pick up all the money and opportunities that other speakers consistently leave on the table:

1. Get prospects to sign up for your newsletter so you can market to them later. You learned how to do this earlier in the chapter.

2. Record every single speech at least in audio so you can turn these programs into profits. For example, you might do a program on networking and then create an audio CD of the program to sell for $39.95 to future audiences. In fact, you might even sell it to that very audience by getting pre-orders before you leave. I did this recently in Toronto and walked away with an extra $1,500 without even having the complete product yet. It does not matter that you are volunteering to speak. Nobody has ever listened to an audio

CD and then complained, "It's good stuff but it sounds like he's speaking for free." If the content is good, you should sell it. Give them a discount for ordering before the product is complete.

3.   Get testimonials from your audience members. Other than someone actually seeing you in action, testimonials are the next best thing for gaining that credibility, confidence, and familiarity with new audiences. The key nowadays is to not simply get the written kind but also the audio and video testimonials as well. You are already recording your speech so it should not be too much extra effort to record testimonials from your audience members. They will go a long way! Visit www.craigvalentine.com to see how I use these audio and video testimonials as marketing weapons.

4.   Transcribe recorded speech and turn it into an e-book or a supplement to a home-study course or training program. I am part of a fusion-marketing product called "Speaking Secrets of the Champions," which is a six CD audio set I did with five other World Champions of Public Speaking. After we sold about 4,000 of these at $69.95, we decided to have it transcribed and turned it into an e-book. Now it can be a separate product or combined with the audio set to add value which increases the price. Likewise you can leverage your free speeches into audio products and then into e-books (or special reports, manuals, etc.) and sell them for a very handsome profit. People spend hours and hours per week in their automobiles and right now your target market should be listening to you.

5.   Videotape your free speech and use parts of it for a demo DVD for prospective clients. My first $40,000 contract came from me sending a demo tape of a full-length 60-minute free speech I gave to a Toastmasters District audience years ago. Although the filming was not at a professional level and all my bloopers and blemishes were left in, the content and connection were good enough to get me hired. Use free speeches as an opportunity to

build your valuable video footage. Eventually you will get professional videographers who can help you leverage your free speech into a full-blown DVD set. You can see my latest demo video at www.craigvalentine.com, and this can give you ideas for yours.

6. Sell your products and services to the audience members right there on the spot. Make sure you get permission from the meeting planners ahead of time because the cultures in some organizations will not allow for it. On the other hand, if you agree to speak for free at an event, they will usually be more than happy to set you up with a table and even provide you with a helper to make your learning resources available for sale.

As you can see, speaking for free is priceless. However, when you start leveraging these speeches by getting testimonials, demo DVDs, and new connections, you will rapidly find yourself commanding healthy fees for your future speeches. That is, of course, as long as you are making your audiences TALL.

Six Strategies for Making your Audience Members TALL (Think, Act, Laugh, and Learn)

1. Start with a bang. The first thirty seconds of your presentation will either make or break you. That is all the time it takes for your audience to figure out whether or not they want to hear more. Do not waste this time on greetings such as, "I am so glad to be here" or "Thank you very much for giving me the opportunity to speak to you today." These are boring and predictable. Instead, start with a bang by immediately going into a story or a major promise. For example, I might start off with an irresistible story and then jump right into this promise: "In the next forty-five minutes, you will learn how to keep your very next audience on the edge of their seats leaning on your every word. You will uncover the secret to generating more new customers with a one-hour speech than most entrepreneurs get in an entire month." Do you think

that promise will grab their attention more than the weather report most speakers open with?

2. Tell a story and sell a process. The late, great Bill Gove (first President of the National Speakers Association) gave us the timeless advice to "tell a story and make a point." As we stated earlier, when people buy into your story and your point, you can sell them almost anything. Stories work because they evoke emotions and people make decisions with emotions backed up by logic. As with any powerful tool, use this with the utmost integrity so that what you sell actually does what you promise.

3. Cater to your visual, auditory, and kinesthetic learners. This means you should use your words and gestures (and an occasional slide) to paint pictures for the visual learners. Speak clearly and with appropriate changes in your stress, rate, pitch, volume, and pausing for your auditory learners. Finally, include activities and other forms of interaction such as asking your audience members questions, physically moving out into your audience for their thoughts, and having them raise their hands occasionally to keep them kinesthetically involved. If you neglect to address either one of these learning styles, then you will find yourself speaking to only a fraction of your audience. This will severely damage your connection and your results.

4. Never end with the question and answer period. This is a huge mistake most speakers make. Audiences remember best what they hear first and last so make sure *your* strong message is the last one they hear. Do not leave it to chance. It is great to have a Q&A period just as long as you follow it with a strong closing, which summarizes your main points and leaves your audience on an emotional high.

5. Do not give "data dumps" unless you want your audience to throw your speech out in the nearest trash can. It is much more effec-

tive to have only three major points that your audience can digest then to force-feed them ten ideas that will overwhelm them. In a paper, you can get away with ten points. In speaking, you cannot. The old speaker proverb is correct: "When you squeeze your information in, you squeeze your audience out." Less is more.

6. Speak conversationally with your audience. The days of oratorical Hyde Park-type lectures will not work for Guerrilla Speaking. Come out from behind the lectern, stand unguarded directly in front of your audience, and converse with them as if you are sharing stories and ideas with a friend. Remember that speaking is a dialog and your audience wants to be heard too. People buy into what they help create so find ways to make them part of your speech. The stronger you connect, the faster your business will grow! Visit www.craigvalentine.com for a free special report on "How to Keep Your Audiences on the Edge of their Seats and then Profit when they Get Up!"

One Final Thought

I completely agree with Jay Conrad Levinson that "marketing is everything." Speaking is a piece of marketing and, if you use the tools from this chapter, speaking can become a huge slice of your profits. You will be thrilled at how fast new leads, customers, and profits come to you with each speech. The only thing you will be surprised at is how much *other* speakers are still leaving on the table.

About Craig Valentine

Craig Valentine is the 1999 Toastmasters International World Champion of Public Speaking. As President of The Communication Factory, he has helped thousands of up-and-coming speakers in seven countries and forty-four of the United States using his process to enhance their presentations and increase their profits. Using this special process, Craig has sold more than $12 Million in educational *learning resources and has received a Congressional Achievement Award from the United States Congress for "Excellence in Communications." He is the Author of the book, "The Nuts and Bolts of Public Speaking" and the producer of several training courses designed to turn your presentations into huge profits. Reach him at* **Info@CraigValentine.com**. *On the Web:* **www.CraigValentine.com**.

CHAPTER 13

OPENING THE DOOR TO OZ

Publishing Guerrilla Marketing Style

Rick Frishman

*"Your attitude, not your aptitude, will
determine your altitude."*

~Zig Ziglar

We all know the scene from *The Wizard of Oz*. Dorothy and her motley bunch of friends finally make it to the Emerald City in the enchanted Land of Oz. They have survived attacks from angry apple trees, a field full of narcotic poppies, and their own bouts of self-doubt. They have made it to the Promised Land, but the little green guy at the door with his shifty eyes and bushy eyebrows bars their way into the place they have fought so hard to get to. But he relents and lets them in because Dorothy has something he wants—*the ruby slippers*. They're magical; they're powerful. They protect people from bad witches, and they hold the key to Dorothy's success.

Most everyone in the world wants to write a book. Really. Eighty percent of the population thinks they have something important to say. And you know what? Everyone *should* be an author, especially if you're a business person. Why? Because a book changes your life. No matter what you do in your business, whether it is taxidermy for turkeys or helping people market themselves on the Internet (both legitimate businesses with books attached to them), you want to be perceived as the expert, and there's no quicker way of getting that "expert" tag than with a book.

So in other words, your book is your very own pair of ruby slippers. When you get to the door at Oz, and you don't have a book, then the little guy says: "Why, you're not allowed in. What business would the wizard have with you?" But when you knock on the door and he pulls back the little peephole and sees you have a book, he says, "Why that's a horse of different color. Come on in," and in that instant you have gained access to the wonderful world of Emerald City, the land of published authors where everyone is rich, skinny, and has great sex—well, at least they have a better life.

With your book, your very own, customized, ruby slippers, you get to play with all the different colored horses. This is everybody in the publishing world: editors, agents, other publishers, people who are going on radio and television and could talk about your book. With a book, you're in. You're now a VIP, and you have all the privileges of a VIP: the networking opportunities, the joint venture and affiliate prospects. You also have access to a variety of smaller wizards: the TV producers, the radio guys, the editors in the top publishing houses. And sometimes, you even get to see the Grand Wizard herself, Oprah!

I know all of this because I am a published author. I've made it into the inner sanctuary of the Grand Wizard, and I've promoted authors for thirty years. I've done all the things that I talk about—hundreds of radio shows, dozens of TV shows, write-ups in the *New York Times* and a front page appearance on *the Wall Street Journal*. My company, Planned TV Arts, helps writers of all shapes and colors publicize their book. I've seen it a thousand times; publishing can change your life. And as a Guerrilla Marketer, it is one of the essential items on your "to do" list that needs to be checked off sooner than later because as a Guerrilla making your way through the minefield of marketing, you want something that makes you stand out from the rest of the folks out there who do what you do or make what you make.

Publishing as a Guerrilla Marketing Strategy

A good Guerrilla Marketer is aggressive in their marketing because they find as many opportunities as they can to get their message out loud and clear to the world. What better medium to do this with than a book? A book presents many different marketing opportunities because of one significant difference. You get on radio shows and even TV shows—arenas that you don't' have to pay for, by the way—because you're not talking about you, you're talking about your book.

Books give you credibility. Think about it. When you see celebrities on a talk show, they're there because they're promoting their latest movie. Authors do the same thing. It's always a much tougher sell to promote yourself. Your book is you once removed, and so it makes you more user-friendly.

Also, Guerrilla Marketing is about using your imagination to develop marketing strategies that will capture your target market. With the advent of Amazon, you don't even need to be in the major book store chains to get your book out there. I know hundreds of authors who made it to the top of Amazon and their book never once graced the aisles of Barnes and Noble. And if you are marketing your book well, you can reach your niche public much more efficiently with a book.

And, of course, the hallmark of any Guerrilla Marketer is to use your imagination; for books, especially small, "how-to" type books, are the best kind of business card you can pass out. You give them out to people just like you do a business card, and it gives your new contact a much better picture of who you are. This helps you to build a relationship with them—another hallmark Guerrilla Marketing principle—even before you sit down with them face to face because they have read all about you.

Where Your Book Comes From

Now, don't start thinking: I'm not a writer, how could I ever publish a book? This is the great part. You don't have to be a writer. If you reread what I've said up to this point, I've been saying published author, not published writer. You hire someone to write your book for you. Ghost writers and editors, good ones, are worth their weight in gold because they take your story and they make it sound good. I'm not actually even the writer of this piece, but I am the author. It is my ideas that are being presented.

To put a book together, all you need to do is gather up your content in some way. Have a friend interview you. If you know anything about Internet marketing, you record a teleseminar, or a series of them, have someone transcribe what you said, and then you either edit it into book form or pay a good editor to do it. Just know you are the expert at what you do. Tell someone about it and then put what you said into a book. Yes it will take time, not a small amount of energy, and definitely a lot of push to get it done. That's the nature of putting a book together, and it's part of being a Guerrilla Marketer.

However, recognizing that the whole publishing process can be a bit daunting, I actually have created a program, *Author 101*, to help authors learn how to navigate through the nebulous world of publishing houses, editors, and literary agents. It takes all of my experience working with these publishing types and gives it to you. While a book lends you instant credibility and legitimacy, and while they aren't too tough to put together—especially with some expert help as I just said—the publishing world is a little bit of a mine field. There're secrets that you need to know, and I'm going to share with you one of the most important: know what kind of publishing route you're dealing with.

There are four different avenues that you can take to getting your ruby sippers, your published book. I'm going to list them from my least favorite to my most favorite.

Publishing Route Number One: Traditional Publishing Houses

These are the Random Houses, Penguin Books, and McGraw-Hills. In other words, the big guys. The problem with this type of publishing house: you don't get in, not unless you have already made it as an author and have a lot of cash to do your own publicity. Now, since Guerrilla Marketers pride themselves on being able to market their businesses on shoe-string budgets, this type of publishing route is not ideal. However, if you insist that this is they way for you to go, here is what you need to know:

1. Write a great book proposal

Like any kind of writing, you can hire someone to do this for you. There's also a ton of books out there on the subject. My *Author 101* and others are all available for free at your local library. No matter which way you go about it, you need to follow the guidelines exactly as we give them to you. Publishers in this category are a stodgy lot. They like consistency; they also get a ton of proposals all the time, and they like a certain format because they can glean what they need to from that format without having to read everything.

Part of what you need in a proposal is your platform. Your platform is both your magic word and your Catch 22. Every traditional publisher wants to know what your platform is because it tells them what kind of a risk you are—and of course the smaller your risk the more likely you are to get published. So the right kind of platform consists of you having an e-mail list with a gazillion names on it and the multiple Web sites to support these lists. These traditional guys want you to own a billion dollar company with hundreds of employees. They want to see that you've been on Oprah at least forty-three times because you've already published ten books, and there are at least one hundred thousand people knocking down the doors at Barnes and Nobles to buy your book the second it hits the shelves. How many of you have a platform? Maybe 1 percent. And this is the catch—you need the book to get the platform. The traditional publishers want no risk with the non-fiction books that they publish. (They will take a chance on a new novelist if they really, really love the book.).

In addition to a strong platform, your proposal should also provide a list of the other books on this subject with an explanation of why your book is different, a marketing plan, and a marketing budget. If all of this sounds daunting, it is. If you have no money, no lists, no prior contact with the publishing world, then you're not in. It's like the college entrance tests, the SAT or the ACT—if you can't frontload your proposal with the keywords that they publisher wants to see, you don't get a high enough score, and so, sorry, you're not going to college—you're not going to have the Random House logo on your book.

2. Get a literary agent

To get into any of the major publishing houses, you need to have a literary agent. I work with about one hundred of them, and know that there are A-,

B-, and C-grade agents. Each agent has contacts in the various publishing houses, and part of what I do at Planned TV Arts is hook up the right agent with an author.

3. Get a literary attorney

In today's litigious culture, this is a must, especially with the major houses. The contracts are so complex that you need an attorney to help you figure out what, exactly, you're signing. My guy is Lloyd Jasin at www.copylaw.com. Whomever you choose, make sure that they've been in the business awhile and have made publishing their specialty.

There are other major minuses when you're looking at the major publishing houses. Once they accept your book, it takes them two years to actually publish the thing. You want your book now so that you can use it to start marketing your business. Who wants to wait that long?! Also, you also lose all control over the whole publishing process. The major houses basically say: Thank you very much, we'll send you a royalty check. You also don't get to be a part of the book design, and, most important, while the book says you own the copyright to your materials, God help you if you ever wanted someone else to publish your book.

Finally, if you're lucky, they might have given you an advance for the book, and that helps offset the wait time for seeing the book actually in print. But you have to have a great platform before they'll cough up advance money. They might even have it in the contract that you will have to buy back the copies of your book that don't sell or you may even have to buy ten thousand copies of your book yourself. You could potentially end up with boxes full of your book in your garage.

So for a Guerrilla Marketer, the traditional publishing route leaves much to be desired. It's very expensive, time consuming, even demeaning at times. They want your book to make money, and while that's nice, we Guerrillas recognize that the book isn't so much about the money; it's about having a product to help you market your business so that your business can make money.

Publishing Route Number Two: Self-Publishing

Any Guerrilla Marketer in their right mind says, "I'm not going to wait two years, hire an agent, and then lose all my control over my book." When Jay Conrad Levinson started the Guerrilla Marketing brand, there was only one other option: self-publishing. The advantages seem to be great—you get to be in total control of your book. However, there is one huge downside to this route. It's very expensive, and it can produce headaches of monumental proportions.

Here's what I'm talking about. You have to do it all: the cover design, the text layout, the paper, printing, and distribution. It costs $15 to $20 grand to do a book right, and that's usually beyond the budgets of most small business owners. Now, if the book takes hold, then you can make money, even a lot of it, down the road.

Lots of well known authors self-published. Richard Nelson Bolles self published *What Color is your Parachute* and John Grisham self published his first book. They marketed their book well, and then got picked up by one of the big guys. This can happen to you when you have a book, but the problem with a self-published book is that you also run the risk of ending up with five thousand copies in your garage and no way to distribute them. That's a problem, and if you're going to spend $10,000 to publish your book, go to the pros. But before you feel stuck, thinking the pros are the big guys, know that the "pros" don't just include the traditional publishers anymore.

Publishing Route Number Three: Print on Demand, or POD Publishing

This is, hands down, the easiest way for you to publish your book. You send your book in and they publish as many copies as you ask for; you're not stuck with the five thousand surplus books in your garage. It's also a very fast way to publish because you can get your book out in about three months, and it only costs $1,000 to get it done. What could be better than that, right?

Point on Demand definitely filled a need when it first came out. It was set up so that anyone could publish his or her book without having to go through all the gyrations a traditional publishing house sends you through. But the problem lies in its strength. Anyone can publish a book—on anything! It could be your mother's recipes or your kid's poems. The credibility suffers a bit because of this fact.

Having your book published through the POD route is kind of like being a baseball pitcher in the farm leagues. You're good enough to get to that point, but you haven't "gone to the show," baseball slang for making it into the major leagues. You might get there if you work hard enough and promote yourself well, and my favorite POD publisher, IUniverse, will even sometimes help you to get into Barnes and Noble or other big chains. But mostly the distribution of your book is left up to you. And distribution is a huge deal in publishing. It's how you get your book out there. While you, as a Guerrilla Marketer, will always be handing out your book as your business card, it is always nice to get your book in the stores because they do your marketing for you! POD rarely offers you that choice, which leads me to the next and final route…

Publishing Route Number Four: The Entrepreneurial Publisher, Morgan James Publishing Company

As you read in the previous section, David Hancock started Morgan James Publishing Company as a way to help authors leverage themselves and their businesses. It was created by a Guerrilla Marketer for Guerrilla Marketers. From a publishing standpoint, it took the best of the traditional publishing world and combined it with the best of the POD and self-publishing routes, and made it into the best way to publish your book.

When your book is published by Morgan James, it has credibility. They receive on average thirty-five manuscripts a year, the same as Random House, and they publish 120 to 150 titles. They also only publish "how-to" and inspirational books—no fiction—so that keeps them focused and on purpose of setting people up to build their businesses. With a Morgan James book, you also have a very professional looking book. The cover design and layout are handled for you, but, unlike the traditional houses, they make you part of the design process. It is your book and so they want you involved in its production. They also allow you to retain the copyright to your book so that when you want to repurpose the content (the marketing term for reusing your stuff) then you don't have to worry about violating any laws.

Most important, they have Ingram, a major book-distribution company, helping them to distribute your book. So you are making it into the big chain stores, and because you're working with people who understand marketing and who really want to work with you as a partner, they help you become more successful in your business. To that end, they also give you a higher royalty rate, much higher, than the traditional houses, even though they don't offer advances. They want to reward you for marketing well, not on what you think you can do. And if you're nervous about how to go about marketing your book, you take classes through the Entrepreneurial University which teaches you many different ways of legitimately making money with your book. (Oh, and one of the best things about Morgan James for me is their high sense of ethics. David will not publish anything that he wouldn't let his kids read.)

Ultimately with Morgan James, you get the best pair of ruby slippers imaginable, and with those slippers, you can click yourself into any scenario you can dream up. I know, because I have always wanted my own imprint. An imprint is the name under which a publisher publishes books. It gives you your own logo at the bottom of a book, but imprints are part of the major house. For example, Alfred Knopf, a well knows publishing house, was bought out by Random House, but Random allowed the Knopf name to continue as an imprint. My imprint with Morgan James is "MegaBook Publishing," and I've teamed up with one of the most-published authors of all time—Mark Victor Hansen, as part of the project. Because I have my own imprint, I get to bring in more people into the Land of Oz. I also have my "million dollar rolodex," the publishing world's yellow brick road. It gives you all the contacts you need to find your way to the Emerald City, the magical place of instant credibility where you are automatically more in demand. What business doesn't want that?

Getting a book published can be daunting. It requires work to get the book done and out. But it's as necessary for your business as breathing because no other marketing technique can catapult you to the big time more than having a book. So get to work. You, too, can have your very own pair of ruby slippers. See you in Oz!

About Rick Frishman

Rick Frishman has been president of Planned Television Arts since 1982. He is one of the most powerful and energetic publicists in the media industry. Rick continues to work with many of the top editors, agents, and publishers in America including Simon and Schuster, Random House, Harper Collins, Pocket Books, Penguin Putnam, and Hyperion Books. Some of the authors he has worked with include: Bill Moyers, Stephen King, Caroline Kennedy, Howard Stern, President Jimmy Carter, Mark Victor Hansen, Nelson DeMille, John Grisham, Hugh Downs, Henry Kissinger, Jack Canfield, Alan Deshowitz, Arnold Palmer, and Harvey Mackay. Rick is also co-author of eight national best-selling books including Guerrilla Marketing for Writers: 100 Weapons for Selling Your Work *with Jay Conrad Levinson and literary agent, Michael Larsen (Writers Digest Books, 2000), and co-author of* Guerrilla Publicity: Hundreds of Sure-Fire Tactics to Get Maximum Sales for Minimum Dollars *with Jay Conrad Levinson and Jill Lublin (Adams Media Corp, 2002). You can contact Rick at **www.RickFrishman.com**.*

PART THREE
Partnering for Profit

The key to successful Guerrilla Marketing is in embracing not the concept of competition but the beauty and advantage of cooperation. In other words, it's fuse for fun & profit. This section delves into one of the most important Guerrilla Marketing weapons: fusion marketing. The purpose of a fusion-marketing arrangement? Mutual profitability. One of the most rewarding, inexpensive, underused, and effective methods of marketing is to tie in your marketing efforts with the efforts of others. This section will help you to realize that almost everyone in your community is a potential fusion-marketing partner, and you will find out how some of the top Guerrilla Marketing Coaches have helped their clients utilize the power of fusion. So spread your wings while reducing your marketing costs. Read this section and be inspired to go out there and fuse?

CHAPTER 14

NIGHT OF THE STARS
Guerrilla Marketing Goes Hollywood

Kip Gienau

> *"Ideas are like rabbits. You get a couple, learn how to look after them, and pretty soon you have a dozen."*
> ~John Steinbeck

"Coral branches had lettering that read *BP Clean*. A school of fish wriggled by, each blinking *Vodafone, Vodafone*. A slithering shark with *Cadbury* curving across the snout. A puffer fish with *Lloyds TBS Group* in black lettering swam over convoluted heads of brain coral, with *Scottish Power* printed along the ridges in orange. And, finally, a moray eel poked its head out of a hole. Its greenish skin pattern said *Marks and Spencer*. Think of the possibilities. We call this genomic advertising."

This scenario is the fictional imagery of Michael Crichton from his latest medical thriller *Next* (Harper Collins Publishers, 2006) where he paints a bleak picture of a world filled with genetic manipulation such that even the realms of marketing aren't left unscathed, as the scene above would indicate.

But is this scenario the marketing of the future? If it is, we are all in serious trouble, because the cost of advertising would be so staggering it would make advertising at the Super Bowl, even with today's advertising prices, a bargain.

While this concept of the future of advertising may or may not be realistic, competing for the buying power of customers may seem just as daunting to the small business or the not-for- profit venture. How can businesses with small or non-existent budgets, compete? How can they stay in business? How can they make a profit when the cost of advertising is so high? The answer is so simple that, as the advertisement for a prominent insurance company says, "Even a caveman can do it."

Overcoming the Problem of Money

Large corporations spend millions of dollars every year (typically 10 percent of their gross income) because they know that their brand needs to be in front of the public constantly, continually, 24/7. For example, Foxwoods Resort and Casino in Norwich, Connecticut spent approximately $25 million worldwide in 2006. Small businesses can't even begin to spend that kind of money. There are bills to pay, inventories to maintain, employees' salaries, insurance, taxes, bookkeepers, etc.; all drain the resources of the small business like a camel drinking water after a long journey through a bone-dry desert.

Then, of course, there is the question of profit. Here is where Guerrilla Marketing can have the greatest impact in increasing—yes, I said *increasing* that evasive little thing every businessperson worth his weight in inventory craves like the "Holy Grail." I'm going to show you how to increase your profits while spending next to nothing on advertising. Impossible you say? Take a look at the following true story of someone just like you—a small business man (or woman). I call it "The Night of the Stars."

The Client

Francis Scott Key Fitzgerald once wrote, "The cleverly expressed opposite of any generally accepted idea is worth a fortune to somebody." Here, in a nutshell, is the most difficult obstacle to overcome: people hate change. Most people cringe at the thought of doing anything outside their "generally accepted ideas"—the way they've always done it. Working outside of their comfort zone can be downright frightening. Business owners, especially, tend to gravitate toward the path of least resistance—the path with the lowest risk. However, risk is often proportionate to success. It can take Herculean efforts to get people to see that the opposite way of thinking just might make them a fortune. It's not money they need, it's ideas.

Mark Grader is the owner of a small chain of jewelry stores. Every year around the same time, he runs a promotion inviting twenty or so of his best customers. He serves them wine and cheese, spends a small amount on advertising, and offers several specials with a modicum of success. He wondered, though, if he could make it more successful without spending a lot of money. The answer is a resounding yes, but it would require Mr. Grader to do something extraordinarily difficult. He would have to change his way of thinking.

Overcoming Prejudices

Graders Jewelers is a family owned business started forty-five years ago by his parents, Peter and Lorraine Grader. They were used to doing business the way they had been doing it for years, and were quite successful. In today's climate, that is commendable since nine out of ten businesses fail in the first two years alone. It is not surprising that Mr. Grader was in his "comfort zone," so how could I convince him that he could do better, *much better*, by employing GM techniques? Could I guarantee it would work with absolute certainty? Whenever there is change, there is risk, as I mentioned earlier. So, no, I could not guarantee it with certainty. However, I could guarantee him it would not cost him a dime more than he had spent in the past. But if it worked, he could see a dramatic increase in profit for spending the same amount of money. It was a win-win situation.

A primary strategy of GM is creativity. My advantage as a certified GM coach is that I have a great imagination. I tend to think in pictures. I "see" solutions unfold in my mind's eye. After five minutes of listening to Mr. Grader describe all the reasons why he did not want to do this, I saw a scene unfolding in my brain in all its resplendent detail. To say I had an idea is an understatement. I was so excited, it was all I could do to keep from jumping up and down. But I politely listened to his diatribe. When he was finished, I told him my revelation. I called it "The Night of the Stars."

This is what I told him: "Imagine the scene. Picture the kind of excitement you might see at an awards ceremony such as the *Oscars*. Bright lights flashing over the entrance, light bulbs from cameras are popping and the crowd leans forward with anticipation as the limos begin to arrive. 'Who is it,' they wonder. Speculation runs rampant through the crowd. Someone shouts, 'It's Bill Murray!' Out rolls the red carpet. A TV camera is trained on the occupants as they emerge and a reporter with a microphone appears. The door to the limo is opened by the driver. A beautiful woman emerges. She is dressed glamorously and is followed by a handsome gentleman in a tuxedo. He waves to the exuberant crowd.

"Inside the jewelry store, the celebrities are greeted and handed a glass of wine. All are given gifts. They receive a ticket for a drawing. The prize? A diamond necklace. Finally, the crowd surges forward as the doors are opened. They clamor for the autographs of the celebrities, who are only too happy to comply. The crowd is treated to hors d'oeuvres as they meander through the store, viewing all the tantalizing jewelry on sale."

Mr. Grader was silent.

"Well, what do you think?"

Mr. Grader finally found the strength to respond. "That…that…is going to cost a fortune," he stammered in astonishment.

I told him, "What if it won't cost you any more than you would normally spend?"

"That's impossible. You could never pull that off."

"But what if I could?"

"Well…I suppose. But I don't see how—"

"That's what I get paid for. That is what a Guerrilla Marketing Coach is trained to do. I know this will work if you will trust me to do my job."

"Well…okay. If you are sure this isn't going to cost me a lot more?"

"That is the one thing I am absolutely sure of," I said with confidence. Indeed, I was confident. I *know* Guerrilla Marketing weapons and strategies work.

Deploying the "Weapons" and "Strategies"

In any war in history, the outcome is usually determined by the weapons and strategies used by the winning army. Guerrilla Marketing Coaches are like Generals as they roll out some of the *over* one hundred weapons at their disposal to win the marketing war. Marketing is, indeed, a war. The Chinese had it right when they used a war strategy called *Bing Fa* in business. The Japanese adopted it to perfection (think "Made in Japan"). They view every business transaction as a war that must be won or lost. Many a businessperson has lost his or her shirt trying to do business in China because they didn't understand this premise. One of the beauties of Guerrilla Marketing is the use of creative thinking in developing a strategy. Also, calling these powerful tools weapons helps us to see that we are in a war, competing for customers. While we may not win the war, we can win an awful lot of battles in that we can win over more customers, and we can do that while at the same time being honest. In today's business climate, *that* is a rarity—but a general principle of Guerrilla Marketing.

My first order of business was to gain allies in this war. In Guerrilla Marketing terminology, this is called *fusion marketing* or *partnering* and is a key element to winning the war. Like I always tell all my customers: What's the worst thing they can say? No? Then ask someone else. I started asking. I contacted a local limo service I had used in the past and explained my idea. I told them about the great exposure and free advertising *they'd* get by providing a limo for the night. In any case involving fusion marketing, you must know what it is your partner wants—what *they* are going to get out of the deal. It is a symbiosis—*mutualism*—both benefit from the relationship. This is a component of another Guerrilla Markting weapon called "giver versus taker" stance—you need to give before you can take. More than half of the marketing weapons in a Guerrilla Marketer's arsenal involve free give-aways. Eventually, this will come back to you down the road if you adopt the idea that you need to be of the mindset of the giver, not the taker.

Winning the War

I started having success with the weapons and my strategy right away. The limo company saw the benefits immediately. High profile clients would mean lots of exposure and draw new clients for them. They loved the idea. A local restaurant agreed to provide the wine and hors d'oeuvres. I also knew they owned a plush red carpet for special occasions, and they were delighted to provide that, as well. After all, we were going to have celebrities. However, I didn't tell them exactly who those celebrities were or how I was going to get them—not yet.

A local cable company agreed to shoot the commercial in exchange for a sponsorship and a small media buy. They also made a connection with *E!* Channel television to air the video on segments of their broadcasting to over thirty thousand homes the week after the event. This laid the groundwork for the following year, should the store agree to run the event again. *E!* Channel supplied an "Emmy" statue, and visitors lined up to have their pictures taken while holding it as if *they* were getting the award.

I also utilized several lines of typical advertising, placing ads in the local newspapers announcing the event. We placed high-quality looking posters inside and outside of the store, as well as distributed them to any place that would put them up. The store's marquee announced an open invitation to the public. Word spread by word-of-mouth rapidly throughout the community— yet *another* weapon of Guerrilla Marketing.

The Night of the Stars

By now, you're probably wondering who the celebrities were and how I managed to get them. No, I don't have any movie star friends or hang out in Hollywood circles, if that's what you're thinking. As I said, I do have a great imagination and that is what it takes to be successful. The stars were the twenty of the store's best customers. They were the ones Mr. Grader threw the party for every year. This year, however, we were *really* going to give them the star treatment. I contacted the customers and told them to dress to the max. I didn't tell them what we were going to do, but I promised them it was going to be a special night they would never forget.

As each guest arrived at the restaurant, wine and a few hors d'oeuvres were served while they waited for the limo to arrive. The anticipation was building. Back at the store, crowds lined up at the door. The red carpet rolled out; spotlights illuminated the whole area. A patrol officer directed traffic, which only added to the curiosity of passers-by.

One by one, the limos delivered the stars. People clamored for their autographs and the customers—the stars of the night—actually complied, as they were caught up in the excitement of the moment.

After all of the stars arrived, the crowd was allowed into the store where they were entered in a contest for a door prize of a diamond necklace. One of the specials was a beautiful watch—buy one get one free! Hors d'oeuvres and wine were served; the reporter roamed through the crowd asking for their opinions. Excitedly they asked, "Am I going to be on TV?" The reporter, by the way, was none other than yours truly. I was dressed in a flashy turquoise suit and held the microphone recording the evening's event. Not exactly Geraldo Rivera, but close enough.

Indisputable Results

Was the event everything I told Mark it would be? Does Guerrilla Marketing really work? Notice Mr. Grader's comments.

"Kip practices what he preaches. Here I am, a conservative second generation retailer, and Kip is trying to convince me to think out of the box. I actually enjoy thinking out of the box and truly have a great respect for it, but—respect can also be translated into a level of 'fear.' So what held me back? My own fear of trying something that in my mind was at the very least 'over the top' and quite improbable. I was thinking of all of the reasons that it couldn't be pulled off successfully and he was seeing a vision of success. So what made me take the leap of faith? The knowledge that you gain after being in business for so many years; I also remembered the saying, 'if you do what you did, you'll get what you got!' We certainly had enough history to see patterns in our business based on our past actions, now was a time to kick it up to the next level!

"I fondly remember the enjoyment of the clients as they sipped cocktails, not quite knowing what to expect next. Their eyes were bright with excitement when they were escorted to the waiting, white limousine. For a brief time they were truly living the life of a celebrity, complete with bright lights and rolling film footage, as they approached the red carpet in front of our jewelry store. We had already accomplished our most important goal: to show our appreciation, in a lasting way, for our very special customers." (Mark Grader, Grader Jewelers, Inc., www.perfectnecklace.com)

What about the financial results, did we achieve our goal of increasing profits? Yes! Profits were up 27 percent over the previous year while spending almost the same amount, demonstrating the *power* of Guerrilla Marketing.

Another Novel Idea

Can this same level of excitement work for a not-for profit organization? Absolutely. The concept of "thinking outside the box"—an idea that has become cliché in our day—is just as effective for an organization with a different financial agenda: the not-for-profit organization. However, regardless of the financial expectations, even a not-for-profit organization needs to exceed their expenses in order to attract a larger clientele. While it might not be *called* "profit," the results need to be positive. They, like any business, need to be in the black. Let me briefly outline the differences and similarities I used in another novel approach to a different set of circumstances.

A good journalist will tell you that a story that begins with a cute little puppy will immediately grab the attention of the reader. In journalism, if you fail to do that in the first sentence or two, you've lost them. The same holds true for marketing. It is with this premise in mind—that is, the thought of the cute dog—that I had an idea.

The Objective

The not-for-profit historical maritime museum was launching a new Web site to attract new customers. With advertising dollars at a bare minimum (no surprise there), they needed a way to track the effectiveness of the site as well as track demographics. In other words, who came to the museum after visiting the site and where did they come from. I had a way to do that *and* entice people to come to the museum. I utilized a Guerrilla Marketing weapon called "the contest," and I called the idea, "The Doggy Spa."

The Concept

It's funny how ideas pop into my brain. I don't always know where they come from—especially this one. I pictured a cute little dog relaxing in an inner tube in the pool of a luxury hotel, sipping on an exotic looking drink with an umbrella in it. The hook was, "Win an all expenses paid trip to a doggy spa for three days for your pet!" Not to be overlooked is what the owners would get: an all expenses paid, three-day luxury cruise on a local schooner. Visitors were driven to the Web site with the lure of a coupon for a $2.00 discount off admission to the museum *with no purchase necessary.*

Perhaps you're wondering what the dog has to do with a maritime museum that displays whaling ships and an old whaling village. The theme the museum was promoting was "dogs of the sea." There were a number of exhibits about famous dogs aboard ship (bet you didn't know there were any). That was where I got the idea of using a dog. One broadcast television station ran with the idea and printed five hundred plastic dog bowls with their logo along with the museum's just to be part of a promotion with this renowned museum.

Another television station shot the commercial and aired it throughout the region as part of the media buy for added value. This also gave exposure to those who provided the prizes as well. They also linked the museum to their Web site. Again, I utilized fusion marketing as I did in *The Night of the Stars.* The cruise, the doggy spa, the commercial and most of the advertisement was paid by fusion marketing, a value of $3,900.

Results

Four thousand visitors to the Web site signed up for the contest. Thirty-five percent of the coupons for $2.00 off were used and the demographics acquired. The visitors to the site had to download the coupon by giving their e-mail and zip code. This allowed for the tracking the museum wanted, and positioned them to follow up for future offers.

Planning Your Next Event

Now that you have some idea how it works, can you plan an event that will shatter your competition and put your business's name in lights? Can you utilize Guerrilla Marketing strategies and weapons and increase your profits while spending little? I think you know the answer, but just in case you missed it—yes! Perhaps you will never be able to afford to have your name blinking on the side of a Blue Whale (and let's hope our species never gets that crazy), but by employing Guerrilla Marketing every day in your business, you will see positive things happen and your business will succeed while others, who spend far more advertising dollars, will be left in your dust. Won't that feel good?

About Kip Gienau

Kip Gienau is the owner of Advertising Works CT, based in Quaker Hill, CT. He has been in the advertising industry for over twelve years, three as a Certified Guerrilla Marketing Coach. One of Kip's greatest strengths is networking. His goal is to have happy, satisfied customers and he accomplishes that with his contagiously infective positive attitude, and his enthusiasm for Guerrilla Marketing techniques. You can contact him at (800) 443-0667 or visit him on the web at www.AdWorksCT.com.

CHAPTER 15

GUERRILLA SPONSORSHIP

How to Get Other People's Money To Pay For Your Marketing, Promotions, and Products

Martin Wales

> *"I love money more than the things it can buy—but what I love more than money is other people's money."*
>
> ~Lawrence Garfield (Danny Devito)
> in *Other People's Money*

I magine if you had a Microsoft paying your marketing bills for you. Picture a multi-billion-dollar corporation featuring you on their Web sites, sharing their brand equity with you, and introducing you to their customers. What if the world's most recognized brand called to offer you over $40,000 for your own exposure, marketing, media and promotion? How long would you think about an offer like that?

Imagine Getting $210,000 in Free Advertising and Exposure

Carolyn Gross didn't have to imagine. That's the annualized, total value of the advertising and exposure she got in a print magazine for cancer patients and survivors. She's a speaker and author of "Treatable and Beatable: Healing Cancer Without Surgery."

Carolyn's sponsor was a magazine that targeted breast cancer women and had over three hundred thousand readers. Every month she got coverage in the magazine with a column and full page ads for her book, as well as for a podcast. After adding up the value of this based on the magazine's rate card (what others had to pay for the same space), she received over $210,000 premium exposure as a result of working with this sponsor.

You can have all this and more—if you understand, participate in, and leverage Guerrilla Sponsorship.

Your Guerrilla Sponsorship Mindset

"Sponsorship" is formally defined as the support, financial and otherwise, of your live events, media broadcasts, and production for *your marketing* and promotion. Similarly, "sponsors" are the organizations or individuals that fund and recommend you and your information for *their own benefit* and profit. (Tip: Don't ever lose focus on *their* interests when discussing funding for your projects, ideas, or events.)

Guerrilla Sponsorship expands beyond these more formal definitions with a more creative and lateral approach—beyond simply seeing sponsorship as money received for displaying logos or paying for a coffee break. But what would it mean to your bottom line if you had others *pay* for your marketing and buy your products too? Because sponsorships are so lucrative, I want you to think of lucrative ways to leverage sponsorship for unlimited profits as you read this chapter. For you, too, can apply what I've discovered over the past fifteen years as an independent professional using sponsors to accelerate my success.

I've have had several major corporations support me through what I've called "Power Alliances" or sponsorships on steroids. These are some major sponsorships I've enjoyed:

Microsoft paid me over $40,000 in airtime to sponsor a series of business talk shows that I hosted on traditional, broadcast radio. It was called *Your Business* on Toronto's Talk 640AM. They paid for my hour of radio broadcast time, each and every week, with my voice and my brand used to invite listeners in twenty to thirty radio ads saying:

> "Hi! This is Martin Wales, The Customer Catcher. Join me each week as we interview a parade of experts and leading authorities to help you grow your business. That's *Your Business*, brought to you by your friends at Microsoft, each week at 2:00 p.m., every Saturday."

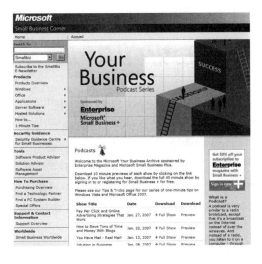

Next, the largest Chamber of Commerce in the country paid for my two-minute network television spots. This was an added value program that aired for over seven thousand business members. Besides the air time, it included all the graphics, post production, staff and camera people, studio and site shoots, and editing too. In fact, the content is still used today at www.CustomerCatcherTV.com.

Another Guerrilla Sponsorship campaign had *Entrepreneur Magazine* support an Internet radio show I produced and hosted, called *The Entrepreneur Magazine eBiz Show*. Entrepreneur is the world's leading brand and provider of content and media to the small business and entrepreneurial communities. The radio show was hosted on wsRadio, the Worldwide Leader in Internet Talk, and home to *eBay Radio* and several other *Entrepreneur Magazine* shows. They are one of the web's most visited business talk radio stations.

Since that time I've gone on to become the Executive Producer of *PayPal Radio*. You've heard of them—the world's leading online payment processors. Are you starting to see a trend here and how one sponsorship effort can lead to more?

PayPal Radio

Finally, a less well-known, software publisher paid $10,000 for just thirteen, one-hour interviews to be podcast online. And radio is just one marketing area for sponsorship. You can use sponsorships for literally any marketing activity from your direct mail campaigns and live seminars to promotional prizes and publicity events. Ask yourself, how could you apply this one, simple, Guerrilla Marketing technique of sponsorship to what you're probably *already* doing?

Choose Your Favorite Sponsorship Method

My success came from working with the radio medium but you can use Guerrilla Sponsorship for almost any marketing activity or event. Without a doubt, sponsorship is strong in a "broadcasting" model like radio or TV because it's something we're exposed to regularly, but don't stop there. The bias you must overcome is only thinking of sponsorship for cash payments. You can utilize sponsors for way more than their money. Think of how you can benefit from any of the following:

Networking: Sponsors are often connected to a large number of other companies, organizations or individuals and if they support you with introductions it's sometimes worth more than cash upfront. Capital is finite while relationships can be cultivated so that they last a lifetime.

Immediate Access: Sponsors can create shortcuts to centers of influence and industry leaders. They can invite you to speak at events they put on and fund. This can put you in front of hundreds or even thousands of your best prospects, all at one time. Just by leveraging the credibility of your sponsors and the recognition that they already have, you become known and you gain access. This tactic has led to me being given the cell phone numbers of chairmen of the boards within five minutes of making a contact. It's about the ability to tie your name and your marketing together with a recognized brand.

Prospect/Customer Database: You can encourage your Sponsors to announce your marketing activity to their customers and their prospect database. And that can be as good as you trying to contact them all directly, right? In fact, it's *better*. Referrals are more likely to read marketing communications, more willing to consider an offer, and less likely to focus on or bring up pricing objections.

Prizes: On several occasions we have had companies donate prizes for our own marketing promotions or contests. Electronics are popular, including mp3 players, digital cameras, wireless keyboards, and GPS tracking software and devices. Thousands and thousands of dollars worth of prizes can be collected directly from the manufacturers, in exchange for mention in marketing materials, on the Web site, and for publicity around the marketing campaign.

Resources: In the past, I've had sponsors who handled writing and distributing press releases for the activities we did together. They already had internal staff or paid on outside PR agency to do this work for them, but now they did it on my behalf at no cost to me!

Social Responsibility: If you offer to make donations based on percentage of net profits, or even of the door's admission tickets, then you gift your prospects with an opportunity to feel good while transacting business. If they can choose between you and another company but you donate 10 percent to your city's Children's Hospital then they may be more likely to pick you.

The most important point is this: you and your sponsors are exchanging value. You provide them with content and exposure while they provide you with what you ask for, be it cash, bartered services, or access to their resources. Don't be afraid to list off everything you need from professional expertise or public relations to practical items like photocopying, spare office space, and airline tickets at their reduced, corporate rates.

Find What Works For Your Industry

Sponsorship works for any profession or industry. Say you're a retailer having a closed-door, customer-appreciation party, an author on a book signing tour, an independent professional, like a Realtor or accountant presenting a local seminar, or a trainer selling promotional products, you can find sponsorships for the event. For any profession, there are potential sponsors you can engage.

When it comes to "saving" money, if you have a hair salon, you could have Starbucks provide one of their mobile coffee bars. If you're a jeweler you can spend less on advertising by having a local fashion designer feature your works on mannequins in her store window. A travel agent could sponsor your coupon program if you sell furniture by offering $100 certificates off flights when a customer of yours buys more than $500 in your store. They do the advertising; you save money. Sometimes, I've had sponsors "pay" me with free attendance at business seminars that cost other attendees $1,000 to over $5,000.

Sponsorship is very familiar to the non-profit arena. If you want to speak on the high school or college circuit to promote special interests, sponsors love it. Nike and other sports gear companies frequently support health, wellness, and physical fitness presentations in many communities.

One of my clients is an eight year old boy who raises awareness and funds for children in developing countries hit by natural or geopolitical disasters, and he has been sponsored by the United Nations through UNICEF.

Organizations, both non-profits and for-profits, have marked funds in their budgets to be spent on subjects and experts, just like you, to share knowledge, skills and positive messages. Mental Health Associations and Public Health Departments are other sources of capital.

What would it mean to your business if you could have a leading company in *your* industry or niche recommend and refer you directly to their entire customer base? Can you imagine how much more credibility (and celebrity) you could gain in the eyes of your prospects? What percentage increase in your sales and profits would you enjoy?

You Can Do It Too

If you develop "power alliances" with recognized brand names, then corpo-rate budgets can virtually underwrite any of your brand building, PR, and marketing communications. Can anybody do this? Yes. And with a few key strategies and the right approach with potential sponsors, you can too!

As an independent marketing coach and consultant, working out of my home and relying extensively on Guerrilla Marketing, sponsorship strategies changed my life. The Microsoft story above makes most think that I come from radio or studied broadcasting.

Far from it. I started out as a high school teacher of geography and science making $35,000 at the time and facing a pension of $40,000 a year after investing thirty years of my life. That snapped me into the realization that the *only* way to get the prosperity, wealth and freedom I desired was through my own enterprise.

Why am I telling you this? Because I want you to know that I've faced similar challenges and obstacles that you might be dealing with now. Even today, I'm not an executive heading up an army of staff, there is no six- or seven-figure marketing budget, and I had no prior training or formal educa-tion in marketing either.

Benefits From OPM

There are millions of dollars in Sponsorship available today in every busi-ness trade. With sponsors, you reduce your marketing costs and eliminate the risk of investing your own, hard-earned money on advertising or live events that *might* work.

Doesn't it make sense to source outside money to promote yourself? Wouldn't it be worthwhile to find ways to conserve your cash flow and have others write the checks for your marketing activities and sales communications? There are many advantages to using "Other People's Money" (OPM) to market and sell much more easily than you ever have before. Let's look at them now.

Sponsorship Brings Cash and Saves Yours

Much of Guerrilla Marketing is based on creating content. This material should be informative and educational, and in true Guerrilla form, it should be produced at a very low cost and distributed through your existing channels and relationships. You don't have to buy expensive, high-end design and advertising placement to get your content out there.

Sponsors are looking for original content to share to both attract new prospects and keep existing customers by "adding value." Therefore, creating good content is one of the best and fastest ways to get sponsorship money for marketing information you're generating anyway!

If you're getting OPM, this content, picked up by a sponsor, saves you money and it reserves your cash flow. You keep it in your pockets and utilize those funds for other marketing or business growth activities.

Sponsorship Gives You Instant Credibility That Lasts a Lifetime

I'm not kidding. When you have a well-known sponsor you get instant credibility that lasts a lifetime. Let me repeat— it's an instant *and* lifetime credibility.

There's no expiry date on your credentials. The "former" U.S. President Bill Clinton makes over $100,000 per speech as he continues to harvest the potential value of a position formerly held. Whether you did it two years ago or ten years ago, you will always be the "former host" of Microsoft's *Your Business*, like I am. Definitely take advantage of this. Create branded content for a set time period and then even when the sponsorship ends you can move onto other projects. On your bio you have all your previous activities listed. This is a unique and defining, competitive advantage.

Sponsorship Reduces Risk

If you're using OPM, then it's not coming out of your cash flow, your bank account and, especially, your credit line. This means reducing risk for you. Typically when buying advertising or renting a conference room, you commit to an investment and sign a contract. You must pay even if the marketing activity or program fails. But when you have a sponsor, they foot the bill!

Often the sponsors promote you directly as well, so they invest in advertising, assign their public relations firm to publicity oriented tasks, send out postcards and other direct mail, and do all sorts of other things that promote you. All this is done with little or no risk to you.

Sponsorship Gets You Extended Exposure

Extended exposure is especially useful and profitable for you through your Internet marketing efforts. You gain extended exposure because sponsors leave content up online for indefinite periods of time. Sometimes it's years—especially with larger corporations. Generally, they're slower to change Web sites and they archive a lot of the information as well. This one point can be significant for your online traffic, back links and search engine optimization strategies.

Sponsorship Attracts More Sponsors.

Once you land one sponsor it immediately multiplies your ability to attract even more sponsors. This is known as the "Tip Jar Theory." If a piano player in a lounge puts up a big wine glass for tips and it's empty, it usually takes a very long time before he gets a tip. If he throws in a couple of bills himself, and the audience sees the money in the jar, they are more likely to tip through example because, they think, other people have rewarded the performer.

Sponsorship Provide Offline Opportunities For Online Traffic

If you do sponsored television, traditional broadcast radio, or a column in a print magazine, that can help to drive people to your Web site. Whether it's to promote your book or increase traffic to your main home page, it's an opportunity to really increase your numbers.

Find offline sponsors that have large pools of customers and have them drive offline customers to view your online marketing. It doesn't cost much money to provide, and it is trackable and measurable. This also allows you to test promotions, copy, and offers and then adjust them for maximum results.

Sponsorship Increases Sales

With the right sponsors promoting their association with you, significant increases in your sales are possible. Sponsors are natural referral sources. They have an existing, trusting relationship with their customers that they've invested time and effort to build. Their clients are responsive to additional recommended products and services. These referrals are often the best buyers and have fewer objections to offers or pricing from recommended suppliers like you.

How to Find a Sponsor That's Right For You

Sponsorship can bring you phenomenal results. Your first step though is to start from seeing this strategy through your potential sponsor's eyes. They are seeking opportunities where they can say, "We're proud to sponsor _____"; or "We support the small business community by providing access to _____"; or "We're proud to be a longtime supporter of the Women's Work-at-Home Movement"; or "We're supporting a non-profit organization that focuses on low-income education in the inner city."

Corporations welcome and have budgets to spend on sponsorship activities. There are millions of dollars available every day. Occasionally, it's as simple as asking for the money. But it's rarely that easy. It's more common to find yourself in competitive situations for finite budgets.

Sponsor Your Success

Hopefully, you're now more aware and have greater insight as to why and how Guerrilla Sponsorship can assist you. Certainly, the number one thing, the most exciting, and maybe the most obvious is using "Other People's Money." You're not putting your cash at risk, and saving a ton of your precious time and effort when sponsors introduce you to their pre-existing list of customers and contacts.

And to get you started, I'm leaving you with this sponsorship action list:

- Make the exchange of value clear to your sponsors.

- Think about all the different ways you can immediately conserve and save your cash for supplies, activities or products you would normally have to purchase with your precious cash or credit.

- Compile a list of the companies that deliver them and target them as your first candidates.

- Have fun and watch what happens to your bottom line when the sponsorships come rolling in!

About Martin Wales

Martin Wales is President of Paradise Publishers, Inc. and e-founder of Customer Catcher Media & Communications, where you can get more powerful, profitable tips today at **www.CustomerCatcher.com***. You can also claim, by e-mail, your free digital audio of an intensive, hour-long, interview on* How to Attract Sponsors and Power Alliances, *at* **sponsorship@CustomerCatcher.com***. Just request the link to download your personal, digital copy.*

CHAPTER 16

GUERRILLA ACCESS

Taking Fusion Marketing to the Next Level

Richard D. Bailey

"If you always put limits on everything you do, physical or anything else, it will spread into your work and into your life. There are no limits. There are only plateaus, and you must not say there, you must go beyond them."

~Bruce Lee

When people talk about fusion marketing, they often think "joint venture"—"JV" in Internet Marketing speak. It's the "I'll sell your stuff if you sell mine," idea. While it's a very workable marketing strategy, and very much a part of what a Guerrilla Marketer is supposed to do, I have always found that it falls short of what I and others have been trying to accomplish in marketing.

I developed my business, *Client By Design*, a web-based coaching and consulting business, during the often-called "Dot Bomb" era where at least 806 dot com companies went belly-up from January of 2000 to February of 2002 (according to Webmergers.com). Money-burning dot com companies were finding out, too late, that making profits were more important to investors than buying beautiful office furniture and flying first class. As these companies desperately begged for one more cash infusion, I watched as their once supportive financial backers cut tether lines in their own desperate acts of self-preservation.

It occurred to me that strong relationships with the right people at the right time could really make a difference, especially when time, powerful connections, and money were in short supply. I wanted to grow my business by finding a way to help others reach their target audience in record time and with minimal expenditure.

That's when I started to develop a method of marketing that helps a person find ways to get others to help you do your marketing for you. As I developed it, I found that it's really a method that brings you to the point where you can create the fusion relationship. What I found, was that it allows any person or company, no matter how small or how new to their individual markets, to rapidly overcome product and service launch barriers entering the market. I developed a series of tightly woven processes that became the building blocks for what I call the "Access Point Marketing Method."

Access Point Marketing, like all Guerrilla Marketing tactics, presents a paradigm shift in the way people think when they go to launch a product or service and also in how they choose to grow their business. It's not really taught in schools and it's not something that big marketing firms want you to know about, especially when they can sell you their services instead for hundreds-of-thousands of dollars per project or campaign.

This marketing method shows you how to get backing from major players, organizations, people of influence, and even big corporations with established credibility to assist in your promotion efforts and with little financial investment on your part. It's called the Access Point Market Entry Process (MEP) and this Access Point strategy allows you to acquire vast marketing resources and instant trustworthiness with little expenditure. The fun part is that when you use it, it's fairly simple to level the playing field once you know how to get started.

It Begins With Finding Commonality

Business that use traditional marketing to launch new products or services often attempt to force their way into the marketplace using big budgets as the key to opening doors to consumer awareness, trust, and eventually the buyer's wallet. This is not the way of the Guerrilla, who relies on time, energy, and imagination to grow his or her business.

Access Points can be compared to mapped-out short cuts, where the idea is to seek out and find companies, organizations, or individuals that will help you reach or enhance the experience of your target audience for free or at a fraction of traditional costs, and then develop a fusion relationship with them. In so doing you create a domino effect that ultimately can quickly give you the necessary credentials into whatever business arena you wish to venture in.

When you look at Access Points, you are looking at who or what is already there, available for you to jump on. It could be a piece of software or service that in turn gives you access to a data base, and then I can use that data-base to communicate to my target audience who can then communicate to their target audience. It could be that you gain access to a data base of media contacts, and by connecting with them, you can now communicate to their audience who in turn communicate to their audiences. It's a new way of thinking. Why send one postcard to one person when I can send one postcard to one organization, and they can then send it out to their members or constituents, and they in turn, if they like what you're selling, can send it on to their lists?

When you acquire the right relationships, you gain access to products and services that instantly give your business the look and feel of a much bigger and well connected business. It could also give you the ability to serve an entirely new clientele. To find the right access points, you have to think "relationships" and make this your primary focus.

With the right relationships, you can achieve the local, national, or global reach of companies with near-infinite budgets at a fraction of what they spend. Imagine getting the right people to sell or distribute your information or connecting to the right products and services that give you an even greater reach or level of distinction within a competitive field. It can all be done through MEP thinking. Consider it a three step or 3W process: where do you want to go and then who and/or what can help you reach your target goals. This will help you in making the right purchases and also the right relationship decisions. You will see in the following real-life examples, anyone can do it.

TIP: Many companies have something called Affinity Programs that allow you access into their advertising forums. Consider Participating or partnering in one of these where you can offer your products to association members as a discounted member benefit through their parent organization. Contact the AAA (American Automobile Association) or Geico (the insurance company with the cute little lizard). Geico has their own membership club, Geico Privileges, that offer Travel, Health, Entertainment, Home garden, Shopping and other related services and products to their member-ship. If you can get your business or service listed, you will gain instant access to thousands of travelers and members who trust what Geico recommends. Better yet, they will even include your product/services in some of their promotional materials. Just contact their affinity program manager for more details and terms. See: www.GeicoPrivileges.com or search for "Affinity Programs" with your favorite search engine to see what else comes up.

Case One: Cars and Food or the Origins of Access Point MEP

I was selling advertising for a media-company and unfortunately one advertiser, a Chinese take-out restaurant, was not happy with their results. Actually, "not happy" is an understatement. The owners were fuming with anger when I paid them an after-the-sale courtesy visit to check on their results. "Not one single customer!" they said had come in to redeem their coupons. Oddly, I had just visited another customer, a car-wash right across from them in a very busy shopping center that practiced this same form of advertising and it was profiting steadily from it.

As I went back to the friendly car-wash to sit and ponder the situation, the Guerrilla Marketer in me just couldn't accept defeat. I was also starting to notice something; the owner didn't mind my sitting in the auto facility's rather spacious and comfortable waiting room where I could peruse an ample stock of car and lifestyle magazines, grab some coffee and tea or watch TV. Anyone who walked in was treated as a new prospect that might shop in their well-stocked auto parts and car-care center complete with a novelty store while their car was being washed. I sat there thinking about the open hospitality of the car-wash, and my empty stomach began to grumble. That's when a thought was triggered.

Joining of Two Worlds

I imagined people stopping at the car-wash while coming from work. The fact that they were using a full-service (non do-it-yourself) car wash probably also meant that cooking was not really something they were looking forward to and so getting a prepared meal would only help to fulfill their need for speed and convenience. I thought about the restaurant owner who wanted to bring in more customers (preferably hungry ones) and it dawned on me that these two totally unrelated entities were a perfect match. Suddenly I felt "the fusion."

It Makes Sense

I quickly asked the car wash manager's permission to allow the restaurant to drop off a stack of take-out menus in their waiting room and he was quick to comply. He saw the value. This ad-hoc relationship would allow his hundreds of weekly customers to truly feel the power, convenience and value of full service. They could get take-out or grab a bite to eat and keep themselves busy while waiting for more time consuming jobs to get done, i.e. oil changes, detailing, fluid changes, wash and wax.

The restaurant owner who was somewhat stunned by my actions and the friendliness of his neighbor (who he once thought of as competition) was more than happy to give it a try. He realized that this new relationship could deliver an almost never-ending supply of hungry and convenience-loving patrons right to his kitchen.

His anger towards me and my company turned into a handshake. In less than ten minutes, the restaurant was able to acquire a powerful access point and an unlikely ally. One complimentary soda later (a peace offering and gift to wash down my meal), a true fusion partnership was born as the owner asked me to get some flyers to handout from the car wash as well. As for me, I felt good as I received my order and looked forward to sneaking a bite of my favorite sautéed broccoli dish before heading home to contemplate ways to really expand on this powerful fusion-marketing-based concept.

Case Two: Krav Ma What? (YorktownFitnessCenter.com)

"Going to market is a combination of talent, plans, and smart decisions that's like dancing—done at 78 RPM— while your competitors are throwing marbles at your feet. It's hard to do, painful and non-stop."

~Jose Palomino, President g2mGroup, Inc.

Davide's Yorktown Total Fitness Center and Krav Maga New York, an official Krav Maga training center in Yorktown Heights, New York, was brought to my attention by a trusted Ad Agency friend who knew of my great love for Martial Arts. He told me about this self-defense system and school that he had just heard of and wondered if I would want to work with this potential client as both a coach and consultant to market and promote their training center. Well, since Krav Maga, a fighting system originally developed for the Israeli Defense Forces and made popular by Actress Jennifer Lopez and Actor Matt Damon in the films *Enough* and *The Bourne Trilogy of films* respectively, was something I was already fascinated with—my answer could only be a resounding yes!

Doors Don't Hit Back

From the very beginning, I could see great potential for community change and outreach, especially once I met the owner, Davide, who impressed me as an honorable and formidable teacher. Yorktown Fitness Center could teach anyone (men, women and children) to defend themselves in life threatening situations by using proven and effective Krav Maga techniques. With the right connections and planning, I would have a chance to help Davide and his staff reach out to more people to increase awareness, gain new enrollments, and teach others how to be both safe and fit. All we needed to do was get some help in opening the right doors—in other words, finding the right access points.

Employing the MEP process, Davide and I quickly analyzed the market to determine and identify who would best benefit from this specialized training and concluded that everyone from law enforcement personnel to small children could actually improve their safety and general well-being with proper teaching. A dedicated Krav Maga practitioner can burn up to nine hundred calories per workout, so anyone can walk into a training center from day-one to get fit and then walk out feeling safer without having to spend years mastering traditional martial arts techniques.

Considered by many to be a "deadly art" with no rules, Krav Maga was also part of an underground movement that was making its mark in pop culture. The system was already getting growing media coverage thanks to celebrities taking advantage of its workout benefits to shape-up and to look and act believable in action film roles: Matt Damon relied on it in *The Bourne Identity* as did Angelina Jolie in the film *Tomb Raider*. It was also getting mixed reviews from those who thought of the system as too violent, preferring the more regimen focused training of traditional martial arts. So positive media involvement had to be an important part of our Access Point Market Entry Process. We had to show a positive, practical, and even fun side of Krav Maga, one that everyone involved—our access points—would be comfortable with.

It's Not Just Who You Tell, but Whom they Have the Power to Tell

When implementing Davide's Yorktown Fitness Center's MEP enhanced seven-step marketing plan, a decision was made to launch special outreach events that would help to bring attention to Krav Maga in the community. These events would need the best access points to be successful, so we set out to identify the best distribution outlets for information that would inform, invite, and lead our intended audience to the events.

After some discussion, we decided that we needed to promote an "abduction prevention seminar" for kids. We called it "Snatch Proof." A strong corporate media access point was required to deliver our message, and it was clear that our best outlet would be a trusted news station. News 12 Westchester, an award winning area news station known for its commitment to reliable news and positive community involvement, was chosen to reach our target audience. They were the perfect access point in this case because we could give them great content and they would give us a platform off of which to communicate our message. We acquired a segment on the News 12's morning broadcast, and the segment served as a foundation to establish area credibility while keeping kids safe.

We also identified additional access points, including the local police department, a children's theater group, youth soccer teams, and local super-markets who volunteered to hand-out flyers to parents with children. All this made it possible to promote the event on a grand scale.

The children's seminar had a fantastic turnout and allowed a community of children and parents to have fun and go home feeling refreshed, safer, and better prepared for emergency situations. It was like having an army of caring people deploying their marketing weapons (e-mail, handouts, referrals, etc) to do something positive, and each group felt good about their contribution in making the event a success and in protecting the area's children.

Right On Track and Give That Man a Coat

We didn't stop with the children's seminar, however. We then identified parking lot safety as an area that needed attention and to which Davide could provide a service. We created another content oriented spot for News 12. Fearing the station would be a little reluctant to air the spot, we had to make sure there was a clear tie-in to something happening in current events and we found it to be "Christmas Holiday shopping." Then something interesting happened. Right after the parking lot safety spot aired, there were reports that a man was running around exposing himself to female patrons in a mall parking lot in a nearby town. Coinciding with media coverage of these incidents, the station decided to air our spot again. These events confirmed that our thinking about parking lot safety was correct, and the mass coverage that News 12 gave us allowed us to activate the other areas of our Seven Step Guerrilla Marketing Plan—a major weapon in the Guerrilla arsenal—with a more targeted focus on community health and safety.

Because of this success with the news station, Davide was quick to adapt the access point concept into his marketing toolkit and has focused his energy on making changes in his community while seeing his business become profitable as well.

To date, hundreds of kids all over the Westchester County area have experienced the "snatch proof" seminar with more to come as we use past successes and testimonials as access points to seek sponsors and to reach out to other schools, companies and organizations. We found a way to give Davide a ton of exposure and not only did he benefit from it, News 12 got great content on timely stories, and the community learned a way to help protect themselves. Truly a "win-win-win" situation.

With the right Guerrilla Marketing Strategies, MEP and coaching—Davide's Yorktown Total Fitness Center and Krav Maga New York is fast becoming an important part of its community and is looking to take its "snatch proof" seminars national through the right relationships.

> **Tip**: Look for what is timely or what kinds of needs your community has. Community as well as national issues can give you great access points. You use what is timely as a way to get your message out. Also, think of who are you trying to reach and what do they do; this will allow you to find the best Access Point(s) to reach them.

Case Three: Global Positioning (LetsJam Music, Inc.—LennyHines.com)

Lenny Hines grew up singing and playing musical instruments. It was his natural love for inspiring people through song that lead Lenny to develop several independent album releases. His first two singles were professionally produced, "Don't Let Me Go," and "My Baby." However, both records were mainly sold or distributed out of his car trunk and given away to a limited audience of family and friends. With no real promotional plan, Lenny would continue to generate new songs simply for the love of his art.

I got a hold of one of his home-brewed albums, *In My Heart*, and I fell in love with several songs. This island, urban, and country-inspired album is a work inspired by love, commitment, and the overcoming of tragedy. The problem was that without proper promotion, history might have repeated itself again, placing this music in a dark closet never to be heard by an audience.

It took only about seven days working with Lenny to create an MEP-enhanced seven- step Guerrilla Marketing plan to launch *In My Heart* on his wholly-owned *LetsJam* Music label. Furthermore, this is what we added to the basic plan that inspired our thinking about access points:

- Identifying his intended audience and needs;

- Analyzing the market to better understand how music is distributed, sold and purchased (both online and offline);

- Acquiring the best access points and resources to reach Lenny's intended audience for effortless sales and promotion.

As any aspiring musician without major label backing knows, it is not an easy task to get your music to the forefront without a lot of "blood, sweat and tears." Armed with a budget of less than $3,000, we set out to get it done. But it's important to know that this project was not about the money; it was about making a difference through music and songs, and we were determined to find the right access points to get the job done.

First, we analyzed the industry in relation to Lenny's intended audience and needs. Once this was complete, we were able to identify several genres where the album would fit in. After re-mastering the album to airplay quality standards and then securing proper copyrights and registrations, the next step was to manufacture slightly over a thousand professional shrink-wrapped CD's filled with songs, professional photography, and personal notes packed with personality, ready for distribution.

Access Points Can Be Revolving Doors

One of the greatest hurdles that aspiring artists face when trying to launch an album without major label backing is distribution. You see it wasn't enough for songs from "In My Heart" to get radio play or to have the whole world talking about it. Consumers and fans needed to have a way to purchase the product, or Lenny's hard work would have been in vain.

Consumers shop online and at their favorite stores because these are the access points to get what they want. Once consumers have heard about your product they will seek you out. Therefore, it is extremely beneficial to streamline the process where consumers can both find and make their purchase. So access points work both ways; they allow you to *push your product* to the consumer while also allowing the consumer *to pull and recognize your product* even in the midst of all the noise of your competition.

Think and Grow Global

Next, the results of our analysis were used to identify and acquire national and international distribution, sales channels through third party labels, and distributors for both digital and physical CD sales. The chosen access point was The Orchard (TheOrchard.com), a global distributor of media content. Working with The Orchard allowed the CD to become available for preview and digital downloads on just about every major music selling point on the Internet (from iTunes to Virgin Digital). It was also in the database of every major retailer including Barnes and Noble, Best Buy, Target and Wal-Mart in just a few short weeks.

We were even able to use another one of our access points, CD Baby (CDBaby.com), to place this CD into the catalogs of over twenty-four hundred neighborhood music stores across the U.S. In addition, foreign distribution made "In My Heart" available to buyers around the globe. How's that for credibility? This entire distribution point creation process (not including manufacturing) took less than sixty days to accomplish and cost less than $200!

Once we activated and launched the rest of the seven step marketing plan, we were able to successfully get multi-regional radio airplay to web and radio listeners propelling "In My Heart" into the forefront of Smooth Reggae and Easy Listening Caribbean music fan favorites, hot picks, and request lines. There have even been discussions with licensing agents for possible movie and television use.

What a Feeling!

I will never forget the feeling I got when I called Lenny and told him to go to Barnes and Noble and type his name into their music database. When he finally saw his CD cover with sample music tracks come up on a the store's computer screen, his reaction was that of a proud and humble man who had finally seen his music get the light of day.

Lenny even teamed up with a local Caribbean Restaurant to distribute music to its patrons. There is also a fusion relationship project between Lenny and a global Children's charity to promote health and support for hungry children throughout the world.

Thousands of downloaded songs later, a growing international fan base and the potential for movie and commercial licensing, it is certain that his music will live on. But more important, Lenny Hines is employing Guerrilla Marketing Methods to make a difference in the lives of others.

> **Tip**: Research "semi or self-liquidator" or "purchase or privilege premium" on the Internet to find organizations that can actually help you to get your product marketed by major brands. Just imagine your product being co-marketed as an incentive on a popular cereal box. The Incentive Marketing Association (incentivemarketing.org) is a great place to start.

Always Think Access Points

It starts with a thought. If you can imagine having the backing of a major player to sponsor, endorse, or promote your product or service, then you have already taken the first step. Instead of just running with the crowd into an even more crowded and competitive marketplace, just think of where you want to go and then find the right relationships. While I've given you three case studies, here's some more ideas to get your Access Point Marketing idea-engine revving:

- **Gain instant credibility**. A real-estate agent could add property management to his/her portfolio by simply partnering with a respected property manager.

- **Develop and connect to local, national and international** sales, information and product distribution points that are willing to work and promote on your behalf. A chiropractor could advertise to thousands of people by partnering with a local supermarket and hosting a health fair, for example, knowing with total certainty that every shopper has a spine.

- **Mirror major corporate acquisitions** by partnering with the right organizations to instantly build your clientele and resource list without spending a dime. Partner with another company and refer to their client list as part of your trusted partner or team client portfolio.

- **Get an instant prospect list**. A new business could joint venture with another established business and then promote to their customer or subscriber list. With an included endorsement from the partner company, this builds instant trust and has the selling power of a referral.

- **Become perceived as a knowledgeable organization** in any field by partnering with experts. A web design firm could add sales conversion expertise to their list of services by partnering with a professional direct marketing copywriter.

The key to Access Point Marketing is to look for established companies, organizations, people, products, or services that can help you get to where you want to go. Then use these resources as access points to find even more open doors and jump to where you need to go with greater focus than you could ever do alone. Do this right and you'll make it a win-win for everyone.

About Richard Bailey

*Speaker, Certified Guerrilla Marketing Coach, technology consultant, g2m Group Panelist, Internet marketing expert and weekend chef, Richard D. Bailey, specializes in the development of methods and technology to attract customers. Gain insight from his over twenty years of combined technology, product launch and marketing experience by visiting his marketing and PR firm Client By Design, LLC at **www.ClientByDesign.com**. You can also learn more about access points at **www.ClientByDesign.com**.*

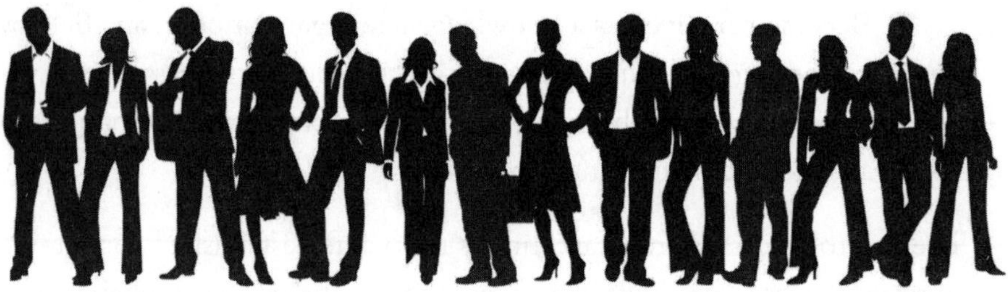

PART FOUR
Grassroots Guerrilla

In the pressure to increase profits, businesses often forget that consumers are first and foremost human beings. The Guerrilla Marketer, however, fundamentally realizes that people are motivated by their hearts and that they eventually take issue with putting profits over people. One important and very honorable Guerrilla Marketing weapon is "cause marketing." It helps you to relate what you do to a cause that people can get behind. This section will motivate you to move your marketing message beyond the sphere of profit and into the realm of helping others. When an overwhelming number of people have said that they would change brands to support a company that embraces cause marketing, can you, as a Guerrilla Marketer, afford not to?

CHAPTER 17

THE GUERRILLA IDEALIST

How Fusion Marketing With Good Causes Can Send Your Profits and Your Spirits Soaring

Amy J. Belanger

> *"Only one who devotes himself to a cause with his whole strength and soul can be a true master."*
> ~Albert Einstein

Traditional marketing is a winner-take-all game that takes out the competition and maximizes profits regardless of any impact on local economies, the environment, families, humanitarian values, and our souls.

In the pressure to increase profits, businesses often forget that consumers are first and foremost human beings. And human beings eventually take issue with putting profits over people. The minute a person connects your company to a deeply held value of theirs—for better or worse—every previous marketing impression can be instantly overturned.

Numerous marketing studies have confirmed this, including the 2006 Cone Millennial Cause Study, in which 89 percent of respondents said if price and quality are equal they'll likely switch to a brand associated with a good cause.

Today's business leaders are marketing to a savvier consumer than they were just a generation ago. Most have witnessed cynical betrayals of the public trust by industry-after-industry: from big tobacco, to HMOs, to war profiteers, to the savings and loans, and so on. Today's consumers expect better corporate behavior and they're saying so with their dollars. Enter the *conscious consumer*, also known as the LOHAS (Lifestyles of Health and Sustainability) market.

Conscious consumers aspire to health and longevity, intellectual and spiritual pursuits, recycling and conservation, peace and human rights, and fine living. They value personal fulfillment over personal fortunes, but they'd like to have both, and many do. They are the market behind the billion-dollar health food and supplement industry, the rise of green business and organic produce, the mainstreaming of yoga and holistic wellness, and the marked spike in charitable giving since 9/11. The spending power of the conscious consumer has motivated companies big and small to adopt cause marketing as a serious business strategy.

Long before the conscious consumer arrived on the scene, Jay Conrad Levinson, counseled businesses to deal honestly with customers, cooperate with other businesses, give back to the community, and partner with causes. This, and his mantra of marketing with time, energy and imagination instead of big bucks, makes Guerrilla Marketing a perfect resource for causes—and for cause-marketing partnerships. As he said in *Guerrilla Marketing, 3rd Edition*: "If you're looking for reasons for people to buy from you, let them help you aid a social cause. If they patronize your business, they'll gain all the benefits you offer; plus they can help save the environment, or stop AIDS in its tracks, or cure multiple sclerosis, or save whales."

When I discovered Guerrilla Marketing early in my cause advocacy career, I enthusiastically added it to my social change toolbox along with grassroots organizing, political advocacy, and traditional public relations. When I met Mitch Meyerson and Jay Levinson in 2006, I enrolled in the Guerrilla Marketing Coach Certification Program and sought Levinson's support for my powerful blend of his tools with mine. Thus, Guerrilla Cause Marketing was born.

This chapter explains the power of Guerrilla Cause Marketing with market studies that show how strongly consumers are motivated by a companies connection to a cause, two real- world examples of Guerrilla Cause Marketing in action, and tips on how you can send your profits and your spirits soaring by partnering with causes.

Fusion for Profit and Prospects

> *"Guerrilla marketing asks you to forget about the competition temporarily and scout opportunities to cooperate with other businesses and support one another in a mutual quest for profits."*
> ~Jay Levinson, *Guerrilla Marketing, 3rd Edition*

The foundation of Guerrilla Cause Marketing is the Guerrilla Marketing concept of Fusion Marketing—joining forces with another organization to benefit both. When Levinson introduced the concept, it flew in the face of the traditional, capitalist business model that says you must obliterate the competition. Yet its use has exploded in the past decade, and can be seen everywhere you look, from travel packages that include airlines, car rentals, hotel chains, restaurants and cruise lines, to solo entrepreneurs fusing to co-create digital products and affiliate programs.

At the local level of the small brick and mortar shop, fusion marketing may involve a local restaurant, limo service, gift shop and dating agency selling their customers tickets to a Valentine's Day dinner. All four companies stand to gain profits and new customer prospects. With fusion marketing, business is taking a page from the nonprofit playbook, and the boldest word on that page is one of the most important lessons of Guerrilla Marketing: *cooperation.*

Fusion for Principles and Purpose

> *"Cause-related marketing is an act of philanthropy on your part, and the world needs and appreciates it."*
> ~Jay Levinson, *Guerrilla Marketing, 3rd Edition*

When you add a charity beneficiary to the Valentine's Day dinner—say, a breast cancer research fund—you turn fusion marketing into cause marketing. The association brings you a whole new list of customer prospects (their members and donors) as well as the organization's publicity power. As a public service, your event becomes newsworthy, so it's publicized in the media and customers have a more compelling reason to attend. You earn more profits, gain community respect, build a new base of loyal customers, and help your community, all at once.

But a cause-marketing relationship cannot be primarily about your marketing goals. Supporters of causes have acute radar for the disingenuous. Partner only with causes you genuinely support, or your best efforts will backfire in what I call "anti-marketing," where people not only avoid you, but they advise their friends and associates to do the same. As Levinson says, "Word will get out that you are in it for the money alone and that will cause you to lose more sales than you'll gain."

This caveat is confirmed by a 2004 consumer survey by Golin Harris, which showed that the *sincerity* of a company's corporate citizenship efforts impacted customers' purchase decisions, the stocks they buy, the companies they support, and the recommendations they make to friends and family. Cooperation for mutual gain is the guiding principle behind fusion marketing. Cooperation for mutual gain *and for the good of the world* is the guiding principle behind cause marketing.

Guerrilla Cause Marketing

If you plunder the entire Guerrilla Marketing arsenal and my cause-marketing tools to promote that Valentine's Dinner and all of its partners, you will turn everyday cause marketing into Guerrilla Cause Marketing. This combination can dramatically expand the visibility of the cause and the marketability of the business.

To show you how, I'll share with you two stories of Guerrilla Cause Marketing in action. The first is from my very first cause advocacy campaign twenty years ago when I first learned the power of partnerships. The second is from my most recent Guerrilla Cause-Marketing campaign where partnerships powered the entire campaign from day one. In both cases partnering saved the day.

The Small Town Preacher Who Slew a Corporate Giant

"Have you accepted Jesus Christ as your Lord and Savior?"

That was one of the first things preacher-turned-activist, Jason Harvey, said to me when we were introduced twenty years ago at the meeting hall where citizens had gathered to talk about a toxic waste facility targeting our town. I immediately surveyed the room for a choking victim to save, or a friend to choke, namely the one who introduced me to Jason and took off.

See, if there was one thing I *thought* I knew then, it was an enlightened college student like me couldn't be wasting her time listening to a small-town Bible thumper when she had a world to save. The toxic waste company had hefty coffers, teams of attorneys, and cash incentives to offer our county commission. We had no publicity experience, no money, and only one County Commissioner on our side. We were outgunned in almost every way. I'd have to stay focused on winning and avoid being distracted by small fries like Jason Harvey.

That was before Jason Harvey got himself accepted as visiting preacher at dozens of churches throughout the region and started explaining to his fellow Southern Baptists how it was their responsibility to protect God's creation from the toxic waste facility. He even quoted scriptures.

Soon after Jason launched his crusade, nearly every public hearing on the subject was packed to overflowing, and citizen comments filled up radio talk shows and newspaper letters-to-the-editor pages. The County Commissioners had to take notice. I did too. Jason hadn't spent a nickel, and he was already outgunning a rich and powerful multinational corporation.

Jason and I joined forces with half a dozen other community leaders and conducted the kind of campaign I would later dub Guerrilla Cause Marketing. Our campaign looked like a demo of the one hundred marketing weapons outlined in *Guerrilla Marketing*, though we had to figure them out the hard way, since the book had not yet been published. We appeared on radio talk shows, distributed leaflets, mailed letters, conducted a direct mail campaign, issued press releases, gave interviews, and so on.

Desperate to give us some measure of defense against the corporation's huge budgets and legal teams, a handful of local businesses donated space for meetings, administrative staff time, and occasionally, money we needed for things like photocopying and stamps. To honor the businesses' support, we promoted them in our fliers and thanked them in our public appearances. We soon built a mass movement that packed public hearings to overflowing, filled the media with persuasive quotes and powerful imagery, won over our public officials, and, in short order, chased the toxic waste facility out of town on a rail. Given the widespread public opinion about the issue, the businesses were numbered among the local heroes.

The Green Pipe Dream Has Gone Mainstream

"The '90's [were] a "green" decade, with more awareness of environmentally safe or damaging products than at any other time in history. And we're getting greener every year. A Roper Poll revealed that consumers said they'd be willing to pay a 5.5 percent premium for green products."
~Jay Levinson, *Guerrilla Marketing, 3rd Edition*

In 2006, a client came to me in a bind. Arizona's Green Building Expo, an annual two-day public event showcasing environmentally-friendly construction, was ten weeks away, and no marketing had begun. The event had hit a plateau in recent years, attracting only thirty to forty local exhibitors, one thousand to fifteen hundred visitors, and thin attendance at its presentations. Frustrated over limited participation and knowing they could do better in the fifth largest city in the nation, the organizers sought out a marketing professional for the first time.

With only ten weeks' lead time, a very limited budget, no media outreach underway, few existing publicity materials, and a city bureaucracy to navigate, Guerrilla Cause Marketing was the only way to turn this event around.

What We Did You Can Do

We followed the Guerrilla Marketing directive to develop a seven-word, ten-second slogan that would be used consistently to motivate a targeted audience through a variety of marketing weapons. Our slogan, "The green building pipe dream has gone mainstream," targeted *niche markets* while simultaneously contradicting the notion that conservation is a fringe idea. Environmental issues were receiving a lot of ink in major business and lifestyle magazines, including *Forbes*, *Inc.* and *Newsweek*. By referring to this mainstreaming trend as often as possible, we instantly broadened the appeal of the event, and our partnership possibilities.

We formed new partnerships, including local activists willing and able to volunteer their time, energy and imagination to get out the word. Their e-mail list-serves became volunteer sources and crucial PR engines, giving us access to hundreds of environmentally concerned citizens who were more than willing to spread the word to their extended contacts numbering in the thousands.

Reviewing the Guerrilla Marketing checklist of one hundred marketing weapons, I equipped volunteers with packets of fliers, bookmarks, postcards, and posters, as well as e-mail announcements of various lengths, Web images, and a page of tips on how to distribute them. We then formed a cause-marketing partnership with Exotic Home Furnishings, a retailer of organic furniture. The company became our top sponsor and hosted an elegant, pre-event party for exhibitors, sponsors, volunteers, and prospects. What was in it for them? Aside from genuinely supporting the cause, they knew the organizers, exhibitors, and volunteers for the trade show were part of a targeted niche market for the store. Exotic Home reported a marked increase in sales after the event.

We formed similar cause-marketing partnerships with dozens of local businesses, environmental nonprofits, government agencies, and solo entrepreneurs. Every new partner was a potential source of new e-mail lists, media contacts, newsletter articles, Web site ads, and distribution points for fliers. And every new partner benefited from public exposure, from on-site banners, to event directory ads, to booths at the event, to television coverage. Although the event organizers had retained publicity help too late for major media deadlines, their new secret weapon of Guerrilla Cause Marketing saved the day.

On the morning of the event, the exhibit corridors began to trickle with the movement and sound of curious visitors, then the trickle became a roaring flood, and the crowds kept coming through that day and the next. Better still, they represented the serious, engaged, motivated niche market that every trade-show exhibitor wants to meet.

The Green Building Expo more than tripled its attendance and sponsorship revenues that weekend, doubled its exhibitors, and enjoyed five-times the attendance at its presentations. These results established the Expo as the largest regional event of its kind in the nation. Throughout, I applied lessons from my Guerrilla Marketing Coach Certification course to coach the event's staff and board to replicate these results in future years.

As the event drew to a close, one of the organizers declared, "This proves that the green pipe dream is going mainstream!" I smiled and met her high-five with a secret smile. Yes, the slogan was true, but with all of the limitations we faced, I knew Guerrilla Cause Marketing had blown the lid off the event's attendance—and would continue to do so for years to come.

The Cause-Marketing Mainstream

> *"Among those who should consider sponsorship are*
> *new businesses that need to establish their identity,*
> *companies that sell items intended for the audiences of*
> *the events sponsored—for example, sporting goods*
> *stores sponsoring any type of athletic team."*
> ~Jay Levinson, *Guerrilla Marketing, 3rd Edition*

Let's face it—the hippie boomers that launched the environmental, peace and justice movements are the retiring developer, homeowner, business leader, agency head and politician of today. As they retire, the values that drove their youthful activism are back on the agenda. Only now, those values are backed by a lifetime of work experience, wisdom and savings. For the smart, idealistically inclined business owner, this population represents a huge market for products and services that are, or can become, green, socially responsible or cause-related. Moreover, the values-driven market spans far beyond its boomer core to people young and old who feel a growing concern for the future and a willingness to back that concern with their purchasing dollars. And there's solid evidence of the trend:

- A 2002 Cone Corporate Citizenship Study showed that 92 percent of Americans have a more positive image of companies that support causes, up from 81 percent in March 2001.

- In a 2004 opinion survey by Golin-Harris, 69 percent of those surveyed said corporate citizenship is "important to their trust in business."

- A 2004 study by Deloitte & Touche found that 72 percent of employed Americans would opt for the company supporting charitable causes if offered two otherwise equal jobs.

- A 2002 Cone Corporate Citizenship Study reported that employees of businesses that support causes are 40 percent more likely to express pride in their employer's values and nearly 25 percent more likely to be loyal to their employers.

- A 2002 Cone study said 75 percent of Americans consider a company's commitment to causes when they recommend products and services to others.

If you still think you would be going out on some corporate cutting edge by taking on cause marketing, think again. The cause-marketing movement, while young, is raging.

- A Chicago trade publication, the IEG Sponsorship Report, projected companies would spend $991 million on cause marketing in 2004, up 57 percent from 1999.

- Last year, the same company reported that cause-marketing spending would rise 20.5 percent in 2007 to $1.34 billion.

- The watchdog Web site PR Watch (www.prwatch.org) points out that cause-marketing sponsorships are now outpacing sports sponsorships, and that large nonprofits are spending upwards of $7.6 billion per year on marketing and public relations.

Gone are the days when cause marketing was considered an expensive luxury of the elite and mega corporations. A motivated core of social entrepreneurs, philanthropists, and socially responsible businesses has been laying the groundwork for a cause-marketing revolution since the 1980's.

Its trailblazers are companies like The Body Shop (supporting the environment, human rights, fair trade and self-esteem); Ben & Jerry's Ice Cream (supporting the local community, global warming action, family farms and the environment); Celestial Seasonings Teas (supporting women's health); and Apple Computer (donating computers to schools and libraries while still a young company).

Contemporary examples include the rock star, Bono, with his Product Red campaign to fund AIDS relief engaging corporations like Motorola, Giorgio Armani, and The Gap; entrepreneur, Robert Kiosaki, conducting fundraisers for PBS; and countless more corporations, small businesses and solo entrepreneurs.

Join the Cause-Marketing Revolution

The key to a successful cause-marketing partnership is finding a cause whose mission is compatible with yours and cultivating an authentic, mutual relationship. You may already feel strongly about a particular cause and know exactly how you would like to support it. If you do, make sure the organization you choose is:

1. Open to marketing partnerships with businesses.

2. Friendly to your business mission.

3. Ready, able and willing to participate without compromising their own priorities.

4. Aligned with your values.

5. Able to reach the markets you want to reach.

If they don't fit these guidelines, trying to "work something out" can create problems. Better to choose a better match with your ideals and business operations. Here are a few examples of good cause-marketing matches:

Business Type	Cause
Success coach, entrepreneur, marketing company, financial advisor, bank	Community economic development agency, poverty programs, literacy programs, Big Brothers/Big Sisters.
Artist, art gallery, or art supply store, most any business	Arts association, art museum, art department of a school.
Outdoor store, nature gift shop, boat maker	Environmental education, nature conservation, pollution regulation
Developer, homebuilder, architect	Habitat for Humanity, energy conservation, homeless shelters, green building education
Bookstore, publishing house, writer/editor, tutoring company, daycare, private college	Public schools, literacy programs, public libraries

You may want to consider the causes the public finds the most important. The 2004 opinion survey by GolinHarris, "Doing Well by Doing Good," showed that the issues companies backed mattered to consumers, and that the following issues mattered most (by rank):

1. Environment

2. Pollution

3. Education

4. Energy Conservation

5. Human Right (e.g.—race, gender, lifestyle)

6. Consumer Rights

"What's in it For Me?"

> *"Although you will be doing your duty as a member of the community, you will also make lots of contacts with people who can give you business and with people who will refer business to you."*
> ~Jay Levinson, *Guerrilla Marketing, 3rd Edition*

You need not feel guilty for caring what you will get from a cause-marketing partnership. If your support is authentic, and you're not exploiting the cause to cover up bad deeds, and your cause is better off with you than without you, enjoying some well-earned publicity is acceptable. Although most businesses do not have a core mission that involves making the world a better place, the marketing studies cited in this chapter prove that adding such values to your mission can increase profits, respectability, employee morale, and customer loyalty. Most every reputable cause will have access to powerful niche marketing resources, and will, within ethical, legal and practical limits, leverage those resources to benefit its sponsors. At the simplest level, for example, a business donating $100 – $1,000 annually to a local charity can expect ads in the organization's printed materials and Web site and acknowledgement at special events.

Businesses that sponsor special events can reasonably expect advertising in the event's promotional materials, acknowledgement from stage, logos on T-shirts and other promotional products, signage on site, mentions in pre-event publicity, and so on, depending on the size of the donation.

If you also invest time serving on the board or volunteer corps of a nonprofit you're passionate about, you will gain free publicity when you speak for the organization, get quoted in the newspaper, publish articles in a newsletter, or appear on radio and television. More advanced levels of partnering can give you limited access to the nonprofit's mailing list, featured status in its newsletters and other materials, joint television and radio ads or programming, incentives for its members to buy your products, and more.

Many organizations will let you customize a high level partnership and the creative involvement can prove exponentially more beneficial for both of you. Although there is plenty of publicity and profit in it for you, you will find that the gains in a cause-marketing partnership pale in comparison to the unexpectedly deep sense of meaning you will experience when you're actively making the world a better place. You will become part of a movement that's setting a higher standard for corporate accountability to the public good. You will literally change the world.

You will also have found the biggest secret of cause marketing: your spirits will soar to heights money can't buy.

About Amy J. Belanger

Amy J. Belanger directed national, regional and local causes for twenty years. She is president and founder of Idealist Marketing, delivering writing, publicity and marketing to nonprofits, socially responsible businesses, entrepreneurs and political candidates. Reach her at: **AmyJBelanger@aol.com** *or on the Web at* **www.IdealistMarketing.com**.

CHAPTER 18

GUERRILLA RELATIONSHIPS
The Power of Face-to-Face Community Involvement

Deborah E. Bifulco

> *"Never doubt that a small group of thoughtful, committed citizens can change the world. Indeed, it is the only thing that ever has."*
> ~Margaret Mead

I started my business in 2002, after closing the door on a long and fruitful career in Corporate America. I spent zero dollars on conventional advertising; however, my Gross Revenue averaged 87 percent increase during the first four years of operation, and my Net Income (Profit) averaged 217 percent! How did I do it? I used Time, Energy and Imagination—in other words, Guerrilla Marketing!

A Dream is Born

When I first had the idea of starting my own business, I was like a lot of other people filled with hopes, dreams, and optimism. As I thought about the next career chapter—being an independent consultant and coach to business owners—I was filled with all of those emotions and many more. I'll also confess to having felt a small measure of good old-fashioned fear, fear that I wouldn't be able to get any clients!

Fear is what drives many to abandon their dreams of business ownership. In my case, however, fear is what *inspired* me to get real about how I was going to build and grow my enterprise. What I quickly realized was that the thought of making "cold calls" filled me with dread. That feeling of dread was quickly followed by panic; if I wasn't committed to making cold calls, how was I going to get appointments with prospective clients?

Referrals, of course! That seemed like a great strategy—but how to get referrals? After all, although I had just left a twenty-plus-year career in the corporate world, I didn't know a single person in my local community. The problem here becomes obvious when you consider that I wanted to build the consulting part of my business locally. I was going to have to figure out a way to get to know people in my immediate area—and fast!

And then it dawned on me. This sounds like a challenge for Guerrilla Marketing! While I was building a killer referral network for myself, I'd also be able to use lots of great Guerrilla Marketing weapons to help me get there.

The more I thought about it, the appeal of my new strategy grew greater and greater. Not only would I be able to build a solid referral-based business for myself, but I'd also be able to get involved in the community, something I had never had the time to do in my past life, which was filled with commuting and long-distance traveling.

My advice to anyone who is considering community involvement as a strategy to help grow his or her business is to make sure that you really *want* to get involved. This may seem like a no-brainer, but community involvement takes time and energy (hey, wait—aren't those two of the three key Guerrilla Marketing requirements!?) So are you committed to investing that time and energy in *your* community?

Getting Started—or Getting Out of Neutral

The first thing to do is to *identify* the community you want to be involved with. Don't be misled by the word "community." In my case that word included the small business *community* as well as the local or geographic *community*. It may be that your involvement will be in the not-for-profit community, or in the art community, or in the teaching community. Your own community may have either a strong geographic component, like mine, or it may not. Either way, your approach is the same.

The key in determining your community is in knowing your *target audience*. At the heart of this is a key Guerrilla dictum which says that we should focus on the 20 percent of the people or organizations which give us 80 percent of our business! That 20 percent becomes your target audience and, in turn, dictates the parameters of your community.

The next step is to select the organizations with which you want to become involved. The criteria for this should be that the organization will get you in front of, or next to, the people you want to get to know; and that it is an association that you truly *want* to be a part of. In short, don't join a group simply because it may get you business. Do it because it may get you some business *and* their mission is one that interests you.

Taking the First Steps

In my case, the first organization on my list was my county Chamber of Commerce. Why? The local Chamber is a robust organization that is actively involved in the small-business community (and since small-business owners are my target audience, that is a good fit). In addition, the chamber is continually seeking improvements in the quality of life for local residents as well as the business owners in the county. Bingo! I found my personal reason for wanting to become involved with this particular organization!

I also put the New Jersey Association of Women Business Owners on my short list. Again, it is an organization that is populated by small-business owners and one that is focuses specifically on the concerns of women-owned enterprises in New Jersey. I'm a woman, I own a small business and I want to do business with other women who own small businesses. Bingo again!

Filling in Around the Core Strategy

Once you've targeted your organizations, what else should you be doing?

There are some Guerrilla Marketing Weapons that just go hand-in-hand with community involvement. Those weapons include networking, public speaking, becoming a member in clubs and associations, saying hello and goodbye well, offering free consultations, serving on boards, creating credibility, writing columns/articles in the local papers, and sending out press releases. You can't really get involved without doing at least some of these other things. Step up, get involved and take a leadership role!

The Importance of Getting Involved

In my case, the first step was to join the aforementioned organizations. My strategy, however, wasn't simply to join, but to get *involved*. How do you do that? My recommendation is that you hand-deliver your membership application and with its fee, meet with the director, president, or person in charge of the group, and ask how you can *serve*. Many organizations have committees or other smaller sub-groups with which you can become involved.

Because I was completely unknown in my local business community, I wanted to gain some visibility and showcase my hard-earned marketing skills. I quickly became the VP of marketing, and a member of the executive board of my local Association of Women Business Owners chapter. These appointments gave me reasons to send out press releases to the local media. They also gave me multiple opportunities to speak in front of small groups, provide complimentary consulting/coaching sessions, network, and further get involved! As well, I became a part of a community that I've really enjoyed.

I used the same approach with the Sussex County Chamber of Commerce. I spent several years working on one of its committees, and I now serve on their board of trustees and executive board. Not only has this been tremendously valuable for my business, I've also met some wonderful people, done some good work, and been able to have a voice in my community. The key to getting involved is to pick activities that play to your own strengths and interests.

The Story of AroundtheArea.com

Another example of community involvement as a marketing strategy is my good friend and fellow business owner, Lynn Lancaster. Her company,

AroundtheArea.com, was started in 2004 by four like-minded women who wanted to develop a community resources Web site for their county. Their vision was to have an online portal where people could go to find out what is happening in the community, from city council meetings to summer festivals to fund raising events. It would also provide general resources to help people know where to go to get various services and products.

Initial funds were raised by business acquaintances of the four women who started the business. They grew the business from there using traditional advertising (with a guerilla spin), networking, press releases, community events, contests, memberships and public speaking. But mostly, they garnered the support of people they knew in the community.

Not coincidentally, all four women had strong roots in the community. Lynn is well known in the community for her involvement. She's an active member of Rotary; is on a Freeholder-appointed to guide the county's growth strategy; gives art lessons to local seniors; and she teaches karate to area kids. She is a stellar example of meshing the things she is passionate about personally with what she does professionally. You can't fake this stuff. This gets to the heart of what I said earlier—you've got to genuinely *want* to be involved!

Some Tips to Getting Started

Any journey starts with that first step. In my case, that involved attending all those dinners *and* breakfasts *and* mixers—initially always walking into a room full of strangers. Frightening? You bet! But there are a couple of tricks you can use to make your debut a little easier each time.

- When you walk into a room full of strangers, take a moment to look around and see if you can spot someone standing by themselves, then walk right over and introduce yourself! It is much easier to approach a "single" than to try to break into a group. And if this person is feeling uncertain, you'll also earn their gratitude.

- Make eye contact and smile—a great big, from-the-heart smile! It's infectious and earns you the right to walk up to someone you've never met.

Having a Volunteer Mentality

Another key to community involvement is that you must be *genuinely* interested in others, and you need to have a volunteer mentality. Good networkers know to ask, "What can I do for you?" rather than, "What can you do for me?" Because networking is such a key part of community involvement, it helps to keep that bit of wisdom in mind. The more valuable a commodity that you become to your community, the more opportunities will come your way. Don't ever hesitate to help others out with a bit of information, an introduction, or even a little of your time.

I mentioned earlier that there are some other Guerrilla Marketing tools that fit naturally with community involvement. A handful of my personal favorites are:

Free Consultations

I hope I am never so busy that I can't find an hour or so to spend getting to know a business owner and understanding what challenges he or she might be facing in realizing their dreams. I've made some wonderful connections this way, not to mention winning clients.

If you offer a product or service that lends itself to free samples or free services, this is a great way to establish yourself in your community. And what better way to introduce people to *your* product or service?

Public Speaking

Public Speaking is an often-overlooked strategy but one well worth pursuing. There are countless clubs and organizations that provide some sort of educational or entertainment component to their monthly/weekly meetings. In my experience, many of these groups have limited (or non-existent) budgets to pay for speakers. However, they're always on the lookout for good content.

If you are willing to donate some time and are a credible public speaker, you can easily find many opportunities to be in front of groups. You just need to contact their program director and offer yourself as a topic speaker.

A couple of important caveats here: make sure that you can tailor your content to the specific audience and make sure to have one or more topics that have fairly broad appeal. The best public speaking is that which educates or entertains *not* which sounds like a commercial!

One of the things I love about public speaking is that you have the chance to become an immediate subject-matter expert. This is a particularly good weapon for service businesses. For example, if a pest control company wanted to employ this strategy, it might offer a short program on five things a businessperson or homeowner could do to "pest-proof" a home or an office. In that same vein, a realtor might team up with a home improvement contractor to offer a talk on the top things a homeowner can do to improve their resale value.

Press Releases and Publicity

This is one opportunity that many people tend to shy away from; after all, it can feel a bit uncomfortable to brag about yourself. I am, however, a firm believer in shameless self-promotion! If you've done something noteworthy, let people know about it by sending a release to your local media.

Exactly what is noteworthy? It could be that you (or your business) have received an award or recognition; or that you've earned a certification; or that you were the guest speaker at an event; or even that your business has celebrated some sort of milestone. Hey, it could even be that you've just written a chapter in the next Guerrilla Marketing book!

And while I'm on the subject of publicity, don't forget to post copies of your press releases on your Web site!

Saying Hello and Goodbye Well

This sounds pretty simple, doesn't it? But it is worth putting some thought behind. Let's take my company. I am a trusted advisor and coach to my clients; I'm always on their side. When I meet someone, whether a stranger or an old friend, I always greet him or her with a smile and a warm "hello." It's part of my identity. I have made it my business to be approachable (and smiling is easy—I really enjoy what I do!)

On a related topic, I always encourage business owners to phone their own company and listen to how the call is answered and how the voicemail greeting sounds. Are they both friendly and inviting? If not, change them right away!

Here's a little tip for recording a winning outgoing message on voicemail: when recording, stand up, look up, and smile while you are talking. You'll be surprised what a difference it makes in the sound and tone of your voice!

Likewise, if you have someone answering your phone, make sure they are doing so with a smile. It doesn't do much good if you're out and about spreading cheer and goodwill in the community and your telephone is being answered by a disinterested, disengaged voice!

Wrapping it All Up

If you believe that Community Involvement is a viable way to grow *your* business, then remember to follow these simple steps:

1. Select your organizations and causes.

2. Make sure you really *want* to be involved.

3. Support your community involvement with other Guerrilla Marketing tools such as publicity, public speaking, networking, free consultations and anything else that fits for you.

From the simplicity of monitoring your business' phone voice, to the more demanding roles of public speaker and publicity writer, by becoming engaged with the people around you will automatically introduce you to future clients.

Community involvement is a *powerful* strategy to grow your business, but it can also be tremendously rewarding on a personal level. Done right, community involvement will result in increased sales along with many opportunities to give something back to your own community. Take the same approach that I have in your own business—and watch it blossom!

About Deborah Bifulco

*Deborah Bifulco, Certified Guerrilla Marketing Coach, works with business owners of small to mid sized companies to help them create results and profits. She founded her business in 2002 after leaving a twenty-plus year career in corporate marketing. Find out more at **www.Bifulco.com**.*

PART FIVE
Innovative Guerrilla Tactics

Guerrilla Marketing is not "business in a box," where you simply follow the formula, one, two, three, and presto, you have a successful business. One of the hallmarks of Guerrilla Marketing is the "100 Guerrilla Marketing weapons," and a good Guerrilla Marketer learns how to use a variety of weapons based on what the individual markets need and want. So if you haven't already done it, fasten your seatbelts now because you're going to learn how eight world-class Guerrilla Marketing coaches have taken high impact marketing strategies to turn visitors into prospects, prospects into customers, and customers into raving fans.

CHAPTER 19

THE GUERRILLA INVITATION

The Most Effective Marketing Strategy on the Planet

Michael Port

> *"Unlike simply selling what we make, 'free' requires creative thinking about how to make money around what we make."*
>
> ~Chris Anderson, editor of *Wired Magazine*

All sales start with a simple conversation. It may be a conversation between you and a potential client or customer, between one of your clients and a potential referral, or between one of your colleagues and a potential referral. An effective sales cycle is based on turning these simple conversations into relationships of trust with your potential clients over time.

We know that people buy from those they like and trust. But as Sir Winston Churchill once said, "It is a mistake to look too far ahead. Only one link in the chain of destiny can be handled at a time."

If you don't have trust with your clients or customers, then it doesn't matter how well you've planned, what you're offering, or whether or not you've created a wide variety of buying options to meet varying budgets. If a potential client doesn't trust you, nothing else matters. They aren't going to buy from you—period. If you think about it, this may be one of the main reasons that so many well-intentioned, decent people say they hate marketing and selling. They may, albeit inadvertently, be trying to market and sell to people with whom they have not yet built trust.

If you want a perpetual stream of inspiring and life-fulfilling ideal clients clamoring for your services and products, then just remember—all sales start with a simple conversation. They're executed when a need is met and trust is assured. So where do you start? By using the most effective marketing strategy on the planet—the always-have-something-to-invite-people-to offer.

The "Book Yourself Solid Sales Cycle"

Your services have a high barrier for entry. To a potential new client, your services are intangible and expensive—whether you think they are or not—especially to someone who has not used the kind of services that you offer or to those who have not had good results with their previous provider. People usually hate to be sold, but they love to receive no-strings-attached invitations.

"The Book Yourself Solid Sales Cycle" begins by making no-barrier-to-entry offers to potential clients. A no-barrier-to-entry offer is one that has no risk whatsoever for a potential client so that she can *sample* your services. I'm not just talking about offering free services, which I don't recommend, and, unfortunately, is still a common practice for many professional service providers. No, the "Book Yourself Solid Sales Cycle" takes this concept much farther with much more success.

I use "The Book Yourself Solid 7 Core Self-Promotion Strategies" of networking, web, direct outreach, referral, writing, speaking, and keep-in-touch, to create awareness for the solutions I offer. However, rather than attempting to *sell* a client, I simply offer them an invitation that has no barrier-for-entry. This is what I mentioned above, the "the always-have-something-to-invite-people–to offer."

Mine is a complimentary teleseminar that I've dubbed the *Think Big Revolution*. I offer it weekly, and it's designed to help people think bigger about who they are and what they offer the world. Sometimes I discuss a topic that is specifically related to getting more clients, and other times I discuss different principles and strategies that will help the callers be more successful in business and in life.

Note that the membership is *free* and has no strings attached. There are no up-sells, no pitches, no bait and switches. If I meet someone who I think will benefit from membership, I invite them to join. In fact, I'd like to invite you. I bet you'll love it. You get an opportunity to participate in something that should add great value to your life and test me out at the same time. And for me, well, it's fantastic because I don't have to *sell* anything. I can offer really great value to the lives of potential clients and customers at no risk to them. And then they have the opportunity to ask me for more business help if they are so inclined. There are tons of ways that you can set up this kind of always-have-something-to-invite-people-to self-promotion strategy. You are only limited by the scope of your imagination.

This strategy works! Of the 93 percent of my clients who successfully book themselves solid, all of them use it. The majority of their prospects become clients after having experienced their always-have-something-to-offer. I earn over 85 percent of my clients this way too.

There is another added benefit of this kind of always-have-something-to-invite-people-to offer. It can serve as one of the most effective ways of establishing your personal brand. Al Lautenslager calls it the tag line, the pithy saying that positions you. For example, while the *Think Big Revolution* is an extension of my personal brand identity, people know me as *the guy to call when you're tired of thinking small.*

Once you come to a *Think Big Revolution* weekly member meeting, you'll immediately see that I want to help you think bigger about who you are and what you offer the world. Your always-have-something-to-invite-people-to offer is the perfect way to integrate and align your *who* and *do what* statement (who you help and what you help them do) with your *why you do it* statement (the philosophical reason that you do what you do).

Consider this example: I worked with a man who is a personal trainer and a healthy-eating chef. When he joined my Book Yourself Solid Fifteen-Week

Intensive Group Learning Program, he hadn't yet created relentless demand for his services. As you might imagine, this caused him to be anxious over what his future held.

After we established the four fundamental elements of his marketing foundation, we created his always-have-something-to-invite-people-to offer: the *Fitness Fiesta for Foodies*. One Sunday evening a month, he would host a party where he would teach his guests how to prepare healthful meals that help them stay fit. There were two requirements for attendance, however. He would put that month's menu on his Web site and each guest was required to bring one item off the menu. Each guest was also asked to bring someone new to the event, thus creating a new audience for his work. After he made his first round of invitations, he barely had to market himself. It was magical. People loved it and they loved him for doing it. Most important, they hired him because of it.

You could do something similar—and better too! All you need to do is look at what you do: are you an entertainer, an artist, a host? You find innovative ways to offer freebies to your target market, something that will benefit them, and you start the process. And here's the best part: you don't need to fork out a ton of money (or any money) for these events either, especially if you collaborate with others. The value you add in your offer meets the needs and desires of the people you serve. Then as you continue to build trust over time through your sales cycle and your follow-up and by offering additional value and creating awareness for the services you provide, you'll attract potential clients deeper into your sales cycle, moving them closer to your core offerings.

You'll notice that the always-have-something-to-invite-people-to offer I profile above is done in a group format. There are three important reasons for this:

1. You'll leverage your time so you're connecting with as many potential clients as possible in the shortest amount of time.

2. You'll leverage the power of communities. When you bring people together, they create far more energy and excitement than you can on your own. Your guests will also see other people interested in what you have to offer and that's the best way to build credibility.

3.	You'll be viewed as a really cool person. Seriously. If you're known in your marketplace as someone who brings people together, that will help you build your reputation and increase your likeability.

Please give away so much value that you think you've given too much and then give more. I had a friend in college who, when he ordered his hero sandwiches, would say, "Put so much mayonnaise on it that you think you've ruined it, and then put more." Gross, I know. I believe that he has since stopped eating his sandwiches that way, and his arteries are thanking him, but adding value should be similar. Remember, your potential clients must know *what* you know. They must also really like you and trust that you have the solutions to their very personal, specific, and urgent problems. The single best way to do that is to invite them to experience what it's like to be around you and the people you serve.

Oh, I almost forgot—if you're a big thinker or want to think bigger about who you are and what you offer the world, then please do join the *Think Big Revolution* by going to **www.MichaelPort.com**. See how easy that was? No selling, just a relevant invitation. If you love it, you'll keep coming. If you don't, you won't.

About Michael Port

Michael Port is the author of Book Yourself Solid *and* Beyond Booked Solid. *He's been called a "marketing guru" by the* Wall Street Journal *and is a renowned public speaker. A slightly irreverent, sometimes funny, knowledgeable, compassionate, and passionate performer, Michael hits his mark every time and leaves his audiences, readers, and clients a little smarter, much more alive and thinking a heck of a lot bigger about who they are and what they offer the world. See videos and read his blog at* **MichaelPort.com**.

CHAPTER 20

GETTING BACK TO BASICS

Eleven Guerrilla Ways to Get Your Marketing to Stand Out

James Dillehay

> *"Good communication is as stimulating as black coffee and just as hard to sleep after."*
> ~Anne Morrow Lindbergh

L iving in our busy world, people have learned to screen out most of the thousands of marketing messages received every day and aimed at selling them something. Guerrillas use tactics that communicate their messages as helpful solutions, rather than sales hype, appealing to the needs and pains of their audiences. Eleven ways your Guerrilla Marketing messages will get noticed are:

1. Identifying Your Customer's Needs

2. Getting in Front of Your Customers

3. Inspiring Trust

4. Banking on Referrals

5. Educating Clients

6. Engaging the Five Senses

7. Social Proof

8. Using Stories

9. Getting a Fast Result

10. Doing Business with Passion

11. Following Up

Identifying Your Customer's Needs

Direct response experts agree that it takes many repetitions of a message to get audiences to respond; more times today than ten years ago, because of the growth in advertising. However, the closer your marketing message appears to answer the needs of the recipient, the fewer times he needs to see or hear it to recognize a potential solution.

Psychographics describes the needs and habits of your ideal prospect to help define his niche world—it's a tool used to recognize him by his behavior. You can also identify your customer by demographic factors like income, sex, color, age, location, and education. Learning who your customer is tells you the niche through which to communicate your marketing in order to get the highest response.

You will usually find more than one niche audience has problems your product solves. This gives you a range of targets at which to aim your messages. Cut your marketing costs by focusing only on those most likely to buy your offer. Aim to be the exact answer your ideal prospects are seeking.

Many businesses focus on their product first by advertising its features. A far more effective and less costly approach is to discover your customer's needs and then highlight your product's ability to fix what's wrong.

Without a niche audience:

1. Customers cannot differentiate your offer from competitors which leads to lower perceived value of your product at best and more often, just being ignored.

2. You won't know who your customers are. Your marketing efforts are then like a hunter closing his eyes and firing a shotgun into the air, hoping to hit something.

3. You will miss opportunities. By focusing your marketing toward a niche audience, you will learn about your audience's specific problems and uncover solutions which will become new products to ease their pain. Listen to your audience and they will tell you what products to offer them.

Getting in Front of Your Customers

Once you know who your ideal customer is and what his unique needs are, position yourself in front of him. Avoid wasting your resources trying to be everywhere and chase everyone—go for the person most likely to purchase your offer by being where he's already spending time.

Identify publications your customer reads. Find associations he belongs to. Learn which Web sites he visits. Answer questions in the discussion groups he participates in.

Get involved with what he does by going where he goes. Learn to put yourself in his shoes and be there waiting when he walks by. Your ideal customer shops at specific stores to buy supplies for his hobbies. He attends consumer expos to learn about the latest trends in his interest area.

Inspiring Trust

Once you know who your customer is and where to find him, give him reasons to trust you. Studies show that confidence is the most important factor in the buying decision; more important than quality, price, convenience, and other influences. Ten ways to inspire confidence in your prospects are:

1. Using testimonials and endorsements from satisfied customers and authority figures like professionals or celebrities.

2. Providing case stories from customers that clearly demonstrate exactly how a person used your product to solve a problem.

3. Getting your product reviewed by associations, TV, or radio allows you to post the reviews and borrow from the popularity of those organizations.

4. Quoting research studies from universities adds credibility.

5. Showing articles printed in major publications provide tangible evidence that your product is worth mentioning.

6. Removing any risk with a money-back guarantee; it's vital to provide this assurance when people are unfamiliar with you and your company. The longer the guarantee, the lower the feeling of risk.

7. Providing your contact information on all your marketing materials. Let prospects know how they can find you in case there's a problem with their purchase.

8. If you belong to the Better Business Bureau, display their logo on your materials.

9. Telling prospects how long you've been in business helps ease concerns about whether you can be trusted.

10. Tying your product to popular media. If your product has been mentioned on TV, include the words "As Seen on TV" on your promotional materials and Web site pages.

Banking on Referrals

When customers are happy with their experience of doing business with you, they'll tell their friends. The $100 billion-a-year direct-selling industry generates almost all of its revenues from referrals.

To insure people spread the word about you, create a quality product, deliver it with speed, and back it up with outstanding customer service. Satisfied customers will then trumpet your praises to their friends.

Don't just wait for word of mouth to happen, make it part of your marketing strategy to ask for referrals. The best time to ask is when the customer is at his peak level of satisfaction, like after they've experienced a benefit that's eased their pain or made them sexier looking or put more money in their account. This is the time when the customer is most willing to pass you a friend's name. Asking for referrals costs nothing.

Word of mouth works online, too. If you aren't already doing so, gather your customer's e-mail address. A 2007 survey by Epsilon reported that 84 percent of people using e-mail said they clicked through to a web page to learn more about offers relevant to their needs. More than 50 percent of these people forwarded e-mail messages about a product or service on to others.

Educating Clients

If you focus on selling, your prospects will perceive you as a salesperson. Instead, aim at educating prospects. You will be viewed as a helpful resource, because you are teaching ways to ease their pains or improve their situations.

Before you can educate others, you must become the up-to-date expert on your industry with your own knowledge base. Make it a regular task to learn all you can about your product, its multiple uses, your industry, and customers who use products like yours. Join trade associations in your industry—they typically produce newsletters with news and current trends. Subscribe to newsletters of independent experts in your field such as consultants to large companies.

Educating your customers has a side effect which can earn you additional profits. In addition to making you the obvious expert in your field, you can create and sell information products based on your knowledge. Information products like books, newsletters, CDs, DVDs, training seminars and more provide multiple opportunities for income streams. The sales of these products will give you more names to promote your original business to.

Become an expert educational resource through the following ways:

1. Create tip sheets with multiple uses for your service or product.

2. Publish a newsletter with industry articles and news informing readers about technology and trends in your area.

3. Sponsor events in your community where you can demonstrate helpful ways to use your product or service.

4. Create a Web site with educational articles, blog, tips and news.

5. Register yourself as an online expert in your field. Sites like www.askanexpert.com; www.allexperts.com; www.suite101.com; and www.authorsandexperts.com seek expert sources to answer queries from visitors.

6. Write a small book as a training manual for your product or service. Authors are perceived as resources. The book will create an additional income stream and you can place an ad for your other product or service in the back.

Educating is a way of showing your honesty, rather than attempting to sell, convince or persuade a prospect.

Engaging the Prospect's Five Senses

Faster than a speeding text message, you can get your prospect's attention through engaging one or more of his five senses. The senses are closely tied to the emotions and since most decisions are emotional, that's where you want your message delivered. Before plastic wrappers and cardboard containers, all products were sold in open air markets where customers could see, smell, touch, hear, and taste goods.

Communicating with product features sends messages about your product— it's *me* marketing Sensory experiences that are about your customer—it's *you* marketing. Involve clients in experiences of how your product makes them feel more beautiful, more entertained, or healthier.

Use lighting and colors in your marketing materials to engage sight. Play soft music in the background. Encourage customers to touch and hold items. If appropriate, lightly touch your prospect's forearm or shoulder when introducing a concept. "Touch your customer, and you're halfway there," said Estee Lauder.

Product demonstrations at trade shows allow you to hook your visitor's five senses right away. You can get them to feel a material. You can provide edibles or drinks people can taste. You can diffuse fragrances that can be smelled.

"The best way to market any offering (goods, service, or experience) is with an experience so engaging that potential customers can't help but pay attention and pay up," says Fortune 500 consultants, Gilmore and Pine.

An added value of creating an experience for the customers is that you get to learn what is important to them. When your business engages the customer, you learn and discover. Customers do business with those who make them feel valued and cared for.

Getting a Fast Result

People are in a hurry and they want their solutions now. Conventional businesses can take a lesson from network marketers who know they have to get their prospects involved with the product right away or lose them to competing providers.

Jack was new to network marketing. His friend Steve had just suffered a bite from a brown recluse spider. The swelling had not gone down, even after a trip to the hospital and antibiotics. Jack recalled hearing a tape where someone got immediate relief from a similar bite. Steve was getting desperate so when Jack offered the product, he grabbed it. After two hours the swelling had gone down. By the next day, the skin around the bite was returning to normal. As a result of his immediate experience, Steve joined the network marketing company and started referring others and earning commissions.

Another way network marketers get immediate results is through home parties. Home parties allow new distributors to demonstrate products in a safe and comfortable environment and collect immediate cash sales on the spot.

Help your prospects experience a result right away and they sell themselves on your product.

Social Proof

One of the ways to heighten your response rate is to communicate how much simpler life is to follow the crowd. Studies indicate that people find it easier to go along with a group than to make a decision on their own, says Robert Cialdini, Ph.D., author of *Influence, The Psychology of Persuasion*. The more that crowd or group resembles ourselves, the more likely we'll go along.

Following the crowd is a form of social proof. Bartenders keep a mug or glass in clear view with dollar bills as a way of prompting customers to leave tips. Collection baskets at revival services start their rounds with cash already in plain view. Network marketers have one distributor after another stand up at meetings and tell their experiences.

Use social proof in your advertising messages like "over ten months on the best-seller list." Describe how long your product's been a top seller and add more proof. Portray images of customers using your service or product, because visual pictures—especially those with human beings—attract the eye.

Using Stories

Dale Carnegie, author of the bestselling book, *How to Win Friends and Influence People* said you will build rapport with your audience faster when making a presentation if you begin your talk with a story about a personal experience that had deep meaning for you.

People are more inclined to remember your offer when it's associated with a story. As the saying goes, "Talk to me and I hear; show me and I understand; tell me a story and I'll remember."

Doing Business with Passion

Regardless of how many tactics you use to market your business, technique alone becomes routine. Passion is far more persuasive than logic. Studies report that eighty percent of our decisions are emotional. Only after we have made an emotional choice, do we then come up with a reason for it.

Excitement is contagious. Enthusiasm generates word-of-mouth referrals. But most of us can't stay *up* all the time. For whatever reasons, we sometimes find ourselves in an emotional slump. When you feel the passion for your business is waning, look to these areas for rekindling your own fire:

1.   Belief in your product or offer.

2.   Motivation to help people.

3.   Enthusiasm for the team of people involved in your business.

4.   Excitement about past marketing campaigns that paid off.

5.   Desire to improve yourself.

6.   Love for the freedom you have to make the decisions in your life every day.

Following Up

Surveys indicate that customers stop doing business with companies more often because they feel neglected than because they are unhappy. Following up with prospects and customers keeps you in touch and helps alleviate their abandonment issues.

Most businesses estimate their chances at 5 to 20 percent when closing a first time sale. However, studies reveal that you have a 20 to 40 percent probability of getting former customers to do business with you again. You will spend much less money by aiming follow-up campaigns at customers who've already bought from you than by going after new business.

If follow-up isn't already in your marketing tactics, write it in, beginning today. Create a follow-up calendar from which you schedule who you follow up with, how you will contact them, when you will reach them, and what the result was. The most effective follow-up is face to face. But when personal meetings aren't possible, use the phone, send something by postal mail, write an e-mail, send a fax, or use instant messaging.

Follow-up that isn't perceived as a nuisance gives the customer news or tips he'll see value in, such as a discount coupon or a useful tip sheet. Demonstrate that you care about your people by solving problems or filling needs relevant to their interests, not your own. Make customers feel valued, not neglected.

About the Author

James Dillehay is a nationally recognized educator helping people with small budgets generate income from their creative ideas. He is author of eight books, a former magazine publisher and editor, a Guerrilla Marketing coach, and co-author of Guerrilla Multilevel Marketing. *For more information, please visit* **www.GMMLM.com**.

CHAPTER 21

BOUNCE BACK PROFITS

The Inside Secret to Getting Your Customers to Immediately Re-Purchase Again and Again and Again...

Blaine P. Oelkers Sr.

> *"Do what you do so well that they will want to see it again and bring their friends."*
>
> ~Walt Disney

Guerrilla Marketers know the power of low-cost and in some cases, no-cost marketing. This is marketing that provides results and returns and results that are not measured in sales dollars, but rather in profits—money in the bank.

To grow your business geometrically, that is the game. In *Guerrilla Marketing, 3rd Edition*, Jay Conrad Levinson said: "Guerrilla Marketers must aim for more transactions with existing customers, larger transactions and referral transactions."

This chapter is all about getting your customers to immediately repurchase from you over and over and over again, making your profits soar. I will show you how to start your next sale by finishing your current sale with what I call the "bounce back offer" that ensures repeat business.

Your Moment of Power

In your business there is just a handful of what I call "moments of power." It's a specific moment in time when you have the ability to impact your business a powerful way. Timing is the key because the ability to impact your business comes at a certain moment and then it's gone. One of the most effective "moments of power" comes at the point of sale. It's precisely at this point you want to let your customer know they made a good decision in buying your product or service and you also want to start right there—in that moment— to market your product or services again. This can be done for little or no cost with *bounce back offers*. It amazes me to see how many businesses let this moment slip away and lose that opportunity forever. An opportunity that could be the difference between success and failure in business. For you it's a great day because you're about to learn how to never miss that moment of power again using the *bounce back offer*.

The American Marketing Association defines a "bounce back offer" as:

> A coupon or other selling device included in a customer-ordered product, premium, refund, or other package that attempts to sell more of the same or another product to the recipient.

Why Bounce Back is Critical—Customers Carry a Big Sign above Their Head

A Guerrilla Marketer knows the long term value of a repeat customer. When I was a franchisee with the world's largest delivery pizza company, we knew our average customer ordered pizza twice a week and spent about $30 a week. That's over $1,500 a year in sales, and more important to a Guerrilla Marketer, it is $300 in profits. So I saw each new customer carrying a big sign above their head saying "I have $300 a year for you." When I examined my business, I also noticed that it did not take many loyal, repeat customers to ensure large profits. With just one hundred customers, I had $30,000 in profits. With just a little over three hundred repeat customers, I had $100,000 in yearly profits. What is the value of a repeat customer in your business? What's the amount in the big sign your customer is carrying over their head? It's critical to know that value and realize the *most important marketing* you do is to your *current customers*.

The secret to marketing to current customers is to leverage as much as possible the moment of power at the time of sale. This ensures your customer returns for more products or services. This can be done for any type of business from restaurants to cleaning services, from dry cleaners to consultants—heck even lawyers can use bounce back offers. Let me teach you through a few real life "Front Line" examples and then conduct a quick brain-storm session to get *you* generating bounce back profits this week.

Front Line Example Number One— Record Profits in Pizza Delivery Business

Let's start with one of my favorite bounce back offers which launched many record weeks in my pizza-delivery franchise. It started out as a low cost promotion that went to no-cost as we added some Guerrilla Marketing creativity to the promotion. Since it turned out to be no cost, it dramatically improved profit since every dollar you save in advertising costs drops right to the bottom line—your bank account!

Bounce Back Basics—Three Simple Things

What you want to do with bounce back offers is to include some type of coupon or offer that is presented to the customer at the moment they purchase something from you. You want this offer to do three things:

1. Thank them for their order.
2. Let them know they made a great decision buying from you.
3. Give them an aggressive, creative Guerrilla Marketing offer to bounce back and purchase from you again and again and again.

For the pizza business we had a good marketing mantra which was to never let a pizza box leave the store without a bounce back coupon offer on the top of the pizza box. Initially, we had simple offers: a free topping, $1 off your next pizza, or a free two liter of soda with your next order. We did make sure to thank them for ordering and reminded them how good we were at delivering their pizza safely and quickly. That's your basic bounce back offer and it was fairly inexpensive to print up the coupons and just glue them to the top of box.

We found the bounce back offers worked well to establish and reward our most important customer—the repeat buyer. You know, the one carrying the big $300 sign over their head. The next step was to direct their buying habits to increase our profits. We did this with *targeted* bounce back offers. For example we knew the average order was under $15 so we created bounce back specials at the $19.99 price point to move the customer into a higher average sale.

The bounce back offer was also used to increase sales during slow times. We used aggressive offers to get customers to order on our slowest day which was Tuesdays. We found that if we offered buy one pizza at full price get one free on Tuesday nights (Two for Tuesday), more customers would order from us two or three times a week instead of just once. But the final two things we did with our bounce back coupon really sent the profits soaring.

Two Guerrilla Tweaks Unlock Bounce Back Power

We did two final things that made this bounce back program the most effective one of its kind. We got into the mind of the customer and introduced fusion marketing. First, we realized that when we glued the bounce back coupon to the top of the box, it would rip and not come off cleanly. We had some customers mention they lost the coupon. When we talked to our best customers, we found that their system was to carefully remove the coupon from the box then put it up on their refrigerator. So we knew there was great opportunity in addressing those issues and learning from our best customers.

What we did was to print up an oversized post-it note bounce back coupon. Then at the top of the coupon it said: "Peel & Stick Me to the Fridge." This not only solved the problem of glue-ripped coupons but also decreased the lost coupons and took advantage of the key point we got from our best customers—get the offer on to the fridge! There was only one drawback to the new coupon. An oversized post-it note cost more than the simple paper coupon we were printing up. Enter fusion marketing to completely remove that cost.

Fusion Marketing Completely Removes Advertising Costs

Fusion marketing is a term use to describe when two businesses are able to fuse together and do mutually beneficial advertising for each other. As Jay Conrad Levinson says in his book *Mastering Guerrilla Marketing*: "In an era of fierce competition, savvy business owners know that they must fuse it or lose it." What we did to actually remove the printing cost was to allow other advertisers like a video rental store to place an offer on our bounce back coupon. In exchange for that advertising, they covered the cost of printing *and* we got our bounce back offers going out with the nightly video rentals—pizza and a movie—perfect! We call that the "bounce over" offer since the video store's customers would then *bounce over* to become our customers. Using the bounce back offer allowed us to leverage the moment of power we have at the time of sale to our customers. We were able to one: thank the customer for their business; two: to remind them they made a great decision buying from us; and three: entice them to repurchase from us again and again and again.

Front Line Example Number Two—
Online Business Built with Bounce Back

Let's discuss another example from an Internet store that I've owned and operated for the last five years. The store sells high-end antioxidant vitamin supplements. I know that the value of a customer for this business is over $1500 in sales per year, but more importantly it's over $600 a year in profits. So I see each customer holding a big sign above their head that says "I have $600 a year for you!" As a Guerrilla Marketer, you know costs six times as much to sell to a new prospect as it does to an existing customer. It costs even far less when you market "at the moment" of sale to an existing customer since you already have their attention and their wallets out. It's important to spend some time thinking and creating the bounce back offers to be used at the moment of sale.

For the Internet store initially the offers were simple like the following bounce back offers you might see from large retailers:

- free shipping with your next order;

- ten percent off your next order;

- ten dollars cash back on your next purchase of $50 or more.

Those offers worked but we wanted to go beyond standard offers. We added colorful stickers to the product. These boldly thanked them for their order and let the customer know there were re-order specials specifically for existing customers that just purchased the product. We created a special Web site location for them to go and a special phone number they could use for re-orders. Then we tapped into a secret that kept the customers coming back again and again and again.

A Secret that's Never Entered Your Competition's Mind

That secret is un-advertised gifts at the time of purchase. This secret got the customer committed to us for their next purchase *while* they were completing their current purchase. It's the "moment of power" that can solidify your customer base. When a current customer would call in to place an order we would take the order. *Then* we would say that we appreciated their business and to show they made the right decision in ordering the product at that moment from us, we would give them a special gift just for them—just because they chose to do business with us. Then based on the size of the order we gave them a free un-advertised gift:

- Surprise—We appreciate you. Free shipping on your order today!

- Surprise—We are going to include a special report on the product you bought!

- Surprise—We are going to include an educational audio CD (normally $9.99) at no charge!

■ Surprise—We are going to include a book (normally $15.99) at no charge!

■ Surprise—We are going to include a new product for you to try at no charge!

Another variation of that special is to extend it to the next purchase. So you say "Thank you for your purchase today. We appreciate your business and when you're ready to purchase again remember us because I have marked your account for a free gift next time you buy from us. We want to build a long term relationship with you." How many times have you had that kind of experience as a customer? You want that free gift with your next order so you'll bounce back!

Okay—Let's Make Your Profit's Soar

Hopefully by now your mind has started to think of some possible bounce back offers you can use in your business. Remember that you're looking for low or no-cost marketing offers that get your customers coming right back to you. You want to thank them for their current order, make sure you remind them of the great decision they made by choosing your product and finally leave them with an offer that gets them coming right back to you. It helps you create an aggressive offer if you calculate and know the value of a repeat customer in your business. When I see the "I've got $600 a year for life in profits" sign above my customer's head, I am inspired to create strong bounce back coupons and offers. With just over 160 repeat customers I've got $100,000 in profits each year. That's profits not sales. That's money in the bank and it comes from good customer service and a strong bounce back offer.

Putting the Three-Pound Tool to Work—Creating Your Bounce Back Offer

It's time for you to create your own bounce back offer unique to your business. It's time to use the most important tool a Guerrilla Marketer has, the three-pound tool. That is the three-pounds of grey matter known as your brain. Along with time and energy, your imagination is the greatest tool you have in creating your marketing and getting profits to soar. Let's get your creative guerilla brain going with your own bounce back offer. Here is a list of sixteen (see my Web site for the top one hundred) different bounce back offers to get your three-pound tool started:

1. **Cash Bounce**: Offer a cash discount off the next order, for example $5 off your next order of $25 or more. Make sure to put a short expiration date on the offer to get your customers to bounce back quickly. You could even make your coupons look like a five dollar bill and have some fun with it.

2. **Percent Bounce**: Offer a percentage discount off the next order, for example 10 percent of your next purchase.

3. **Free Shipping Bounce**: Free shipping on the next order. This offer can help to remove barriers for customers, especially when ordering online. You could also get customers to bounce back again and again by offering them free shipping for the rest of the month or for all orders during a certain time.

4. **UAG Bounce**: An un-advertised gift at purchase time. Make it surprising and something unique they will remember and even freely tell friends about which brings you the added bonus, the referral bounce.

5. **Loyalty Bounce**: Offer free products or services to encourage loyalty with repeat orders. To track purchases, use things like punch cards or track it for the customer via a customer number or telephone number. Many grocery stores provide you with a discount card to get you to bounce back to their store. A bounce back program for one of the world's largest coffee houses worked so well in the grocery stores that they had to discontinue it because it was taking business away from the stand alone stores. The grocery store was giving a free coffee for every so many purchased. The best part was that the grocery store kept track of the sales for you. This made it easy for the customer and each time they were reminded: "Only x number of lattes till you get one for free!" This offer had customers bouncing back to the grocery store locations much more frequently than the stand alone stores.

6. **Time Bounce**: Service industries can offer some free time. "Thank you for your business. Here is a coupon for fifteen minutes free on your next visit." This works well for things like massages, consultants, and lawyers!

7. **Information Bounce**: This is a great one for doctors, lawyers, consultants and service people of any kind. Offer an article, report, or perhaps a chapter of a book you've written. This builds the relationship with the customer and increases repeat business. For example as a lawyer you could provide a bounce back kit on creating a will or even better provide a short article on how to prepare for a meeting with your lawyer to ensure it goes as quickly (and inexpensively) as possible. How many lawyers have ever given that out? You will have more business than all the other lawyers in town. Or, how many times have you gone to the doctor and he or she gives you an article on how to take better care of your body at the end of your appointment?

8. **Survey Bounce**: Provide the customer with a short survey to complete and tie it to an aggressive discount. This gets them bouncing back and providing you with some great information. I recently ate lunch at a restaurant that gave me a coupon for 15 percent off my next meal—all I had to do was call in and take an automated survey to receive my validation code. It worked well— I did the survey and returned the next week for lunch!

9. **Receipt Bounce:** Print up a bounce back offer on the back of your sales receipt or invoice. Some stores provide nice bounce back offers printed up on the back of the sales receipt. Some even have a separate machine that prints up specific offers based on what the customer buys. You have to provide the receipt anyway; why not turn it into a marketing tool?! I recently received a shipment in the mail for a few things I purchased online. On the back of my invoice were four deeply discounted offers. These were unadvertised specials ranging from 40 percent to 70 percent off the regular prices. It was a great offer and people tend to keep their receipts and invoices so the offer has a shelf life.

10. **Fast Bounce:** Offer your largest possible discount with a very short window of availability. For example: 50 percent off your next order *if* it's within the next twenty-four hours. Getting a customer to bounce back that quickly can dramatically increase the retention, placing you head and shoulders above the competition.

11. **Timed Bounce:** Use the bounce back offer to increase business at specific times or seasons for your business. For example: 25 percent off any order on Tuesdays or buy-one-meal-get-one-free Monday nights only

12. **Gift Bounce:** Offer a gift certificate to try a free product with next purchase. I recently got a catalog with an order I placed. In big bold letters on the front of the catalog was: "Thank You For Your Order. We'll Send You A *Free Gift* With Your *Next* Order." Then there was a special code to ensure I got the free gift.

13. **Fusion Gift Bounce:** Give away a gift at the time of sale that's free from a cooperative business partner. Get a local business that's looking for more customers to give your customers something for free.

14. **Bounce Over:** Create an offer with another non-competing business that they give out to their customers to get them to "bounce over" to your business. Like the video-rental store and pizza delivery example.

15. **Referral Bounce:** At your "moment of power" when a customer has just purchased from you, they are usually at the height of their emotion for your product since they just traded some of their money for it. This is a great time to get referrals. You can include some type of bounce back offer for them but give them a few extra to share with friends.

16. **Pre-Bounce Profit**: There are ways to make a profit with bounce back offers even before your customers buy. You can actually sell part of your "moment of power" to others. You can actually get companies to pay you, to deliver their offer to your customer at the

time of sale. There are many businesses doing that today. My last order of books from an online book seller included a whole package of "special offers." Every month when you get your credit-card bills, there are a bunch of other offers inside with your bill. As your customer base grows, so can your pre-bounce profits. Those companies pay you to have their advertisements given to your customers.

Do not miss one of the greatest and most often overlooked "moments of power" in your business—the bounce back offer. Remember if your customers are not bouncing back, they're bouncing away.

Now get those bounce back offers going *this week* in your business. They are the secret to getting your customers to immediately repurchase again and again and again.

About Blaine Oelkers

*Blaine Oelkers is a Certified Guerrilla Marketing Coach and Bounce Back offer specialist. For the last twenty years, Blaine has been using Guerrilla Marketing principles and practices to create highly profitable businesses. A graduate of Purdue University, Blaine has owned and operated a computer consulting firm, a franchise with the world's largest pizza delivery company, and four health and wellness businesses. One company he built completely online using bounce back offers to build a loyal customer base. For a free copy Blaine's top one hundred bounce back offers visit his Web site at: **www.BounceBackProfits.com**.*

CHAPTER 22

GUERRILLA MARKETING USING A SINGLE SHEET OF PAPER

Six Ways to Cut Costs and Increase Profits

Roger C. Parker

> *"Be daring, be different, be impractical, be anything that will assert integrity of purpose and imaginative vision against the play-it-safers, the creatures of the commonplace, the slaves of the ordinary."*
>
> ~Cecil Beaton

One of the major themes that Jay Conrad Levinson emphasizes throughout his books is that marketing success is based on ruthless efficiency, achieved by using creativity and technology to keep marketing costs as low as possible while—at the same time—leveraging maximum sales out of each marketing message. He even said that a single sheet of paper may be all that's separating you from Guerrilla Marketing success!

In this chapter there are six ways you can use a single sheet of paper to wring maximum sales out of every sales and marketing opportunity. Here, you'll learn how to:

1. Promote your competence for free, month after month.

2. Capture the names and e-mail addresses of Web site visitors.

3. Make sure interviewers ask you the right questions.

4. Find out what prospects are thinking.

5. Quickly create an effective marketing plan.

6. Prepare proposals that get the business.

Promote your Competence for Free, Month after Month

In the third edition of *Guerrilla Marketing*, Jay Conrad Levinson wrote: "The ultimate winners in the future will be companies that are totally accessible to buyers at the time the buyers want to buy."

The negative way of saying the same thing is: "Out of sight, out of mind." Your marketing message has to be consistently visible, so that you will be there when your prospects are ready to buy or your clients are ready to re-buy.

Think of the heart monitor in the hospital melodramas that take place in emergency rooms like *E.R.* Each time the patient's heart beats, the trace appears at the top of the screen. But it doesn't stay there! It immediately begins to decay. Soon, the trace has dropped to the bottom of the screen.

Your marketing is like that. Each time you communicate with clients and prospects, you enter top-of-mind awareness. But this awareness quickly dissipates. *Soon, you're invisible!* If your competitor, however, is visible when your client or prospect is ready to buy, they're likely to steal the sale from you!

Why Traditional Newsletters Fail

Newsletter marketing has always made sense in theory, but rarely in practice. Four and eight page newsletters have frequently failed because of the time and costs involved in preparing and distributing them. As a result, multipage, printed and mailed newsletters simply don't work!

Not only do conventional newsletters take too much time to prepare and cost too much, but too much time typically goes by between issues. As a result, consistent visibility suffers.

The One-Page Solution

Taking advantage of advantages of technology, which Jay has always endorsed in his Guerrilla Marketing books, it is possible to redefine newsletter marketing. The new model of newsletter marketing success is based on five key points:

1. **Content:** One relevant, educational, topic per issue.

2. **Frequency:** monthly, announced via e-mail.

3. **Length:** front and back of a single sheet of paper.

4. **Distribution:** primarily electronic file (i.e., Acrobat PDF, FlashPaper, etc.), delivered as a Web site download or e-mail attachment. (Copies can be desktop-printed for face-to-face delivery or distribution at networking events.)

5. **Layout:** formatted for easy reading and to promote a professional image that differentiates the sender from their competition.

One-Page Newsletters that follow the above formula avoid the costs and delays of printing and mailing, take just a few hours to create, provide a relevant reason to contact clients and prospects each month, and provide a meaningful reason to sign up for your monthly e-mails that announce each new issue.

Case Study

Like many important advances, my One-Page Newsletter was created almost by accident!

In early 2001, I was contacted by the Ford Motor Company and asked to speak about readable design at their upcoming Ford International Newsletter Editor's convention. As a first-time speaker, I wanted to have a packed room!

Accordingly, four months before the conference, I invested a few hours creating my first One-Page Newsletter, which I sent as an Acrobat PDF file to the individual organizing the event. I asked the event organizer to pass it along to anyone who might be interested in attending my workshop. The issue discussed headline formatting for recognition and easy reading. My goal was to fill the room by pre-selling the information I was going to communicate, as well as build comfort and familiarity among those who might attend. I committed to sending a similar newsletter every thirty days until the event.

I was so pleased with the way my newsletter came out, I sent three additional PDF copies to clients I had previously worked with, but not presently working with. Within two hours of sending three PDF's for free, I received an e-mail reply from a program manager at Microsoft complimenting me on the content and layout of the newsletter, asking me to call her that afternoon and to visit Microsoft the next week to help with a major project!

Imagine: something I created and sent *for free* generated a week's consulting plus a free trip to Seattle! That's the power of a One-Page Newsletter.

Lesson

Clients and prospects judge you not by the size of your marketing budget but by the relevance of your marketing message and your ability to deliver the right message at the right time. The above newsletter succeeded because it arrived on a day when there was a need for my service. If I hadn't been visible that day, I probably wouldn't have been contacted—and a competitor who was visible that day probably would have profited!

Remember the formula: one-page/two-side, one educational topic, attractively formatted, and delivered electronically each month. That's a winning formula for One-Page Newsletter success!

Use Tip Sheets to Build your Opt-in E-mail Marketing List

E-mail marketing is one of the bargains of our age. E-mail permits you to promote your competence and your professionalism to Web site visitors over and over again *without* incurring the costs of printing and mailing. For free, you can send as many relevant communications to your prospects as desired.

However, successful e-mail marketing depends on an incentive, one strong enough to persuade first time visitors to your Web site to submit their name and e-mail address as well as permission to receive e-mail from you in the future.

A simple tip sheet can provide the bonus—or incentive—necessary to tip the odds in your favor, encouraging reluctant Web site visitors to sign-up for your newsletter.

What is a Tip Sheet?

A tip sheet communicates *relevant information, distilled to its essence,* displayed on a *single side of a single sheet of paper.* Tip sheets communicate professionalism by providing concise information that communicates experience.

Tip sheets succeed to the extent they help prospects and clients achieve a successful task. They are popular incentives because they help prospects avoid mistakes, make better buying decisions, or show how to make the most of a previous purchase.

Case Study

One of the most successful tip sheets was for Guerrilla Marketer Gene Paltrineri, a local photographer who needed a way to help entrepreneurs prepare for formal business portraits, i.e., portraits that could be used over a long period of time in their marketing materials as well as distributed to the press.

Reviewing his previous experiences, Gene noticed that the same problems often occurred: clients would show up stressed over traffic, wearing the wrong clothes, or concerned about a recent haircut or new hair style.

Accordingly, Gene made a tip sheet which emphasized the importance of leaving early, described what to wear—and what *not* to wear—and emphasized the importance of not trying a new barber or hairstylist the day before the portrait session.

Although the tips were basically, "common sense," they were only common sense to a professional who had seen these mistakes made over and over again. To his clients, the tips were both helpful and relevant. The casual style of the tip sheets also helped relax clients before the photo shoot.

Three years after it was first created, Gene is still distributing his original tip sheet as a sign-up incentive, a presentation hand-out, and a confidence builder for new clients.

Lessons

You as the business owner are the authority. You have an overview of the factors that contribute—and undermine—your client's success. Simply translate your knowledge into one side of a single sheet of paper that summarizes your knowledge into topics like:

- How to Avoid the Eight Biggest Mistakes Made When …

- Ten Things to Look for When …

- Eight Steps to Success When …

Use Talk Sheets to Ensure Successful Interviews

Always prepare a "Talk Sheet" before you are interviewed. A talk sheet consists of a single sheet of paper that contains questions you want to be asked during a teleseminar or radio interview.

Talk sheets put you in control of the interview. Talk sheets not only make sure that the interviewer will ask you the questions you want to be asked, talk sheets also reduce the likelihood that interviewers will inadvertently blindside you with questions that are either irrelevant or that you're uncomfortable asking.

Case study

The importance of talk sheets was driven home to me earlier this year when I was being interviewed on a network radio program that was not only broadcast live but was archived on a very active Web site.

I was discussing my latest book, *Design to Sell*, which shows how non-designers can profit from design concepts like white space and tools like Microsoft Publisher that professional designers use to create effective print communications like newsletters, postcards, and small ads. Not having read the book—which is not an unusual situation, unfortunately—the interviewer started asking me questions about using Publisher to create Web sites which is not Publisher's strong point.

This put me in a very difficult position. With less than five minutes to go, I didn't want to waste time talking about what the book didn't cover, nor did

I want to annoy the interviewer by correcting him on the air. As a result, the interview was effectively, if inadvertently, totally undermined.

Lesson

A talk sheet, printed on one side of a single sheet of paper, could have prevented the above debacle. By including the following elements, I could have ensured a successful interview. The one-page talk sheet that I've since created includes:

- **a one paragraph summary** of the book, the problem it addresses, and the solution it offers;

- **a single paragraph summary** of my background;

- **twelve suggested questions** that I am comfortable answering.

Most important, my talk sheet concludes with a subheading entitled, "What this book is not about," and three points that should *not* be addressed. (Remember, unless your testifying before Congress, your interviewer is likely to be more interested in creating a relaxed and interesting segment, rather than trying to trip you up.)

Talk sheets should be posted under a "media" section of your Web site. When potential interviewers encounter your questions, they will be pre-sold on your courtesy and professionalism—which will pre-sell you as a desirable guest.

Find out What Prospects are Thinking Before you Try to Sell Them

A one-page assessment can make the difference between introductory meetings, or telephone calls, that succeed or fail.

A pre-call or visit assessment helps you ask the right questions and pre-sells your ability to solve the prospect's problem by communicating a competent, professional image. Assessments show that you respect your time and the prospect's time. Assessments also drive home the point that the upcoming conversation will revolve around the prospect and their problem, rather than being a sales pitch for your services.

And best of all, like all Guerrilla Marketing tools, assessments offer maximum payback for a minimum investment of time and money.

Case Study

After delivering a successful Microsoft Leadership Forum Webcast, I received the names and addresses of everyone who had signed up for the event, as well as those that had asked me to contact them. I immediately sent participants a "Thank You for Attending" postcard offering a free thirty-minute introductory call to discuss their marketing challenges. Soon, we were scheduling several calls a day.

To make maximum use of these calls, I used Assessment Generator at assessmentgenerator.com to send a *pre-call assessment* a few days before every scheduled call. There was *no cost to this program*, as I was already an Assessment-Generator client and there are no charges for additional assessments. The completed assessment provided me with the information I needed to ascertain the individual's responsibility, the size and type of business, the firms attitude toward marketing, and—most important—the individual's perception of their major challenges.

During each call, I was able to focus the call around the prospect's responses, encouraging them elaborate on their original responses. As a result, the assessments encouraged a healthy dialogue, based on the prospect's needs and how I might help them reach their goals. Because I had "done my homework in advance," the calls were lively and paved the way for future relationships, even if the first call did not result in a sale.

Lessons

In addition to pre-qualifying prospects and paving the way for successful calls and meetings, assessments make it possible to not only obtain a Web site visitor's e-mail address and permission to re-contact them, but also to *find out what they're thinking!*

A carefully-prepared assessment helps you answer questions like:

- ■ Who are your Web site visitors?

■ What are you're their major problems?

■ What is the magnitude, and urgency, of their frustrations?

■ What solutions have they tried before?

■ Do they have authority and resources to hire you?

Although there is little or no cost involved creating assessments, make sure that your questions are open-ended enough to encourage your prospects to respond in detail. Avoid asking questions that sound like a large, impersonal corporation, or a controlled circulation publication that asks too many qualifying questions. Instead, use your assessment as a way of promoting your expertise and empathy, to spark a healthy dialogue.

Create a One-Page Marketing Plan

Many firms operate without marketing plans, because they think that marketing plans have to be long and detailed. Nothing is further from the truth. An effective marketing plan can be as simple as one side of a single sheet of paper. It can be created as a three-column table created in Microsoft Word! Resize the columns, so that the third column is the widest:

■ In the **left-hand column**, list the names of the next twelve months.

■ In the **center column**, enter the topic you want to focus each month's marketing on. Topics should reflect the *benefits* offered by your new and existing products and services rather than the names of the products and services.

■ In the **right-hand column**, list how and where you can promote each topic.

Look for opportunities where you can recycle and reuse the same information in various ways.

Case Study

Next month, for example, newsletter marketing will be my topic. My One-Page Newsletter will focus on a single aspect of newsletter marketing, I'll offer a free follow-up teleseminar for prospects who want to discuss the topic with me, and I'll be offering a three week Newsletter Marketing Master Class.

The following month, I'll feature online presentations, i.e. Webcasts, etc. My newsletter will describe a single aspect of online presentations, i.e. creating presentation visuals. I'll follow-up with a free online teleseminar for those that are interested, as well as a Presentation Master Class.

Often the hardest part of an effective marketing plan is choosing the topics to focus on each month. Once you have identified your next twelve marketing topics, doing the work is the often the easiest, and most enjoyable, part!

Convert Prospects to Customers with One-Page Proposals

Most proposals fail. The reason is often that the proposals are too long, take too much time to prepare, and take too much time to read. Often, the proposals focus on the seller's background, rather than the prospect's concerns. Worse, there often is no urgency to encourage prospects to take immediate action.

In these time-crunched days, you don't have time to devote to preparing multi-page, detailed proposals. Likewise, your prospects don't have time to read long, detailed proposals. If your proposals are so long that clients put off reading them until "later," you're in danger of losing assignments that might be awarded to competitors who submit short, relevant, and on-time proposals.

The point of a proposal is to *not* to focus on your background and experience, or a detailed description of *how* you are going to solve your prospect's problem. Rather, the proposal is intended to summarize the benefits of the solution you're offering, spark dialogue, and communicate a sense of urgency. *If prospects have specific questions, they will ask them!* (When prospects ask you questions that you already answered in your proposal, it's a sign that your proposals are too long and they are not being completely read.)

The best way to communicate urgency is to include a *timeline* that emphasizes how delays now, in accepting the proposal, will create even greater costs and delays in future months. By visually communicating the penalties of procrastination, your proposal can encourage prospects to take immediate action.

Case study

Jeff, one of my twenty-year clients, owns a video security system in the Pacific Northwest. He is a sole proprietor and salesperson for a firm that installs security systems to reduce vandalism, employee theft, and frivolous lawsuits.

Jeff is successfully competing with larger, more established firms, because he can prepare and submit a proposal weeks ahead of his competitors. By submitting a short, benefit-oriented proposal and letter of agreement with a computer-generated itemized list of parts and labor, he often closes sales within hours of meeting a client for the first time.

His competition, however, often takes *up to three weeks* to prepare a proposal!

Lesson

Your proposals are not "graded" on the number of pages or detailed descriptions of what you are going to do. Instead, your proposal's success rests on how well you articulate the benefits the prospect will enjoy, the competent image you project, and your ability to persuade your prospect to sign on the dotted line before one of your competitors can get the order first.

As always, conciseness and on-time delivery are the keys to success!

Conclusion

The above six single-page projects share several attributes in common:

- **Their length encourages focused and concise writing.** Long documents encourage sloppy writing. When you're limited to a single page, however, you're forced to focus on what's important, write as clearly as possible, and eliminate unnecessary detail.

- **They save you time.** As a Guerrilla Marketer, you try to prepare as much of your marketing yourself. It's common sense that it will take less time to write a one-page newsletter than a four- or eight-page newsletter. One-page newsletters contain just 625 words. That's a provocative headline, an introductory paragraph, three or four main points, a conclusion, and a call to action.

- **They save your prospects and clients time.** Your prospects and clients are as busy as you are. Prospects and clients lack the time or the motivation to read long documents. In today's time-pressed business environment, conciseness is a virtue. One-page documents can be easily read at a traffic light or while waiting for an e-mail response. One-page documents can also be easily shared with co-workers and superiors.

- **They stimulate dialogue**. A long, detailed communication stifles dialogue. Instead of asking questions to clarify specific points, your prospect may decide to search for the missing information at a later date, i.e. "tomorrow." Yet, "tomorrow" may be too late!

- **They can be automated.** Jay Conrad Levinson has always endorsed technology. Today, it's never been easier to harness technology like e-mail and autoresponders to deliver newsletters as Web site downloads, or use shopping carts to simultaneously deliver sign-up incentives and add the visitor's name and e-mail address to your opt-in mailing list. Likewise, it's only recently that self-scoring online assessments have become easy to prepare and automatic in their delivery.

The history of Guerrilla Marketing has always been focused on promoting your competence to your prospects and previous clients as efficiently—easily and inexpensively—as possible. Jay's decades-own vision of entrepreneurial marketing success has never been as easy to achieve as it is today.

About Robert C. Parker

*Roger C. Parker invites you to visit **www.DesignToSellOnline.com** where you can test your Design Marketing IQ at and sign up for his Guerrilla Marketing & Design newsletter.*

CHAPTER 23

LOAVES AND FISHES

A Guerrilla Marketing Coach Teaches Three (Formerly) Starving Artists to Reel in the Profits!

Leslie Hamp

> *"Determine that the thing can and shall be done,*
> *and then we shall find the way."*
>
> ~Abraham Lincoln

It's a common belief that creative artists are destined to struggle. This case study shows how a painter, photographer and writer conquered the barriers that every small business owner faces and turned their "blank slates" into successful ventures, thanks to Guerrilla Marketing coaching.

My artists, in order of appearance, are:

Gailyn. Creative, skilled, and unsure how to prepare for her upcoming solo art show featuring 40 oil paintings.

Ros. Driven, successful, and longing to shift her graphic design skills to large photography prints exhibited in art galleries, businesses and homes throughout the United States.

Debra. Big-picture, energetic, and determined to transform her local writing and editing business into a global venture that attracted a higher caliber of writers.

All were longing for a new path. All were at a loss as to how to proceed. All sought out Guerrilla Marketing coaching to convert their dreams to reality. Here are their stories.

Gailyn Holmgren, Painter, St. Paul, Minnesota

Gailyn Holmgren had a looming deadline. With just three weeks to prepare for her solo art show at the Art and Invention Gallery in Nashville, Tennessee, Gailyn was beginning to buckle under the pressure of marketing herself. Uncertain of the next steps to take, she turned to coaching. Our focus: developing a step-by-step action plan while eliminating roadblocks to marketing success.

You see, Gailyn was a master painter, not a businesswoman. She landed the solo show because of her expertise in painting with oil. Some of her pieces were edgy; some, traditional; some, a collage of mixed media. Painting was not her challenge—marketing was.

"I remember being scared when I got the solo show," Gailyn said. "I knew I had quality art and framed pieces ready to go, but I couldn't get my head around all the marketing details related to the show. I worried that I'd fuss, have nothing concrete done, and look foolish at the reception. I worried that I'd feel regretful that I didn't present my work, and myself, as well as I could have."

Our coaching program focused on two basic Guerrilla Marketing principles: begin with the end in mind and create SMART (Sensible, Measurable, Achievable, Realistic and Time- bound) goals.

I asked similar questions to those used in Guerrilla Marketing Coach Certification. How did Gailyn want her art to be displayed on the walls of the gallery? What did she want to write in her artist statement for each painting? How did she want to present herself and interact with others at the reception? What were her sales goals? The clock was ticking and we only had three weeks. We hit the ground running with a step-by-step action plan that set the stage for big results.

Gailyn's Action Plan

- Step One: Develop gallery contract, including purchaser's reproduction rights.

- Step Two: Define categories of art.

- Step Three: Develop print materials—artist statement for each painting and postcards with a surrealistic image on one side and contact information on the other.

- Step Four: Send framed art to gallery owners.

- Step Five: Define success at the reception and in terms of sales.

- Step Six: Visualize the exact outcome desired, from leaving Minneapolis to flying to Nashville to dressing for the reception to conversations with patrons to closing the sale.

- Step Seven: Celebrate.

The big day arrived. There were jitters, but Gailyn embraced Guerrilla Marketing sales tactics to sell herself and her art by focusing on relationships more than sales. By engaging her prospects in casual conversation, asking relevant questions and personalizing her responses, Gailyn felt at ease and created a positive first impression. She conveyed pride and confidence through facial expression, tone of voice, and selection of words. She believed in herself, and her optimism positively affected relationships and sales.

"The reception was exactly as I had visualized," Gailyn said. "I walked into the space and saw my work on every wall. I connected with the gallery owners and patrons and had fun describing my work, discovering what others saw in it, and selling for a price that surprised me. For the first time I had the realization: I am a professional artist. I have a gallery representing me. I have people who want to buy my work. That is what all artists want."

Before she knew it, Gailyn closed three sales and boldly set ten sales as her ultimate measure of success. She kept her eye on the prize, and within a few short months her wildest dreams became reality.

"Okay, I'm sold on coaching," she told me. "When I got to Nashville to pick up my pieces from the art show, ten pieces had sold, I was invited to send art to two shows next year, and I can count on a solo show next year."

But the sales didn't stop at ten. Two more paintings sold, including one that Gailyn had nearly tossed into the garbage. That $1,000 sale eliminated another roadblock. Gailyn now realized she could earn a profit expressing herself on canvas. And it sent her back to her easel. She finished two new paintings, sent them to the gallery, and voila! One sold before the show even opened.

"The good news is that the paintings are priced higher than they were last year to the point that even I can't afford to buy them," said Gailyn. "I just completed another piece with another on the way, and I get ideas lying in bed at night."

Roadblocks to marketing success? No more, for this artist now living her dream to make money through painting. She overcame a lack of understanding of marketing and sales. She mastered a process she can use again and again, and she conquered her fear of talking about herself and her art work. Gailyn Holmgren created her success with the help of Guerrilla Marketing in action.

Ros Nelson, Graphic Artist, Bayfield, Wisconsin

Ros Nelson had a big vision when we started coaching. She visualized her photographic-based images printed four to eight feet tall, installed in a large, gray, marbled lobby with plentiful space and light to showcase the work. She realized that she wanted big results!

The puzzle of how to bring fine art to market brought Ros to coaching. While she had a successful graphics business helping others market their products and services, she had no idea how to market herself. She didn't know how to define her audience, and she had no selling or follow-up strategies. And the challenge of selling something with such personal meaning made it even more complex.

From the standpoint of time alone, her challenge seemed daunting. "How could I make a living, make art, fund the prints and frames, and then have time left for marketing? Yes, time was an issue, but feeling overwhelmed because of my lack of clarity was the real problem," she admitted.

We reviewed her projects in light of the 80/20 rule—the Guerrilla Marketing principle that urges entrepreneurs to focus on the 20 percent of their business that generates 80 percent of their sales. Ros quickly discovered that, like many entrepreneurs, she was spending 80 percent of her time on projects that produced only 20 percent of her income. To be profitable, she needed to focus on the 20 percent that generated 80 percent of sales.

"Coaching helped me see that I try to do too much, that I need to choose core tasks that stimulate me and are profitable emotionally or financially—whether graphics or fine art," she said.

To place marketing fine art into a profitable category, Ros needed a focused plan. She completed the "Where Do You Need to Focus?" exercise in the Guerrilla Marketing Toolkit. "My scores were very low in defining my audience, seeing opportunities that were right in front of me, identifying action steps, and implementing follow-up," she said. "I yearned for this new venture and had an unwavering commitment, but I needed someone to bounce ideas off of and who would hold me accountable."

Our actions were modeled after the Guerrilla Marketing plan and calendar found in the Guerrilla Marketing Toolkit, and results were measured against specific, quantifiable goals. We built her marketing success through market research, building relationships with art galleries, entering competitions, applying for grants, developing fusion-marketing partners, creating a unique business identity separate from her other business and displaying her work.

Gradually, her efforts began paying off. She began selling prints to a surgeon who embraced her calming, vivid images for waiting rooms and exam rooms. Then, she won a statewide competition sponsored by the Wisconsin Arts Board. And recently, she established a relationship with a gallery in Rochester, Minnesota.

"Laying groundwork also created a sort of energy and momentum," Ros said. "Through coaching I learned focus, how to describe prints to buyers, and how to evaluate galleries. I developed follow-up that included a letter, disk, e-mail and phone messages, and when possible, a face-to-face visit. I became more direct when asking for exhibition space. And the more confidence I developed, the more success I experienced."

Ros was pro-active and dauntless. She created a Web site, www.glacialdrift.com. She turned her studio entry into her own gallery. She incorporated her art into products used by design clients. She attended seminars and paid attention to her goals on a regular basis.

"I put myself on my own list," she said, "began to learn which venues fit me, and leveraged my successes."

Niche Marketing

Ros embraced a Guerrilla Marketing lesson that many artists and small business owners shy away from. She defined a niche based on her purpose, benefits, and target market. "When I got clear on my niche, presenting work to a target audience got much easier," she said. "I'm now better able to understand what my customers want and help them visualize one of my prints in their home or business and how that will make them feel. I am on their side now, instead of feeling insecure about presenting myself."

Knowing that it costs six-times more to sell a product to a prospect than it does to sell that same thing to a customer, Ros embraced the Guerrilla Marketing concept that existing clients are your best prospects.

She began to personalize her services, exceeding the expectations of customers, giving more than they anticipated and caring more than they're used to sellers caring. Handwritten notes and phone calls made customers and gallery owners feel appreciated. By using the customers' and gallery owners' names, talking with them of non-business topics, alerting them to special new products or services and responding instantly to their calls and e-mails, Ros stood out from the competition.

Mastering these Guerrilla Marketing tactics unleashed fresh creativity for this visual artist, and she's reaping the rewards: more ideas, more confidence and clarity, more connections and more sales. Ros Nelson is now a quintessential Guerrilla Marketer.

Debra Marrs, Editor and Writer's Coach, Riverview, Florida

Debra was steadfast in her determination to grow her local business well beyond the borders of Riverview, Florida. She outlined a plan: establish a solid brand, create a Web site with products, and publish a book. Debra knew her path. What she didn't know was a surefire way to get from Point A to Point B. She turned to coaching for direction and accountability.

When we first met, Debra was teaching creative non-fiction writing at the University of South Florida and, from there, attracting private clients who wanted to continue working with her. "My goal was to establish a global business within the year," she remembers. "I needed help, help, help as to where to begin. I knew it was essential to set the overall goal then break it down into manageable chunks. I needed to find helpful people and resources in order to launch my planned products—e-books, tele-classes, and coaching."

"First things, first," I thought.

Debra needed an unmistakable brand identity, first and foremost. She was falling into the entrepreneurial trap of serving everyone who came her way. And because those clients did not motivate her to do her best work, she experienced the pitfalls of procrastination. We set to work identifying her ideal business situation, client interaction, and income streams—all methods taught in Guerrilla Marketing.

What followed was dramatic. "I notified my clients that it was time for me to step up to a new level in my work," she recalls, "and that, in order to manage my business growth, I had to take a look at what I do best, what I enjoy doing, and what I can do to help other writers grow too."

"The areas of my strongest expertise include memoir and autobiography; non-fiction books including how-to, spiritual, business, and professional, where the writer is the subject matter expert; how-to articles for magazine or Web site publication; non-fiction book proposals; and short stories, flash fiction and flash memoir.

"I told clients that I would no longer be editing novel length works of fiction and recommended a new editor. I doubled my fees in the first month and tripled them within the year."

Debra was accelerating her results via a Seven-Step Guerrilla Marketing plan, a model that's also part of the Guerrilla Marketing Coach Certification course.

Debra's Seven-Step Guerrilla Marketing Plan

- **Step One:** She defined the purpose of her marketing—creation of a global venture.

- **Step Two:** She defined the benefits of her products and services—helping others get published.

- **Step Three:** She defined her target audience—highly motivated writers with the goal of publishing in certain genres.

- **Step Four:** She defined her niche—editor and coach for writers.

- **Step Five:** She defined her marketing tactics—creation of a Web site, targeted advertising in writing publications, and offering coaching samples, to name a few.

- **Step Six:** She created a new business name and identity—Writing Together stands for high quality, integrity, and a focus on publication.

- **Step Seven:** She defined her budget—This included resources to establish a Web site and shopping cart for international sales.

"Defining my target market was huge," Debra says. "Focusing on ideal clients made things easier and less stressful. I feel so much more joy now working with high-caliber writers who produce manuscripts that I look forward to reading. I only work with those who are serious about publishing as well as those who take instruction and apply it."

By narrowing her niche and target audience, Debra also found more ease in launching new products. She added a one-half dozen e-courses, audio products, and tele-classes into her product mix, and she automated some of these programs for 24/7 interaction from her Web site. She adapted her Web site to better reflect her expertise and how she is different from the competition, what Guerrilla Marketing calls her "unique selling proposition."

As a business owner who walks her talk, Debra is now in the midst of writing her own book. "I've developed a unique approach to memoir writing through experimental forms," she said. "It's given clients and students more freedom in their life-story writing and they're experiencing amazing results. This technique is so powerful; I am pulling it all together in book form and expect publication within the year. Coaching has helped me see how essential it is to leverage my time, and this will give me a way to reach more writers easily."

Through savvy Guerrilla Marketing, Debra transformed her business into the global venture that was just an idea eighteen months ago. She now enjoys clients throughout the United States and around the world. She has created multiple streams of income through e-courses, tele-classes, and coaching programs, and she is attracting prospective clients at her Web site, writingtogether.com.

Debra Marrs mastered the secrets of Guerrilla Marketing and propelled herself into the land of her dreams.

*****

Three real-world stories. Three real-world successes. Three more entrepreneurs who reached for their highest vision and reaped the rewards with the expert guidance of a certified Guerrilla Marketing Coach.

About Leslie Hamp

Leslie Hamp, Certified Guerrilla Marketing Coach, shows small business owners how to boost business and marketing success. Leslie holds a Master of Arts degree in Mass Communications, is the recipient of a Bronze Award for feature-article writing from the National Council of Marketing and Public Relations, and serves on the USA Today *Small Business Panel. Find out more at* **www.BoostYourBottomLine.com**.

CHAPTER 24

THE WONDERFUL WORLD OF WOW! WINDOWS

Achieving 500 percent growth in Eighteen Months with Guerrilla Marketing

John Williamson

"To business that we love we rise betime,
And go to 't with delight."
~William Shakespeare

April 2006

"YEESSSSS!" John punched the air as he put down the phone.

His wife, Shirley, looked up in surprise.

"Joyce has just landed that big new client I was telling you about," he beamed. "Not only did she take over this new client from a competitor who had been servicing that client for many years but the client has agreed to pay her three times as much as he had been paying her competitor. That makes 500 percent growth in her client base in eighteen months! In fact, when she told the prospective client 'We're not the cheapest...' he replied, 'Well, of course you're not.'"

"Brilliant," Shirley smiled, "considering she almost gave up the business when they lost half their clients eighteen months ago. You obviously had something to do with her success."

"Just a little," John agreed grinning.

Shirley smiled at his mirth. "Stop giggling and tell me *how* she managed to increase her client base by 500 per cent in eighteen months," she insisted. "*And* increase her prices."

John thought back over the two years that he had been coaching Joyce Ozier and her Vancouver-based business, WOW! WINDOWS

*****

In Vancouver, Joyce replaced her telephone, reflecting on the ups and downs of her amazing business journey. For Joyce, it had all started in 2000, the millennium year...

How clearly she remembered ... It was midnight. The orange glow of the street lamp illuminated Joyce and her son Doug as they sat in her car. Joyce had given Doug a lift to his flat, and he was trying to persuade her that she would be happier work-wise if she returned to her creative roots by applying her theatre set design skills to creating stunning retail windows.

Joyce, who has a Masters Degree in Theatrical Design, had led her own experimental theatre company in her youth before moving into arts management. She had managed several Canadian dance companies and was the first Executive Director of the Vancouver Dance Centre for professional dancers. Now, in her late fifties, she'd been happily married for over thirty-five years to her physicist husband, Irving, who would be retiring soon, and it didn't seem like a good time to reinvent herself.

The spark of excitement that her son had ignited faded as she drove home across town, and common sense returned. But two days later, Doug challenged her again by suggesting she approach their neighborhood bank to create an exciting new display in their window *free of charge!* She surprised herself and accepted the challenge; her offer to the Bank Manager was accepted, and her other son David took some photographs to use for her first brochure.

Within a couple of days of sending out a few brochures, Joyce had her first paying client. That was when she panicked and phoned her friend Olivia for help. Olivia had risen to become Western Canadian Head of Visual Merchandising for a large retail chain, and eventually retired to become a well-respected professional painter.

Olivia had laughed, but had agreed to help her and teach her all she could about retail visual merchandising. Joyce started to create her own unique style by marrying her own theatre set design skills with what she learned from Olivia. She withdrew $5,000 from her savings as start-up capital and WOW! WINDOWS was born.

Three Years Later—June 2003

While visiting a regular client, Joyce was struck by the outstanding window displays in a small boutique. James Williams, the talented man responsible, was later to become her creative partner. James had held senior positions in Visual Merchandising with Birks in Montreal, and Harrods, Jaeger and Alfred Dunhill in London, England.

Joyce had more work than she could handle that year, so she asked James if he'd like to help her. The rest, as they say, is history.

Six Months Later—January 2004

Clients were consistently delighted with the excellence of the WOW! WINDOWS team's designs and installations. But the business was growing very slowly. They were working long hours, taking minimal remuneration, and Joyce was still subsidizing the business from her savings. Although Joyce loved working with James and respected his creative genius, the business had ceased being fun, it wasn't really paying off, and she was seriously considering giving it up altogether.

The year before, she had joined an Internet marketing forum and had lurked, reading and learning. She soon realized that one person in particular was responsible for getting that forum off the ground and its rapid growth of member participation. It was a man named John Williamson. John, although not the forum owner, was effectively the resident "guru." He answered questions from anybody and everybody, not only about marketing, but any business subject, revealing wisdom and knowledge that was both deep and wide.

Acting on an impulse, Joyce e-mailed John. To her delight, John not only replied to her e-mail, but telephoned her from England. She explained her predicament to him and was excited when John offered to coach her.

Almost immediately after they started working together, Joyce realized that this coaching was at a different level entirely from her past experiences with business coaches. She felt she was getting a "street-wise MBA in a month," month-after-month-after-month. This time business coaching was certainly "raising her game."

They discussed exit strategies and quantified them, which enabled them to set financial objectives for the business over the next few years. Their first Guerrilla Marketing Calendar was based on these initial objectives.

Joyce explained to John that while the business was basically sound with happy clients, both she and James—whom she had now taken into partnership with her—were working at full capacity but weren't really making much money. They were barely profitable with a 'feast and famine' type of cash flow supported from Joyce's savings. The business had hit a ceiling and they didn't know how to get past it.

If both partners were working up to their capacity, there was no point in marketing and taking on new clients until they had increased their working capacity.

John agreed, but explained that these problems were common to creative and service businesses; they tended to overspend on materials, and consume excessive amounts of time trying to produce near-perfect work. However, the extra 20 percent of work required to meet their 'perfection' standard often consumed 80 percent of the time and costs of the job, making it uneconomic.

John reassured her that this could be controlled even by a sole-proprietor by implementing simple budgeting, job-costing, and quality control procedures, thus freeing up valuable resources to market and to take on more clients.

John asked Joyce to list all the functions she currently performed—then they focused on ways of increasing performance efficiency, eliminating or delegating these tasks.

In addition to exercising greater control over the design, prop creation, and installation process, they could also increase their capacity by employing additional part-time and full-time staff—as cash flow would allow—and delegating more. They drafted employee recruitment and selection procedures and documentation, ready for use when required.

Joyce implemented these ideas and quickly found that they were now doing high-quality client work much more efficiently and cost-effectively. And they truly had realized surplus capacity. They couldn't take on more clients.

John and Joyce reviewed and created systems for the business. "You can't make a money machine work faster, if it's only partially built," explained John.

Realizing that the information produced monthly by the book-keeper's accounting package was not particularly useful for management purposes, John created a new, easy to understand, Monthly Reporting Package. This enabled Joyce and James to understand exactly how the business was performing. Now they could more easily co-ordinate and measure their Guerrilla Marketing results from their Marketing Calendar together with the other functions of the business.

As part of the review of the sales systems, Terms of Business and Client Agreements were introduced. John explained that securing a regular and consistent business cash flow depended upon agreeing to proper Terms of Business with clients. It also enabled any misunderstandings or disputes to be resolved more easily. "Only amateurs run businesses without specifying the terms on which they will do business," John advised Joyce.

From the beginning of working together, they had discussed Guerrilla Marketing techniques. One of the topics John emphasized was "Positioning." The Positioning of the business affects many other aspects, including how much you can charge (pricing) and your sales closing rate. If you are recognized as an expert it is much easier to close new business than if you are unknown—and the clients are prepared to pay more.

At that point in time, WOW! WINDOWS was little known except by their existing clients. They were charging very little for their services, barely enough to cover their time and materials. John's energy and enthusiasm sparked a similar response in Joyce. Together they started brainstorming numerous no-cost and low-cost ways to promote and increase the market awareness and the positioning of WOW! WINDOWS.

To take advantage of retail windows' 24/7 exposure, Joyce had some decals made. And she included in her Terms of Business the right to "badge" WOW! WINDOWS' work by affixing the decals to the shop windows of clients. Passers-by, including other store owners—potential new clients—would now recognize their work. They hired a professional photographer to take photographs of their installed displays. They started to build a collection of quality photographs of their work—a collection of case histories—which would later be featured on their Web site.

Joyce joined some retail trade associations and began to network. She had some new business cards printed and collaborated with John to formulate her "thirty-second introduction" to use at networking meetings. She started writing and contributing articles to retail trade newsletters and magazines. Encouraged by John, she also entered several competitions for retail displays—and won! This enabled her to start issuing Press Releases and use such by-lines as:

> "Award Winning Designers! Winning Design! 'Outstanding Window Shopping in Vancouver' Awarded by Visitor's Choice—the leading Tourist Guide"

Their Positioning was gradually increasing, resulting in an increasing trickle of enquiries—some of whom were converted into clients—but more needed to be done. John taught Joyce a sales system that would increase her sales closing rate, thus saving a great deal of time on abortive sales calls and producing more effective results from their Guerrilla Marketing.

She learned from John that one of the objectives of effective positioning was to have the prospective client "buy" you before you even walked through their door. Then the majority of work required for the subsequent sale was almost done—if she handled it in the way John had taught her. Joyce was cautious at first but soon grew in confidence as her average sales closing rate improved to recruiting eight new clients per ten qualified prospect interviews.

The first few months working with John flew by with many innovative ideas and changes being introduced. John had encouraged her to position her services as an *investment*, not a cost, but Joyce was still undercharging and was not overly confident of being able to charge more. This all changed as a result of one of the exercises John encouraged her do. Joyce commissioned a survey of passers-by outside several of her clients' stores. The results were impressive, and she was able to use them in her marketing:

> *"Results!*
>
> *In a recently commissioned street survey, 85 percent of respondents questioned stated that the WOW! WINDOWS display they were being questioned about got their attention enough to go into the store. Seventy-five percent of those people were not usually regular customers."*

These results helped bring home to Joyce the real value her WOW! WINDOWS team was bringing to their clients' businesses. With her confidence increased, she started to implement John's advice about Pricing on a value basis.

Joyce was confident of WOW! WINDOWS quality and value to their clients, but prospective clients needed more proof. So Joyce started to seriously assemble testimonials from her satisfied clients which was something she had not done before in a systematic way. They devised and implemented a referral program, and Joyce was delighted when it resulted in more new clients.

John taught Joyce that sales communications are most effective if they are sent periodically in a series. Together they designed a series of postcards and sales letters. Joyce had the postcards printed and tentatively sent them to a small initial list of prospective clients she had targeted.

Next, the testimonials and photographs were brought together to create a new high- quality brochure which was professionally designed and printed. John was teaching Joyce to use all available resources for marketing and business building. He suggested that Joyce's son, David —an award winning film-maker—be asked to create a video "business card" for WOW! WINDOWS.

The video was shot and only the final editing remained to be done when the time came for Joyce and Irving to take a long awaited month's holiday to celebrate Irving's retirement.

Joyce recruited a business manager to look after the clients and collect any outstanding accounts while she and Irving were on holiday. Apart from stopping off in London to spend a little time for a first meeting with John in September 2004, they spent a wonderful month holidaying in Malta before returning home to Vancouver—to a business disaster.

October 2004

While James had been carrying on as usual, creating wonderful displays for happy clients, the business manager that Joyce had employed had effectively done nothing—apart from alienating and losing half of their clients. No cash had been collected and the business bank account was virtually empty.

Joyce frantically tried to recover the situation by contacting the lost clients but to no avail. Whatever that manager had done, those clients weren't coming back. Sadly, Joyce phoned John. "I'm seriously considering closing the business," she said. "It took us years to build that client base, and now the half that remains can't support the business."

John listened sympathetically. "If you wish to close the business, you have my full support, but we can turn it around if you want to."

Joyce knew that John was an experienced "turnaround man," but she'd lost hope that she could save the business. "How?" she asked.

"Your first job every day is to chase outstanding accounts and get that money in. Talk to your bank about what's happened and get their agreement to support you while we recover the situation.

"Your second job every day is sales and marketing activity. We've spent the last few months building the infrastructure, the systems, and the Guerrilla Marketing Weapons we need to build the business. We've built a money machine. Now all we have to do is load it and increase the rate at which it works. By the way, how many of those postcards and brochures do you still have?"

"Most of them," admitted Joyce.

"You've invested good money to acquire these marketing weapons. Now it's time to get a return on that expenditure. Let's revise our Guerrilla Marketing calendar. Use me as an accountability partner; report to me every day on what cash you've collected and what sales and marketing activity you've done."

"If you believe we can turn this around, John, I'll trust you. Let's do it."

From that day onwards, Joyce monitored her sales and marketing activity and it increased dramatically. As her daily activity increased, so did the number of new clients. The DVD video "business card" David was editing was finally completed. The new brochure and DVD video "business card" formed part of a new appointment confirmation pack which was sent to prospects whenever Joyce confirmed a first sales appointment. This created a positioning effect whose purpose was to help the prospect "buy" Joyce before she even walked through the door.

Before Christmas, Joyce had one of her "How To..." magazine articles published. With the publisher's permission, she had copies of the colorful article printed, rolled into a tube, and tied with silver ribbon. An actress was employed at a nominal rate to dress as Santa's Little Helper and distribute them as gifts to retailers outside the store of a retail supplier she had met through her networking. This resulted in one new client in particular worth an additional $40,000 of income.

As part of John's wacky sense of humor, he had suggested that Joyce and James dress up as super heroes to attract attention while they were working in clients' windows. It inspired Joyce to tap into her earlier experimental theatre experience and the result was "Living Windows." The concept was to stage live events in and around a client's store windows, fusing street theatre with retail display, attracting attention and encouraging customers into the store. This entertaining and theatrical approach differentiated WOW! WINDOWS from its competition.

Their clients and surprised pedestrians enjoyed Living Windows events, which featured such "happenings" as a bride shopping for honeymoon shoes—the 'bride' was basically a Pied Piper with shoppers following her down the street and into the store; lovelorn window washers; models; stilt-walkers, etc.

These "happenings" proved great for attracting media attention, great for client sales figures, and greatly improved WOW! WINDOWS positioning. New clients started seeking out Joyce and James from both sides of the Canadian/USA border—and further afield.

WOW! WINDOWS niche market was high-end retailers, but they decided to "widen the net" and introduced highly acclaimed training seminars for smaller retailers. As a result of these seminars, they attracted the attention of a large shopping mall and a retail association who became clients. Joyce and James were also commissioned to run a series of their seminars for smaller retailers in the mall.

"John, I've got a problem," Joyce started one conversation with her coach, "I told you the mall wanted us to provide four prop statues. Now they've told us they want to auction them and give the proceeds to charity. This creates a real problem for us because display props aren't sufficiently durable, and we aren't charging enough to provide real quality statues. It's a really high-end mall and we need to ensure these are high quality statues. Any ideas?"

"Fusion marketing, Joyce," John laughed, "Do you know any local quality sculptors who would like to raise their profile and the marketability of their work?"

"No, but I know how I can find one," she'd replied—and she did.

The sculptor was happy to charge only for materials for which she received six-months exposure for her work—that was the length of time her sculptures were on display in the mall. Everybody benefited, and that's a good way to do business.

*****

Irving looked in through the door of Joyce's office. "Did I hear you mention HGTV to John?"

Joyce smiled her infectious smile, "Yes, apparently they've heard about our Living Windows and are considering featuring us in one of their shows. But what I'm really excited about…you know how we lost all those clients while we were on holiday? Well, we've already replaced them, *and* we've increased our client base by more than 500 per cent in the last eighteen months. We now service almost one hundred store windows, excluding the mall, *and according* to our latest accountant's figures, we just earned more last month than we did in eight months of last year! John believed in me, encouraged me, and showed me how to do it, even when things looked really bad. He made me believe that *anything is possible*—and that's turning out to be true, isn't it? Onwards and upwards. I'm having the time of my life. Isn't it wonderful?"

*****

"...So that's how we did it. We had a sound foundation of Joyce and James' combined talents to build with. But it was really possible because of Joyce's persistence, positive attitude, remarkable energy, and creative follow-through. It's a real success story. I'm proud of her." John finished telling the story to Shirley, just as his telephone rang.

He picked it up to hear a familiar voice saying, "Hi John; it's Mitch Meyerson here. Jay and I are thinking of putting together a new Guerrilla Marketing book called *Guerrilla Marketing On The Front Lines*. It's to include only real-life stories from the World's Greatest Guerrilla Marketing Coaches. Do you have a story we could include?"

"Do you know, Mitch?" John smiled, "I think I might."

About John Williamson

John Williamson is the UK's Original and Most Distinguished Wealth Coach. He is regarded as a "business and wealth-creation heavyweight," with multiple professional business qualifications plus business experience described by his growing international following as "long, deep and wide." **Retailers**, *to collect your* free copy of Joyce Ozier & John Williamson's Mini-Course, "Professional Secrets of Profitable Retail Displays," please go to the following website:* **www.RetailDisplaySecrets.com/gm1**. **Readers**, *to collect your free copy of John Williamson's Mini-Course, "Guerrilla Marketing Wealth Secrets," please go to the following website:* **www.MarketingWealthSecrets.com/gm1**.

CHAPTER 25

DIRECT MAIL GUERRILLA MARKETING STYLE
"Stuff" They Can't Miss

Debbie Ann Newhouse

"Drive thy business or it will drive thee."
~Benjamin Franklin

Direct mail is one of the most effective ways of reaching a large number of people in a very targeted way. It is a staple for a Guerrilla Marketer because compared to traditional marketing methods, it is relatively inexpensive and with imagination you can come up with something that your customers will respond to. In fact, you are very much in control of your expenses because you are using your own labor time, and you can estimate the other expenses prior to execution. It also allows customers to contact you in whichever way they prefer, whether by phone, e-mail, fax, or even snail mail.

And lest you think that the Internet is usurping direct mail's territory, think again. Because of e-mail filters and the enormous amount of traffic on the Internet, it is becoming increasingly more difficult for your Web site to be found. Direct mail provides you with the opportunity to invite potential clients and customers to your Web site. In fact, direct mail allows you to start relationships off-line and then maintain them online. Most of all, direct mail gives you an unbeatable platform to creatively introduce your product or service to a business customer visible outside of the computer.

While I am a certified Guerrilla Marketing Coach, I deal primarily with Business to Business, otherwise referred to as B2B. B2B is defined as a business that markets and sells its products or services to other businesses and doesn't traditionally sell directly to end-users—clients and customers—otherwise known as business to consumer sales or B2C. B2B type businesses generally have much higher marketing budgets than entrepreneurs looking for ways to expand their businesses because instead of selling lower priced merchandise and services, they build relationships with contracts worth thousands or greater. And this is where Guerrilla Marketing comes in.

Guerrilla Marketing refers to unconventional marketing strategies that are designed to generate maximum results from minimal resources. What "maximum" and "minimum" look like in real dollar figures is highly relevant to what I'm about to tell you. Let me give you the following example as an illustration:

Many B2B products require in-person sales calls and many B2Bs use this vehicle to introduce their products to potential customers. Any sales call requires the expense of travel, food, and many times lodging. Most B2B companies also find that their business customers are located miles apart making it difficult to see more than one in a day trip. The average sales call in 2001 according to Reed Business was $392. This same study revealed that it took 5.1 in-person sales calls to close the sale. Which means the total cost of sales visits required to close an average B2B sale was close to $2,000—and that was in '01. Think of what it would be now with the increased cost in fuel! Now, the Internet has helped to reduce this cost by allowing photos and videos of a product to be easily available. However, most customers still desire an actual sample prior to sending in their purchase order, and because their orders are high dollar, they want to make sure that they're doing business with someone they trust. That's where direct mail has become a Guerrilla Marketing friend to B2B accounts.

What we have found is that a unique direct mail or delivered piece with a product can produce a response rate quicker even than a sales call and definitely with fewer resources. These unique pieces have warmed up the customer to your product or service, and they have saved you funds by defining the relationship quicker.

Although some of our direct mail pieces presented in the following pages may strike you as being too pricey for Guerrilla Marketing tactics, they qualify as Guerrilla Marketing because I have definitely used my time, energy, and imagination to develop them, and because they shorten the sales-cycle time, are less expensive per piece than a commonly used sales call, and they don't end up on cancelled flights and no-show appointments.

One of the key objectives when marketing is to place your product in the hands of the decision makers or influencers and assist them to take note of the benefits and why they should care about it at all. With all of today's marketing noise coming at us, this can be rather difficult. What makes it even tougher is when your product isn't "top of the mind" like the popular Xbox or exciting on its own. However, we can't all market game systems and such, so we have created some unique ways via direct mail and delivery to generate prompt interest in this client's product line with success that continues today.

Direct Mail Response

Before you embark on any direct mail campaign, you need to be armed with some knowledge. You need to know what you can expect from a direct mail campaign.

According to the Direct Marketing Association (DMA) 2005 Response Rate Report, dimensional direct mail receives an overall response rate of 3.67 percent and flat mail receives a 2.77 percent response rate. DMA also reports in their 2005 Response Rate Report that catalog and retail stores are among the most successful direct mailers with response rates averaging over 7 percent while professional services came in at 3.98 percent. Post cards came in at 2.19 percent slightly lower than flat direct mail. Recipients of catalogs and other direct mail pieces have a combined online purchase rate of 28 percent according to USPS, The Multi-Channel Catalog Study, 2004.

Seventy-three percent of wired households prefer to get information on new products and promotions by direct mail, in the ICR Research Group

Survey, 2001, icrsurvey.com. While these guidelines can help you budget for your promotional mailing, know something—with Guerrilla Marketing you can easily exceed these averages. Such was our experience with Cornerstone Specialty Wood Products, LLC.

This company develops and manufactures specialty wood flooring panels for mezzanines in distribution centers throughout North America. This is definitely not razzle-dazzle stuff, but they need to market their product just like the rest of the world, so they started working with us in 2001 on a small scale and then challenged us to bring awareness to their product line by using a highly-targeted list of potential customers in 2003.

Before we started on any large scale direct marketing campaign, we did some solid pre-planning. This can help you increase your success rate with a promotional mailing or delivery. We constantly use Jay Levinson's advice to help us organize ours and have inserted one of his direct-mail recommendations from chapter 21 of "Secrets for Making Big Profits from your Small Business," *Guerrilla Marketing 3rd Edition*.

According to Levinson, Guerrilla Marketing's eight direct-mail advantages are:

1. The most important element is the right list.
2. Make it easy for the recipient to take action.
3. Letters almost always out pull mailing packages with no letters.
4. The best buyers are those who have bought by mail before, a rapidly growing number.
5. Do anything to get your envelope opened.
6. Keeping good records is paramount.
7. Testimonials improve response rates.
8. Remember nothing is as simple as it seems.

Although not all of these listed fit our particular situation, several did and we found that numbers one, two, five, six, and eight assisted us with getting Extreme Response Rates, which we define as double-digit response rates. This is how we did it:

Free Lunch

Our initial product we wanted to promote through direct mail was the ResinDek® product line. ResinDek® flooring/decking panels are engineered specifically for mezzanines in distribution centers and warehouses to provide an alternative to the traditionally used products such as plywood, bar grate, concrete, and metal plank. ResinDek® is less expensive flooring than the more traditional options and easier to install.

Now, we could have just sent pictures of the product or even samples of it in the mail with a great sales letter. That's pretty typical. However, we wanted to make our marketing stand out, so we introduced the product to a targeted list of people with a Free Lunch. Everyone loves pizza, right? We had hot pizza delivered to fifty highly-targeted prospects, all over the country, and with it came another pizza box loaded with mezzanine flooring panel samples cut in the shape of pizza slices. We had a label on the 'wood' pizza box that read, "Anyway you slice it. We deliver," and included literature about the ResinDek® product line with benefits.

Of course, we couldn't have done this for a large number of prospects, and we didn't want to. We targeted our list of recipients to potential customers whom we already knew were a perfect fit for this product—we just needed to get their attention long enough to explain it. We delivered over fifty piping-hot pepperoni pizzas with floor samples in the USA and delivered gift certificates to those located outside of the USA. Cornerstone Wood Specialty Products was immediately barraged with response. There were phone calls, faxes, and notes thanking the owner for the lunch and that opened the door to communication. The owner was able to talk directly to these customers and the customers were willing to listen. Remember the typical response rate of 3.67 percent? The response rates to our free lunch were well over 50 percent and in some cases provided the all-important introduction we had been looking for.

The additional benefit of this promotion is that it has not been forgotten and has provided the vehicle for easy going conversations. At trade shows and other venues, those who received the pizza want to know "where's the beer," or tease "guess what's for lunch?" It continues in 2007, four years after the initial promotion, as the pizza recipients at the trade shows shout across the aisles: "hey pizza man, I need some product information."

So yes, delivering pizzas may be a somewhat pricey attention getter, but the response more than made up for the initial cost. It landed product samples in the hands of the decision makers without sending a direct sales person on the road to each location. It occurred within a couple of days, which caused the customers to contact our client, and it is still being recalled today. To be remembered in today's busy world is a great compliment and to have fun teasing about it provides some energy that isn't always easy to build in new relationships. And while you may not have the budget to deliver pizzas, it's the idea that counts. I invite you to model what we did in the pizza campaign. Make the gimmick specific to your products, and have fun!

A New Take on Post Cards

You have heard it said before—marketing is addressing an immediate need of the customer's. And one tried and tested direct mail form for doing this is post cards. Cornerstone Specialty Wood Products, LLC, liked the response they got with the pizzas so much that they hired us to do more. Our next direct mail piece combined a post card with the necessity of the customer receiving a sample of the actual product. We made the product sample the post card and then added one more fun twist that satisfied addressing the immediate need of the customer.

Here's what we did. We cut the ResinDek® flooring panels into post card size panels and attached a label to them so they looked like a post card. We then addressed the customer needs by having copy that concentrated on the high price of plywood at the time by exhorting the benefits of ResinDek® over plywood for mezzanine flooring. And we added one more twist. Instead of a sales post-card, we made it look like a travel postcard—something every one loves to receive. Our copy on the full size label read: "Greetings! Having a great vacation with the savings I got from using ResinDek® LD unfinished instead of plywood, because ResinDek UF (unfinished) is competitively priced, bears 2X the pallet jack load of plywood, has a 5-year warranty, 2x tighter tolerances and never delaminates! Hope you can join me soon! (This is an actual product sample of ResinDek® UF, ResinDek® is manufactured by Cornerstone Specialty Wood Products, LLC).”

This mailing resulted in an *immediate* reorder for an additional 60 percent of flooring panels because it caught the eye of the customer and addressed a need they easily and quickly related to. Jay Levinson, in *Guerrilla Marketing for Consultants* tells us to:

> Mail only to highly targeted lists, preferably a list you have created, not rented. Use caution with rented mailing lists because you have no idea if they will reach your target clients. Focus the subject of the mailing on a timely, specific and urgent matter, not just your firm's qualifications. Be sure you can quickly follow up with every lead that the mailing produces. Handwrite some part of the mailing. Test the results of a small mailing before committing to a mass-mailing campaign.

We had addressed a timely, specific and urgent matter with our plywood message and tested our piece prior to the mass mailing to make sure it could be processed by mail and received in good condition since we did not package it. We followed his advice and the results were spectacular. The key here is that we took something that is known to work, and applied our imagination and creativity to come up with something that was fun, eye-catching, and that hit a nerve with everyone who received it. While you probably don't have a flooring sample to make up a postcard, I bet you can find something that would make an unusual postcard and get your audience's attention.

The Louisville Slugger® Give-Away

We had so much fun with the postcard that we looked forward to our next challenge. What could we create that could top that. Well, we took the phrase "hit them over the head with a baseball bat" literally and created the following multi-faceted promotion.

It's important that the ResinDek® flooring panels be associated with quality. When you're spending thousands of dollars on flooring, you want it to last awhile. Since we understand that as a key interest of our target market, and because we live in Louisville, Kentucky, our next promotion became very clear. It makes sense to consider Louisville Slugger® Bats as a quality partner. We sourced a clear carton normally used for greeting cards and inserted a piece of ResinDek® with a baseball type card that read, "Hit a Home Run with ResinDek®, enter to win a personalized Louisville Slugger® baseball bat!" The backside of the card was titled, "Put the Power Hitter on Deck" and the product benefits with specifications of strength were listed. We also included a short survey. Entries were encouraged on the Web site, but we also used fax and traditional mail to get as many entries as possible.

This is what happened: the Web site entries increased traffic to the Web site and provided an opportunity for visitors to sign up for our newsletter for future contact. The presentations of the baseball bats allowed for press releases and ResinDek® partners were provided an opportunity to team up with ResinDek® to promote their brand identities.

The response rate for this sweepstakes was 4 percent—just slightly above average. However, the newsletter by e-mail sign-ups increased by 133 percent and 5 percent requested additional product information with appointments. We were very pleased with our experience with Louisville Slugger® and received several compliments from customers regarding how easy it was to order their personalized bats on the Web site or to call them directly with their gift certificates they had won. Louisville Slugger® simply requested that we run our promotional piece by them prior to production for their approval, and we were off with a great reputable name to be mentioned with our client's brand name in quality. And this is exactly what this promotion was designed to do. Jay Levinson reminds us in *Guerrilla Marketing 3rd Edition* that "Direct mail doesn't always make the sale all by itself, but it obtains crucial leads that result in sales. A huge 89 percent of marketing directors use it to generate leads, while 48 percent use it to generate sales."

If you are planning a direct marketing campaign modeled on this promotion, here are some other advantages to consider (also by Jay Levinson):

- ■ You can achieve more accurately measured results.

- You can be as expansive or concise as you wish.

- You can zero in on almost any target audience.

- You can personalize your marketing like crazy.

- You can expect the highest of all response rates.

- You can use unlimited opportunities for testing.

- You can enjoy repeat sales to proven customers.

- You can compete with, even beat, the giants.

What Else Can You Do with Floor Samples?!

As you know it's always nice to be associated with the "big dogs," and that's exactly what we did with our next direct mail piece that tied in with the Cornerstone Specialty Wood Products' tradeshow booth for that year.

It started with the idea that the best testimonials come from highlighting your well-known brand name customers. ResinDek® flooring panels have been installed in some significant brand distribution centers in the apparel, technology, sporting goods, office supplies, bookstores, online retail, automotive, health care, business services, manufacturing, and other industries. These all provided us with a wonderful opportunity to connect to others with these major brands.

In order to send this message to others we created a pre-show mailing post card that listed these major brands and read, "Leave it to the Experts to Select ResinDek®. Come by booth #___ to see why." Several that received this post card were mentioned or saw their major competitor's name on it and wanted to see what and why they had selected this product for their distribution centers. We then reinforced the post card and message in recognition on a serpentine wall in the booth at the show.

As you know, well-known brands associated with yours can assist you with gaining creditability quicker and easier in new industries and situations; however patience is still involved. As Jay Levinson put it in "How Long Till Marketing Works": "Keep in mind that people are attracted to businesses that have established credibility. You get it with superb marketing and commitment to a plan. Marketing continues to be a blend of art, science, business and patience. It works. But it rarely works instantly. That's why the most crucial ingredient in the blend called marketing is your own patience."

And that wasn't the end of our efforts. We had built brand identity at that trade show. We had customer recognition because of the other direct mail campaigns. A recent assignment was to find a permanent home for these samples in customers' offices and get them delivered without damaged edges. This is a big deal—product samples need to be shipped cheaply but safely because while you don't want to over-pack a product that you're touting as durable, you also don't want it to arrive damaged because that, well, damages your credibility.

Now, any good direct-mail marketer dislikes barriers such as boxes or envelopes concealing the product. We took up this challenge first. We wanted to find an existing packaging option so that we could avoid paying for tooling costs or low volume specialty items. We ended up using VHS cartons—remember those? We cut the flooring panel to fit the box and labeled each with its own specifications. They fit nicely in the VHS box and we then inserted it into the VHS carton which had a label on the outside promoting the product and brand. And here was the fun part. Instead of ignoring the fact that it was a VHS box, we played that up. The label copy read: "In Live Performances Across North America in Distribution Centers." The entire package was shrink-wrapped with clear wrap to encourage the receiver to open it or to minimally read it since the label was in color and prominent.

Several recipients commented on how nice it was to receive a sample that could easily be stored on an office bookshelf or desk. We also solved the problem of protecting the product; the edges had been protected while the product remained very accessible from a bottom entry VHS carton in clear packaging.

Greg Doppler, President of Cornerstone Specialty Wood Products, LLC received several compliments and commented to us, "We love this package for our product and have implemented it as our next sample kit in vinyl VHS cases because of the positive response it has received from this recent promotional mailing." The new sample case includes actual product samples inside, color insert for front and spine while the back contains numerous tabs inserted between the vinyl cover and case.

How to Deliver a Winning Direct-Mail Promotion

No one said direct mail was easy. The direct mail campaigns we showcased here required imagination, some legwork to find various items, coordination, organization, and definitely some funds. However, as I said earlier, the cost is well worth it because they generate leads, orders, and relationships without the cost of numerous sales trips.

If you are considering your own Guerrilla Marketing direct-mail campaign modeled on what you learned here, here are some tips we have learned throughout the years of doing Guerrilla Marketing in the B2B segment.

First, know that all of these direct mailings I just told you about required samples or proto-types to be shared with all individuals involved and everything that we sent out required auditing to ensure the quality of the mailing matched our expectations.

Here are our other recommendations and tips for a direct-mail campaign:

- Don't allow your product to fall victim to "stereotype" presentations.
- Communicate with all involved early to avoid setting up difficult to execute direct mail pieces, early suggestions might save money and time.
- Check with your mail specialists or post office for regulations.
- Audit the package prior to completion to insure they are assembled properly.
- Test mail or ship to ensure they arrive in good condition.
- Measure your results by setting up a unique e-mail, phone number or inquiry from incoming leads.
- Obtain estimates from suppliers for printing, labor to assemble, shipping/mailing, and check out mail house companies that can provide bulk discounts as well as labor to assemble large quantities.

- Use packaging that is no longer in high demand and easily available to reduce costs, such as VHS cartons.

- Check to see if you can secure gift certificates for convenience or as a backup to those that cannot receive the actual promotional products. We found Louisville Slugger's Web site and customer service easy and pleasant for our winners. Pizza Hut gift certificates were shipped to those with the wood pizza samples outside of pizza delivery areas.

- Make sure the package and message fits your target audience's personality.

- Check printing inks to make sure they are waterproof, since some packages may get wet during certain seasons.

- Check adhesives to make sure they stay put on your materials and don't change with temperatures or humidity.

- Quality is important, because this is your first impression to some. Labels should be adhered straight, etc. If someone is packing and shipping, perform an audit early and provide a sample of what the end result should look like for a clear understanding of expectations. Don't take anything for granted.

- Consider back-up plans or alternatives if problems arise. The pizza promotion required us to be available across numerous time zones for several hours.

- Test the communication, e-mail, etc. prior to the implementation to make sure the inquiries are delivered promptly and easily. Pretend you are the customer and put yourself through the experience and process to verify smooth operations. Send an e-mail and see if it shows up in a timely manner and if you receive the response as planned. Do this early so glitches have time to be eliminated.

- If possible keep the same team of people involved from the beginning of the concept to the end to reduce errors.

- Provide a sample for comparison and checking.

- Review lead times with all involved to plan accordingly and make note of the suppliers' business cycles for planning purposes since some are busier at different times of the year.

- Creative concepts can come from humor in the industry, unmet needs, windows of opportunities and product pairing. Using the obvious that customers can relate to works well and quickly establishes a rapport with them.

- Don't allow your product/service to take a backseat to your giveaway.

- Involve the client in the beginning for input that is critical to the industry and product. They know the unique industry and customer's idiosyncrasies.

- Use existing vehicles for your products promotion to avoid start-up tooling and other unique expenses.

- Don't over protect "tough" products because this will make them be perceived as not being tough enough for the job.

- Repeat direct mailings in creative interesting formats, so people look forward to receiving your information.

- Always immediately verify your various components involved for quality and that they are what you ordered, don't wait to do this until it's time to assemble; by that time it's too late to exchange and fix the problem without upsetting the entire schedule.

Cornerstone Specialty Wood Products, LLC, not only uses direct mail or delivery in their marketing arsenal, they engage in several ongoing Guerrilla Marketing tactics to keep their product line ResinDek® in front of the decision makers and are always seeking unique avenues to those targets. So work by the Guerrilla's Manifesto: "In order to sell a product or a service, a company must establish a relationship with the customer. It must build trust and rapport. It must understand the customer's needs, and it must provide a product that delivers the promised benefits as stated in Guerrilla Marketing Excellence" (Taken from *The Fifty Golden Rules for Small Business Success*).

Direct mail can be a highly effective form of marketing. It helps to build relationships as well as brand identity. Several of Cornerstone Specialty Wood Products' customers have told them that they look forward to receiving their promotions because they are unique and add fun to a product that could be rather common. However, just because your product might be in the "boring" category doesn't mean that it's not unique. ResinDek® is a unique product in its field, and the marketing is geared to promote those benefits in order to differentiate it from other mezzanine flooring panels.

So take a look at your product. What is unique about it? What kinds of fun, creative ways can you position that product in a direct mail campaign that gets attention? While I know that you've heard this often in this book, it holds true here: while there may be a limit to your budget, there never is a limit to your time, energy, and imagination.

About Debbie Ann Newhouse

Debbie Ann Newhouse is a certified Guerrilla Marketing Coach who was intro-
duced to Guerrilla Marketing by Jim Woodhouse while working for a small company
whose major competitors were well-known brand names with larger marketing
budgets. She has worked for a Fortune 500 company as a marketing manager prior
to starting her own marketing company in 1999. She now has a cliental list of
companies that range in size from two people to companies listed in the Fortune 500,
matching specific programs to each customer's needs. Debbie Ann Newhouse is the
president of Newhouse Strategic Marketing, Inc. and a managing partner of Rev Up
Now, LLC and can be reached at www.NSMktg.com.

CHAPTER 26

GUERRILLA SALESMANSHIP

How a Vintage Airstream Trailer, Chocolate Chip Cookies, and Artful Questions Turned a Startup Tech-Support Company into a Market Leader

J. Sheldon Snodgrass

> *"Nothing in the world can take the place of persistence. Talent will not. Genius will not. Education will not. Persistence and determination alone are omnipotent."*
>
> ~Calvin Coolidge

I showed up to my first sales training appointment at Tech Cavalry wishing I had brought sun block. Bug repellent would have been useful, too. It was a beautiful but scorching summer day, and I was meeting four computer technicians in the backyard of Jef Sharp's house.

Jef Sharp co-owns Tech Cavalry with Jeff Hausthor. They started their computing support business in the garage of Jef's house on a lovely country road in Northampton, Massachusetts, a perfect community for Jef. He is a big thinker, and a serial entrepreneur, having started four other businesses before Tech Cavalry. He's also community conscious, progressive, and fun. His tousled hair, easy manner, and warm smile invite a relaxed informality.

Jeff Hausthor is the master technician. While equally warm and approachable, Jeff is quiet, tidy, and has a modest demeanor that belies his impressive corporate résumé. He's the technology genius who screens all new hires to ensure they can both solve complex technical challenges and delight customers at the same time. Jeff conceives and develops many of the systems that allow Tech Cavalry to save time, energy and money while selling more and serving better.

Jef and Jeff are the perfect pair to lead Tech Cavalry. From a Guerrilla perspective, they embody two important competencies: market sensitivity and enthusiasm. The sensitivity comes from adopting the customer's point of view at all possible junctures. Everything is customer-centric: from their telephone protocol, to their brand promise—"Help is on the way"—to their scope of services. Their enthusiasm is infectious. Their positive energy radiates across the company, revealing a truly likable cast of characters. Working with Tech Cavalry is easy and fun.

When they called the Steady Sales Group for help, Tech Cavalry was three years old with two part-time and two full-time technicians. Jef managed daily operations and was responsible for driving sales. Although he is Guerrilla minded, Jef generated new business mostly in a non-Guerrilla way. He relied heavily on advertising in the local paper, the *Daily Hampshire Gazette*: circulation nineteen thousand in a city of thirty thousand people.

The advertising worked. Jef was a masterful, though unwitting, user of three Guerrilla advertising principles: he was consistent, compelling, and committed to the long haul. His simple, benefit-oriented message appeared week after week. "PC Troubles? Your place or ours, help is on the way!" his uncluttered ads would trumpet.

By its third year Tech Cavalry's revenue had plateaued and Jef was eager to push sales to the next level. Just tweaking the advertising strategy wouldn't be enough. "I need more customers," Jef declared. "I've considered hiring a sales rep, but the thought of it makes me cringe. I'd love to get my technicians selling more, but they're not salespeople—they're technicians."

"Jef," I replied, "whether you see your technicians as salespeople isn't half as important as how they see themselves. They actually *are* your sales force. Your technicians are your feet on the street, your representatives, your uniformed, mobile ambassadors. These guys face customers and prospects every day. Let's get them to think like sales professionals. That's where we should spend our time, energy, and imagination. After all, a Guerrilla Marketer invests in those three assets before investing money."

Jef was all ears. He had a vision of Tech Cavalry with multiple branches, ultimately leading to a regional, then national franchise. He knew that any model of growth would have to be sustainable, repeatable, and affordable. The idea of training technicians to sell while they served appealed to Jef. The big question was, how?

Artful Questions

To answer Jef, I pulled two words right out of the Guerrilla Marketing lexicon: *intentionality* and *measurement*. My sales training plan was simple. Whereas I often teach my classic seven-step sales process[2] to other clients, I planned a two-pronged approach with the Tech Cavalry team.

First, intentionality: I would focus on reprogramming the team's thinking about what salesmanship truly is. I would help them see that they are salespeople by virtue of their roles, thereby empowering them to better serve their customers. By coaching each employee to simply ask strong questions and focus on rendering delightful service, I would tap into what made them excellent technicians, as a means to boost sales.

Second, measurement: Being savvy entrepreneurs, Jeff and Jef were well aware of the importance of tracking vital business metrics. Indeed, they easily

---

2 1. Product Knowledge. 2. Prospecting. 3. Approach (close). 4. Needs Assessment (close). 5. Presentation (close). 6. Final Close. 7. Follow-up.

provided five important statistics that I asked for: 1) number of service calls; 2) average length of appointment; 3) billable time per consultant; 4) average revenue per appointment; 5) monthly profits. What I proposed, however, was to measure a process as well as the results. In other words, I would focus on the behaviors that drive the metrics. "Target the sales-related behaviors," I advised, "and excellent results will follow."

On the first training day I was not surprised by the team's resistance to salesmanship. "I'm not interested in selling" was a typical early admission.

Others followed: "I'm called to provide a service, not sell."

"Our customers don't want to be sold to. They call us for help."

"I'm a tech, not a salesman."

"Selling feels pushy."

"I didn't get hired to sell. I got hired for my technical expertise."

"I don't like salesmen, and I don't want to be one."

Thus did my sales training with the Tech Cavalry team begin.

We spent considerable time examining team assumptions about what sales, selling, and service really are. We explored the experiences, prejudices, and fears that each technician harbored about sales. Clearly, sales had a bad rap.

A sale made with integrity is a worthy goal; at its best, everyone wins. But rather than preach the gospel of sales to a jaded crew, I crafted specific questions as a way to model what I hoped to teach the Tech Cavalry team.

"If you are called to repair, say, a virus problem, and you notice there is no surge suppression in place, do you owe it to your customer to suggest it?" I asked.

"Of course!" was the unanimous reply.

"What about suggestions for data backup, closing security vulnerabilities, enhancing efficiency, freeing network bottlenecks, protecting privacy, and so on? Do you owe your customers a chance to benefit from such services if it fits their needs?" I probed.

"Yes!" came another unanimous response.

"Well, then, if you owe it to your customers to provide a deeper level of service, what sorts of questions could you ask your customers to politely probe for need? How could you comfortably weave such questions into your dialogue? What tools could you develop, and what systems could you put in place, to help you deliver on the promise of deeper and more delightful service?"

Out of this dialogue some important tools emerged. We crafted a handful of semi-scripted questions that each technician could massage and memorize to suit his style. We also developed a leave-behind packet that included a checklist of services. The checklist served double duty as an *à la carte* menu for the customer and a cue sheet of talking points for each technician.

Problem solved, right? Wrong! Old habits die hard: two months after we implemented our process of friendly, probing dialogue coupled with a presentation packet, half of the technicians admitted to failing on the agreement. The other half of the team admitted to inconsistency at best. Bless them for their honesty.

Among the major coaching observations I've made since starting the Steady Sales Group is that significant behavioral change requires three elements: a vision of a more desirable future, the resources (both material and intellectual) required to move forward, and a system of accountability. The technicians at Tech Cavalry had the vision. Resources and understanding were accumulating nicely. It was the third element, accountability, that needed more attention.

So we explored every possible barrier, objection, or difficulty, and then set about removing them. We role-played the sales conversation. We practiced the simple, "scripted" sales questions that each technician could comfortably integrate into his service calls. We built a reminder system into the service call logout process that prompted everyone to probe for additional ways to add value. We created periodic incentives. And perhaps most important, we published results and regularly met to discuss how everyone was doing. We reinforced, again and again, the importance of following through on our new sales ethic.

Gradually behaviors changed and, sure enough, results followed. When I began coaching the Tech Cavalry team, the average length of appointment was one-and-one-fourth hours. After six months, the average rose 20 percent to one-and-one-half hours. One year later the average length of appointment peaked at one-and-three-fourths hours. This 40 percent increase in billable time came from focusing on one thing: viewing service calls as sales opportunities.

But increasing the average length of appointment could be a deceiving measure of the team's success. What if customers felt that the technicians were working too slowly or inefficiently? What if, heaven forbid, the customer felt manipulated into a longer, more expensive service call than they had bargained for?

The Tech Cavalry team knew these risks existed if they made extending the service call more important than building a long-term relationship. "Those two objectives are not mutually exclusive," I reminded them. But the team did not need much reminding. Deep down, everybody knew what all Guerrilla Marketers know: get consent, be generous, and delight customers at every turn. That is what creates customers for life.

The Guerrilla mindset came easily to the technicians. The challenge was to ensure that behaviors were repeatable, consistent, and measurable. Some things, like customer delight, are hard to measure, but we knew a metric was needed. Lo and behold, the answer came to us while we were eating leftover chocolate chip cookies.

ACE Moments

Over the years, Tech Cavalry had developed the practice of handing a logo-wrapped cookie to the customer at the end of a service call. But like many things that go unmeasured, or are left out of an established protocol, the practice remained inconsistent; hence the leftover cookies. Yet nagging the technicians to always remember the cookie seemed, well, petty. After all, it wasn't the cookie itself that mattered, it was what the cookie represented— an attempt at delighting customers and exceeding their expectations.

Exceed customer expectations. That was it! That's the attitude we wanted to cultivate among the technicians in addition to a sales mentality. Certainly, each technician cultivated a service orientation, but we wanted to surpass competent work with a cookie and a smile. So Jef and Jeff coined the term ACE, which stood for Always Exceed Customer Expectations, and it became a mantra.

The push was on: at every encounter ask opportunity questions, speak to the menu of services, give the customer a cookie, and always look for "ACE moments."

ACE moments became the stuff of hallway conversations, staff meetings, and bragging rights. Small touches such as cleaning a customer's monitor and leaving behind a few Tech Cavalry branded swabs were encouraged. To give an extra cookie or three to family members, or offer a free computing tip, or anything that might exceed a customer's expectation, became as much a part of a service call as fixing a PC.

In true Guerrilla fashion, Jef and Jeff made outstanding customer service part of the culture at Tech Cavalry: not by mandate but by facilitation. Freshly baked and bagged cookies were always on hand. Promotional packets were stuffed and stacked by the office door. The Web-based log-out screen accessed by technicians to close service calls contained an ACE prompt. And, of course, the question "What ACE moments did you create today?" was constant.

The Best Billboard Ever

Such measures may seem trivial, but in the words of one of my mentors, "The little stuff drives the big stuff." Cookies, screen wipes, referral coupons, and friendly computing tips are certainly "little stuff," but consider the impact on the "big stuff" at Tech Cavalry.

Eight months into the "ACE moments" campaign, we boasted these results: customer referrals as a source of new business increased 10 percent; repeat business from existing customers jumped from 45 percent to 65 percent; additionally, customer complaints, while always low, dropped another 6 percent.

With the "little stuff" in hand, Jef and Jeff turned to something big—*really* big: twenty- seven-feet long, eight-feet wide, and nine-feet tall, to be precise.

"Guess what, Sheldon?" Jef asked me during one of our planning sessions at a local coffee house. "You finally hired a uniformed cavalryman to trot around town, blowing a bugle and waving the company flag?" I asked, remembering an idea we had previously discussed.

"Nope. Better than that; I don't have to worry about all the horse manure," he continued with a grin. "I bought a vintage Airstream trailer for $4,000. It's in great condition, shines like a mirror and will make a perfect rolling billboard."

Jef's print advertising was effective, but he was always eager to try new media. Billboards, he imagined, would be ideal for Tech Cavalry: massive exposure, tens of thousands of weekly impressions, bold, localized and fun to boot. It sounded great until Jef heard the deal: $1,000 per week with a four-week minimum. Billboard advertising was not only financially unsustainable, but also, I pointed out, untargeted and inflexible.

A rolling billboard, on the other hand, would enable Jef to crisscross his service area with an eye-catching, buzz-generating, sustainable advertising medium. But towing Tech Cavalry's branded Airstream trailer around town was only the beginning. We hatched a scheme to station it at key road crossings and parking lots throughout the territory. "What about parking the trailer outside of selected event venues, throughout the year?" I offered. "The fairgrounds, the function halls, and the conference facilities all host events that attract your ideal customer."

"I love it," Jef replied.

As if we didn't have enough to ponder, Jef continued, "Wouldn't it be cool to outfit the trailer with a few laptop stations and remote wireless Internet connectivity? This way we could have sort of a mobile command post to provide support and training anywhere at any time." "Absolutely!" I exclaimed. "We could announce things like: coming to a school, or church, or office complex, or event, near you: free tips, free consultations, free troubleshooting from the Tech Cavalry mobile command post."

"Not only that," Jef added, "I bet we'd get tons of great press exposure."

"No doubt about it," I said giddily. "Plus, if we play our cards right we can get our hosts to promote us in their e-mails, newsletters and flyers."

The next cup of coffee we ordered was decaf. I wanted to slow down and consider that essential Guerrilla Marketing fundamental: execution. "Let's save that conversation for our next meeting," Jef offered. It was easy for me to agree. I was pleased that, like true Guerrillas, we had transformed Jef's idea for a rolling billboard into a flexible, relationship-building, long-term, brand-trumpeting asset. A four-thousand-dollar investment brought the Tech Cavalry team hundreds of thousands of dollars' worth of year-round exposure.

The rolling billboard is one of the many tools that make Tech Cavalry's marketing toolbox a potent collection. For it is marketing combinations that yield lasting impact, which is what we were all after. During our three-year collaboration we shared many pizzas and smiles. The combination of Steady Sales' and Tech Cavalry's unique strengths made our relationship enduring, fun, and effective. Revenue increased by 120 percent. While profits soared 76 percent, the marketing budget, as a percentage of revenue, went down by half: from 15 percent to 7 percent. And as final testimony to the value of behaving like a sales professional, revenue per employee jumped 22 percent; music to this sales coach's ears.

Oh yes, the team, which doubled in size, moved out of Jef's garage to new digs just down the road. Tech Cavalry, after all, needed a place to park its Airstream and stable the horse that I suspect is coming soon.

About Sheldon Snodgrass

*J. Sheldon Snodgrass served as an Airborne trained officer in cold-war Berlin, ending his tour dancing with the Germans in the streets the night the wall came down. Back home, Sheldon advanced through sales and marketing leadership roles in franchise travel, public utilities, and information technology. Inspired by his successes, he launched **SteadySales.com** to help ambitious people profit in the turbulent waters of the entrepreneurial adventure. A motivational speaker, consultant, coach, and white-water guide, Sheldon holds an MBA from the University of Massachusetts and is a certified Guerrilla Marketing Coach. He resides in Williamsburg, MA with his wife, and two daughters. You can contact Sheldon at **www.SteadySales.com**.*

PART SIX
The Guerrilla Organization

Now that you have some key strategies and tactics in your Guerrilla Marketing arsenal, you need to concentrate on building the right kind of organization that will support your Guerrilla Marketing efforts. This section introduces a brand new Guerrilla Marketing weapon: how to build and effectively utilize a masterful Guerrilla Marketing team. Learn how maximize your sales force. Get rid of the dead weight that's holding you back by building a finely-honed team that will "war-proof" your organization so that you're ready for anything.

CHAPTER 27

BATTLE CRIES FOR THE MARKETING UNDERDOG

How to "War Proof" your Business—Literally

Monroe Mann

> *"You are always in the right place, at the right time, successfully engaged in the right activity, whether you know it or not."*
>
> ~Shakti Gawain and Leonard Orr

This is a story of overcoming odds, and turning the most sour of lemons into the most delicious of lemonades. I took a situation that most would consider bad luck of the highest order, and turned it into one of the greatest experiences of my life. You see, on May 23, 2004, I was busy running my business school for artists, playing with my band and acting in films, and producing the world's first wakeboarding feature film entitled, "In the Wake." On May 24, Uncle Sam changed all that with a solitary phone call: "Lieutenant Mann, pack your bags. You're going to war." I was scared out of my mind.

Lesson One: Prepare for the unexpected. I joined the Army National Guard in 1999, two years prior to 9/11. While I knew that war might happen, I certainly didn't realistically think it *would* happen. Well, I was wrong, and I learned my lesson the very hard way. I'm hoping you will learn from my mistake: *Plan for the unthinkable. It actually might happen!*

So yes, I was scared out of my mind. Not scared so much about *going to battle*—for I was trained for just that event. No, ironically, I was more scared about leaving my civilian life behind. About leaving everything behind. About my dreams being shattered, destroyed, and thrown to the wolves.

Breaking the lease for my Union Square office in Manhattan—on Broadway!—was probably the worst. Or maybe it was my band breaking up. No, wait, it was the fact that I had to tell everyone that my feature film, *In the Wake* was no longer in production. Or quite possibly, it was the gut-wrenching feelings of disappointment when I had to shut down my business and tell my clients and students I would be incommunicado for quite some time.

Depressed? That doesn't even come close to how I was feeling. I was absolutely miserable. And sure, I'll admit it: I cried. Proud to be serving my country sure, but jeesh, do my career and business have to get thrown so far into left field as a result? That's how I felt the entire first three weeks of my training up at Fort Drum, NY.

But wait! If I allowed this deployment to be a problem, then it *would* be a problem. So my first step to recovery was simple: I just stopped thinking of this deployment as a problem. After these few weeks of depression, I suddenly realized that if I continually looked at this as a setback rather than as an opportunity, then it would be the worst year of my life (if not the death of me). Not only would I have a loaded weapon in my hand every day, but I'd be depressed too. Probably not a good combination!

If I chose to look at my service to my country as a problem, rather than a challenge—and in fact a solution—then possibly I would become just another could've been, would've been, should've been. Forget that. I decided I'm a *going to be*!

Rather than give up on my ambitions, I decided to heed my own advice. I decided to practice what I preach and live by something I call the Break

Diver's Creed: No Rules, No Excuses, No Regrets.® What is Break Diving, you ask? Simple: instead of waiting for opportunities to float to the surface, Break Divers dive right in and find those opportunities themselves.

Why does fighting in a war have to be only a bad thing for me personally? Says who? Why can't I help the Iraqis and help myself at the same time? Why does my career have to go on hold and my businesses get shut down? Where does it say that? Why couldn't I—like a true Guerrilla—use this deployment *to my advantage?*

Well, using this chain of thinking, I forced myself to look at my eighteen-month combat sabbatical not as a setback but as an opportunity and a blessing. I became determined to make this experience something I would be grateful for, and benefit from. I became determined to make my deployment—my deployment into a *war zone* where I just might die—not only an educational playground but a veritable potpourri of possibility.

And so I did.

> **Lesson Two**: Refuse to be a victim of your circumstances. Life is what it is, and people who are successful do great things with whatever hand they are dealt. It's too easy to be a victim; it's a lot more impressive to be a master of your circumstances. You are not a victim unless you allow yourself to be. In my opinion, a victim is someone who allows bad circumstances to overshadow the good things in life, and who forgets to seek the good that can come from the bad. Don't let that happen! It's difficult, I know, but the alternative is failure. And truly, there is nothing more disgusting than someone who has accepted his fate. Here's the solution: *Look on the bright side and realize success is your fate.*

The transformation from depressed victim to conquering victor began for me at Fort Drum by writing out the "Top Twenty Benefits of Me Going to Fight in the War in Iraq." That list included things like, "Serving Your Country," "Great Ideas for Screenplays," "Great Ideas for Books," even "Makes Me a More Interesting Person." I kept that list in my pocket during our unit's entire deployment.

Perhaps you might find it even more interesting to discover that not only did that list keep my spirits up, but to my surprise, those inspiring words actually came to pass. I actually *did* most of the things I wrote on my list.

Sure, I served my country, but while there in Iraq—working twelve-hour days as an advisor to the fourth Iraqi Army and dealing with the daily stress and anxiety of mortars, rocket fire, car bombs, and rifle shots—I also wrote a book inspired by these experiences called, *Battle Cries for the Underdog—Fightin' Words for an Extraordinary Life*. The book has recently been released and has been recognized as the first self-help book to come out of modern combat. I even managed to get a blurb from the man himself, Jay Conrad Levinson. He writes:

> Monroe Mann gives readers an almost too-vivid vision of immortality through success. In *Battle Cries for the Underdog*, Mann energizes classic words that have been uttered since the beginning of conflict on earth with his own insightful, encouraging, and relentless inspiration. Yet, these are timeless words, and Mann deserves special commendation for his restraint in still allowing the classics to speak for themselves. A profound work.

Did I mention that I also managed to keep my business alive and breathing by sending a weekly tip, called a RoeTip, to my e-mail list every week. From Iraq. From a war zone?

Oh, yes, something else. I kept a video camera in my cargo pocket the entire time I was there. I have over one hundred hours of original miniDV footage that I am now turning into the world's first comedic documentary about the war in Iraq, called *Fobbits—and Other Tales from the Lighter Side of Combat*.

Perhaps I should also point out that while in Iraq, I enrolled in an online novel writing class, and in my spare time, began tapping out the beginnings of my first John Grisham-like thriller. I also hired a script doctor to help fine tune the script to my film, *In the Wake*, and got a write-up about the film in *Wakeboarding Magazine*. I also managed to get interviewed by a number of publications about the film, the book, and my school.

How did I do all this? Nine simple letters: G.U.E.R.R.I.L.L.A.

Lesson Three: Do not limit yourself! Among the many lessons I learned from the military, the strongest is this: you have *no idea* of what you are capable, so stop trying to put a limit on what you can accomplish! That is defeatist. Don't do it! Stay away from that negativity. Don't get depressed when something goes awry or when up against an 'insurmountable' obstacle—instead, ask yourself, "If I had to make it work, how *could* I make it work?" Then, when you get the answers, the next step should be clear: *Make it work! Your life truly does depend on it.*

Some of you might be wondering how I met Jay in the first place. Well, before I left for Iraq, I decided to go out on a limb and try to contact my hero, Mr. Levinson himself. If I were to die in Iraq, at least I would let Jay know what an impact he had on my life before I had no life. Logical, no?

So I launched online. I found the e-mail address for his webmaster. Expecting to hear nothing, I sent the webmaster an e-mail with a request to please forward my message on to Jay. Well, ladies and gentlemen, the next morning, you'll never guess whose return address I saw when I heard AOL happily say, "You've got mail!" I received an e-mail from the great marketer himself, Jay Conrad Levinson! I was the happiest man alive!

Turns out Jay—go figure—is also a US Army intelligence officer, and—again, go figure—he actually read my book *The Theatrical Juggernaut*. He actually knew who I was!

Long story short, we became e-mail pen pals and as my training continually moved closer to the imminent flight to Kuwait, we became friends.

By the time I left Iraq, we were far more than just friends: we teamed up to write one of the newest books in the Guerrilla series entitled, *Guerrilla Networking*. Co-written by Jay Conrad Levinson and (ta da!)... Monroe Mann.

Lesson Four: If it weren't for the war and my thoughts of impending death, I would never have felt such an urgency to get in touch with Jay. If it weren't for the war, I would probably not be co-writing a book with him, and you certainly wouldn't be reading this story. Facing death is certainly a wake up call, but please, don't wait until death is staring you in the face to find the courage to reach for your dreams; to do what you should have done yesterday; to say the things you know you should be saying; and to say thank you to the very people who change and impact your life. *Tomorrow could be the last day your have to live. Act accordingly.*

Ladies and gentlemen, the bottom line message of this chapter is to use setback to your advantage. I'm not sharing my story with you to brag. I am instead, as I like to say, just *sharing the vibe*. I am sharing the vibe with you to inspire you. To help you realize once and for all that there truly are no obstacles, except those we set up in our mind. To help you realize once and for all that there is opportunity right in front of us at every waking moment of our lives, and that it is our own self-imposed limitations that prevent us from seeing them. I am sharing my story with you to help you realize once and for all that if you fail then it is—brace yourself—*your fault!*

You see, you cannot blame your circumstances! I think my situation has proven this. I could easily have used Iraq as a great excuse for why my career went down the drain, why my business "went under," and why I never "made it" in show business. Gosh, and every one would have felt so sorry for me.

But that's too easy. I refuse to be a victim. Because I am a Guerrilla. And a Guerrilla Marketer to boot.

One of the clear reasons why I was able to keep my dreams alive in my own head and my business alive for my clients and fans is through the use of Guerrilla Marketing principles: low-cost, high-impact marketing. That is Jay's philosophy in a nutshell and one of the secrets to my success while stationed in a combat zone.

I kept my business alive and even expanded its reach from the most unlikely place on earth. How so? The list of weapons I used—beyond my rifle and pistol of course!—is endless: mailing lists, Web sites, testimonials, referrals, press releases, advertising, word-of-mouth, a newsletter, e-mail, and on and on. And of course a stubborn refusal to give up in the face of defeat.

The writing is on the wall: I'm a Levinson disciple through and through. Like a *true* "guerrilla," I decided to beat the odds and turn the war and my unlikely odds to my advantage. Not only did I help the Iraqi people in their drive for freedom and security, but I helped myself at the same time. And truly, if I was able to keep my dreams alive from Iraq, then certainly you can keep your dreams alive from wherever you may find yourself as well. Get what I'm saying? I'm not trying to minimize your problems. I am simply trying to put what you *think* are problems into a different perspective in hopes of making us all realize that our "problems" aren't really that problematic after all.

As they say in my business—the show must go on! It doesn't matter if the lights go out, if you aren't rehearsed enough, or if the lead performer fails to show up. The show must go on. This principle applies as equally well to your own business endeavors: the marketing must go on! Business must drive forward! There is no alternative but success!

It doesn't matter what your own personal situation is, you must—as Jay points out repeatedly in *Guerrilla Marketing*—be consistent with a capital "C." In other words, no matter what comes your way, you must continue to be a Guerrilla. You can't let the odds against you diminish your determination and momentum. You must not allow your own personal "deployment to a combat zone" allow you to slow down, give up, or worse, *quit*. You need—read *absolutely need*—to use anything that happens (or doesn't happen) to your marketing advantage. Get up! Fight one more round! You are three feet from gold! And four feet from stardom!

Bottom line: whatever your own "war situation" may be—get over it! We all experience them. The winners overcome them. As my drill sergeants would say to me every day at basic training, "SUCK IT UP AND DRIVE ON, PRIVATE! I DON'T WANT TO HEAR YOUR EXCUSES!" Take solace and comfort in the undeniable fact that you are not the only one experiencing difficulty in the running and expansion of your business. You are not the only one!

I know that each of you reading this can—and are going to—become a great success, and that you are soon going to be the future powerbrokers in this great nation. I salute you. I applaud you. I support you.

And I look forward to meeting you—*at the top!*

Lesson Five: Opportunity is knocking wherever you may find yourself, no matter what your station in life may be. No matter what life hands you, there seems to always be a silver lining of opportunity for those who are looking for it. You, as a Guerrilla, need to look for it and exploit it. Life often gives us more upsets than it gives us victories; therefore, doesn't it make sense to search for many of those opportunities in the upsets since we seem to get them in such abundant supply? If there's one overarching lesson I learned while in Iraq, it is that the vast majority of people do not take advantage of the freedoms they are given. Most in fact take for granted the economic freedom, the freedom of the press, the freedom to work, the freedom not to work, and the freedom to enjoy the fruits of our labor that we are afforded each and every day. Don't squander that freedom. Take advantage of it—every single day. Ladies and gentlemen: *Opportunity is knocking. Are you listening?*

P.S. One last question. Each week, someone new is going to be on the cover of *Entrepreneur Magazine*, *Fast Company*, *Forbes*, etc. Either you—or someone else. The question is simple: Who is it 'gonna be?

About Monroe Mann

Monroe Mann, a certified Guerrilla Marketing Coach, is the founder of Unstoppable Artists, a business, marketing, financial, and strategic planning firm for up-and-coming actors and artists, located in Manhattan, New York City. His clients have produced their own films, directed their own shows, started their own bands, written their own books, signed with major agencies and management firms, and been written about or been guests on Carson Daly, Inside Edition, Good Morning America, ABC News, Glamour Magazine, NY Times, NY Post, Boston Globe, Premiere Magazine, Entertainment Tonight, and the list goes on and on. He is the author of Battle Cries for the Underdog; To Benning & Back—the Making of a Citizen Soldier; *and* The Theatrical Juggernaut—The

Psyche of the Star (2nd Edition, Director's Cut). *He is also the co-author of* Guerrilla Networking *with Jay Conrad Levinson (2007), as well as* Guerrilla Marketing for the Arts *(2007). If you'd like to receive Monroe's inspiring business newsletter via e-mail, visit* **www.UnstoppableArtists.com**. *Better yet, call him at (914) 481-1641for a free career consultation by phone or fax him at (914) 939-2162. He can also be reached at* **roe@UnstoppableArtists.com**.

CHAPTER 28

THE MASTERFUL GUERRILLA TEAM

Growing Your Customer Base by Capitalizing on the Power of Diversity

Bea Fields

> *"The old adage "People are your most important asset" turns out to be wrong. People are not your most important asset. The right people are."*
>
> ~Theodore Roosevelt

The very essence of Guerrilla Marketing is stealth, versatility, and adaptation. But no Guerrilla Marketer fights every battle alone. Sometimes, we have an internal team structure built into place, but even if we are truly a "sole" proprietor, working on our own, we must have a strong team of partners working together to make our goal a reality. However, we've all experienced "death by committee," and have seen the ripple effects of something I call "death by team." This is when a leader who is built for speed—and that would be all good Guerrilla Marketers—has the wrong team members who can slow down progress. So how do we bridge this disconnect between doing what we do best, a solo mission, and taking a team of diverse individuals along with us?

When battles on the front line of business rage and ideas heat up, the only way to combat the competition effectively is with a closely-knit team of members acting out of their own unique properties. You can have two equally talented teams, and the one that has strong leadership will thrive, while the other team will either just slide along or fall apart. With an effective team in place, you can save time by trusting your team to be the backbone of creativity, aggressiveness, and service that separates the masterful Guerrilla marketer from the mediocre one. Coaching, training, and development are all investments in building strong teams and even stronger leaders.

To lead an effective team of diverse individuals and still move as swiftly as a lone Guerrilla through the front line trenches, it is vital that you and your team share the same marketing values and strategies. I am a leadership coach who has worked with large corporations and small business owners. I help people to become strong leaders so that they can build strong teams that will fuel their company's success. You are about to read three case studies where three separate owners of very different businesses had to face some very typical challenges developing a solid team. However, Elyse Hillegass, Pam Gantt, and Greg Hiebert aren't just Guerrilla Marketers; they're masterful Guerrilla *leaders*.

There are few in this industry I trust as much to help guide me through the principles of leading teams through diversity as these three. Each of these amazing people, strong leaders in their own right, embodies the three steps that I'm going to share with you, and each person had a particular challenge that they had to overcome. Elyse had to recognize where the strengths of her individual team members lay and then strategically place those members in the right positions to get the outcome that she wanted. Pam had to deal with a communication gap in her team that was keeping her from realizing her goal, and Greg merely had to tighten up the culture that he had built around building respect and rapport for all his team-members and his clients so that his team could work effectively with their existing clients as opposed to getting too dispersed chasing after new clients.

After reading their inspiring stories of Guerrilla success, I hope you'll agree that these three really are the "best of the best," and that you are able to take these strategies and build your own masterful Guerrilla team.

Elyse Hillegass: Standing Room Only on a Bus Full of Leaders

Many business leaders focus on *what*; Guerrilla leaders focus on *who*. In other words, Guerrillas put team-members before tasks. This process creates not just a leader-team relationship, but a true "team of leaders."

Jim Collins, author of *Good to Great* (Collins, 2001), is a true believer in the "First *who*, then *what*" philosophy of team-building. Collins' line, "To build a great company, you must get the right people on the bus," became a battle cry for the subject of my first case study, Elyse Hillegass.

While CEO of the Moore County Chamber of Commerce, Elyse took the wheel of a bus that held some great people who weren't necessarily sitting in the right seats. At the time, the Chamber had a member retention rate of 76 percent, but Elyse had aspirations of increasing retention rate by 10 percentage points. Elyse, a master of transition leadership, knew that she had to not only get the right people on her team but had to get them in the right positions. And she didn't stop there. She quickly dedicated her efforts not only to making sure that her Chamber stayed on the road, she had the goal to put the Moore County Chamber "on the map" for customer service.

When I met Elyse for the first time, I knew that I was in the presence of success; she was eager and committed to growing the Chamber through building a highly-effective team. Instinctively, Elyse realized that despite the diverse nature of her team, getting the "right people on the bus" and "getting them in the right seats" would be critical to the Chamber's ability to increase their retention rate by providing top-flight service to their members.

Says Elyse, "For any business to survive…training existing employees to be customer service-driven is a requirement, and…can be a time-intensive, monumental task."

Diversity was an issue right from the start. Elyse knew instinctively that her service-oriented style of leadership needed to align with her team's diversity. We quickly set to work designing a custom-built, 360-degree feedback interview process involving thirty key employees, board members and volunteers. Using the 360-degree feedback tool, we focused on fifteen key leadership competencies, including:

- effective communication;
- organizational ability;
- executive presence;
- decisiveness.

Assessment is worthless without action. After a thorough review of the 360, we formulated a plan to support the team in shifting their mindset to a "first-in-class" customer service culture, a talent acquisition plan designed to "get the right people on the bus and in the right seats" and strategies for enhancing team trust.

As Elyse recalls, "Good customer service at the Moore County Chamber was key to improving the retention of existing customers, as well as attracting new ones." The team development plan worked, and member retention gradually increased from 76 percent to 87 percent over a period of two years, surpassing her original goal of a 10 percent increase!

How did she do it, and what leadership skills does Elyse have to offer the Guerrilla leader in us all? Here is her list:

1. **Communication is key**. Diversity causes gulfs not because of lack of talent but because of lack of communication. Knowing the communication style of each person inside your business can mean stronger customer relationships.

2. **Embrace diversity.** A diverse team can attract a wide variety of members. When you have a team that is all of one mind, the network can become too tight and closed off. Elyse focused on recruiting a mix of skills and talent—from her team to volunteers to board members—so that they met a wide variety of needs in the community and attracted business owners from all walks of life.

3. **Who first, then What.** Getting the right people on the bus is imperative for creating a team that can then tackle the what. Elyse looked at the positions that needed to be filled and then found the best person to fill them. She was able to leverage the unique strengths of her team. She put the right people on the

right jobs and her strategy worked. Her members received a "first in class" customer experience.

4. **Trust yourself; trust your team.** Through rigorous assessment and constant team-building, Elyse developed a process for strengthening internal trust. This trust-building ensured that the diversity she was dealing with would not slow her down. This is particularly important for any Guerrilla Marketer as he or she approaches the front lines. Establishing trust establishes a bulkhead there.

5. **Visibility is vital.** Elyse consciously engaged in a highly-visible approach as ambassador for the Chamber. This visibility brought the Chamber back into the mainstream public and exponentially raised its value to the members.

6. **Streamline for success.** Through practicing *follow-up*, Elyse streamlined tasks for her team so that she could become one of the *best* connectors between the Chamber and the small business community in her town.

Elyse was able to get her retention rates up because she was able to recognize what positions needed to be in place for her to accomplish that goal, find the right people to fill those positions, and then strategically use her team to reach that goal. Get the right people and put them in the right position—that is the mark of a strong Guerrilla leader building a strong Guerrilla team.

Pam Gantt: Acknowledging Communication Skills

To the Guerrilla Marketer, risk is just another reason to get out of bed in the morning. We view risk as opportunity and opportunity as profit. Pam Gantt of Key Mortgage in Southern Pines, N.C, took an extreme risk several years ago when she decided to do no advertising of any sort. Instead, she made a goal to have 99 percent of her business come from referrals.

In order to make that happen, she needed to identify her team's strengths and figure out the gaps. She knew that communication was key to this strategy, and good communication would offset her risk. Says Pam, "By knowing the communication style of your employees—and your culture—you can attract referral partners and team members who are a perfect fit for your company."

On the surface, it looked like Pam's problem would be in the number of employees she had. However, that was not the case. By being able to understanding each team member, she was able to nurture their unique talents more effectively. There is an "unspoken communication culture" that drives most teams. It is important to *define that culture* and then to be able to understand how both internal and external players are *responding to that culture*. This is exactly what we did with Pam.

Assess the Problem First

Pam bills herself as, "Your Mortgage Loan Consultant for Life," and in order to serve her customers better, she wanted to build her business exclusively on a by-referral-only basis. Because of her willingness to truly get to know herself—and her team—Pam was the ideal candidate for a DiSC Assessment. The DiSC model, available through Inscape Publishing, is a tool that describes communication and behavioral patterns of four human tendencies.

D.i.S.C. stands for:

- **Dominant**. These people are fast paced, direct, decisive, and to the point. They are the visionaries, natural goal setters. They make things happen. They focus on getting things *done*.

- **influential**. This style keeps their pace fast, making things happen in a timely fashion, but they are more "touchy-feely," freely embracing and sharing their feelings. These are often your salesperson types.

- **Supportive** people are warm and friendly folks that are emotionally open, but their pace is deliberate. They like to collect information from others by asking questions about people's feelings.

- **Conscientious** is deliberate. This type takes pride in being the perfectionists, and when they do a job, they do it *right* the first time. These are your detail oriented people.

Assessment tools can be a critical factor when you are building your team. When a person takes the DiSC, he or she receives an extensive fifteen-page report explaining her communication style, including what factors motivate that person, the preferred working environment, how they respond to conflict, their approach to marketing and selling and how to be more effective in all life areas.

We did both a DiSC assessment for each team member at Key Mortgage and then a DiSC culture assessment. The report revealed that the Key Mortgage culture was most in alignment with a high "i culture," which values creativity, optimism collaboration, passion and spontaneity in work. The DiSC assessment also revealed that even though Pam's team was small, it was diverse. Pam was a very high "i" and a high "D" leader, meaning she was more social and more results-oriented. This communicated well to her high "i" sales staff. However, even though she is a strong visionary, her approach was not what every person responded to, especially employees who were more detail oriented, or a high "C."

Because she is a masterful leader, Pam quickly implemented what she learned from the DiSC assessment on her company, and she developed a team who respected each other's style of communication based on their DiSC behavior. This wasn't too hard to do with the people who where already most like her—namely her sales force. The main communication gap was between all the "i" types and the high "S" and "C" types. Some of the communication strategies she implemented with the "S" and "C" types were:

- Communicating more openly when changing directions;
- Providing written documentation when requested;
- Writing scripts for employees who were not as comfortable with the sales process.

Make More out of Less

In Guerrilla Marketing, the fleet-of-foot beat the-big-of-budget every time. Because Pam now had the tools to help her team members communicate more effectively, she knew how to turn the liability of fewer team members into a positive trait. Because everyone on her team was communicating effectively, that led her straight to the front lines—and to increased referrals. She did this using the same tool that she used to build her team into a more cohesive group. She trained her team on how to leverage their different communication styles so that they could best interact with a select group of five to seven key "champion" clients.

In choosing to specialize in the "less is more" school of marketing, Pam was able to effectively roll out the red carpet for her champions, not just because they were great referral partners but because they were also close friends and colleagues of Key Mortgage.

Building a business on referrals only saves tremendous time and money. Says Pam, "You are talking to five people who are perfectly suited for your business and who are ready to do business with you, because they have been referred to you. If I can work with each person on my team and their unique communication style to make it easy for them to ask for referrals, then I will feel as if I have been successful with this process."

Because Pam's team knows they are building a business based on referrals, they know to talk to each person in a way that builds relationships with them. Each one of her team members is trained on how to identify the various DiSC behaviors, and that is a huge plus because the clients feel that they are being communicated to in a way that they can understand.

Pam's referral-only policy of Guerrilla Marketing has paid off. Key Mortgage was the 2006 US Chamber Small Business Blue Ribbon Award winner. But for Pam, the only award she ever needs is that next referral.

Greg Hiebert: A Road Map from Success to Significance

Tiger Woods, one of the greatest golfers of all time, is also one of the game's greatest students. Even at the pinnacle of success and achievement, Tiger takes input, feedback and criticism from his coach; he takes advice from a coach that he would most likely beat on the course. Greg Hiebert, one of the world's top leadership consultants and trainer—the Tiger Woods of his game—was actually asking for a partner when he called me for coaching. He wanted someone who would provide him with the support and accountability he needed to lead his company, Leadership Forward, from success to significance. His story is an example of what can happen when a strong team is in place.

Greg Hiebert is senior partner in Leadership Forward, a professional services company that focuses on helping topflight businesses transform their leadership development into an integrated business discipline that produces breakthrough leaders.

Greg not only directs his company's culture; he embodies it. He also recognizes the disparity between writing a mission statement and living it: "Our core values are trust and respect," explains Greg. "We were so proud of these values that we are tempted to tell our clients about them all the time." But Greg also recognized that the clients don't care what you say, they care about what you do. In other words: "you have to live them."

Greg is a leader at the top of his game. He regularly mentors some of this country's top leaders from organizations including the US Air Force and Orlando Regional Health System, making "Leadership Forward" both a company name and a goal. Greg's focus is on customer retention and relationship-building, two of the key pillars in his masterful Guerrilla leadership strategy. These just happen to be two successful strategies for working with a diverse and multi-faceted team. As a result of his relentless commitment to excellence and uncompromising passion for service, Greg not only keeps his team intact over the long haul, he has a staggering 93 percent retention rate among his very, very satisfied customers!

Not surprisingly, Greg espouses the Guerrilla Marketing competency of *relationships* to tackle diversity, not only in his team but in his clients. Greg recognizes that relationships are built on a strong sense of rapport, and took the conscious step to train not just himself but all of his team members in the foundational principles of NLP, (Neuro-Linguistic Programming).

While NLP has various benefits and applications, Greg's priority focused on modeling the behaviors and beliefs of his clients who have achieved excellence. By modeling, his team members can match the tone and pace of their clients, no matter how diverse, to build a greater, deeper connection.

This connection becomes the essence of building rapport—meeting people and creating, then maintaining, a strong connection. This is the secret to his success of keeping both his team and his clientele in tact. To help you strengthen that connection and underscore the importance of building rapport, Greg shares his Seven Principles of Building R-A-P-P-O-R-T:

1. **R-eal behaviors:** At the heart of Leadership Forward is a core set of values that truly make Greg's company stand out. But Greg cautions, "You can't just have conscious and deliberate discussion about team values; they must have teeth. Value statements must become real behaviors that can be observed, measured and lived."

2. **A-cting the part:** Service is a performance; Guerrilla leaders must be part actors. Explains Greg, "When I walk into a client's organization I am mindful that just the quality of my presence can positively or negatively impact our clients."

3. **P-acing:** One of the principle techniques of building rapport is pacing. Greg urges team members to meet the pacing of the client; "… to be in the same wavelength of your clients so that they sense your support and connection and allow yourself to be a greater resource for them."

4. **P-ersonalize yourself:** "I have found no quicker way to connect with a human being," explains Greg, "than for me to be vulnerable with them about my shortcomings and my failings." The client must get to know you as a person; you must personalize yourself and be vulnerable to entering into a relationship of mutual trust and respect.

5. **O-n all the time:** Every comment and every movement is often recorded by clients. "You must be 'on' all the time," reiterates Greg, "you can't treat a senior executive one way and those who are on a different part of the corporate ladder another."

6. **R-ecognizing the client's needs:** Part of staying in great rapport with clients is to understand their needs and to be patient and attentive to what is really going on well beyond the spoken

words. Greg says, "I have had to let go of some of my bad habits as a consultant where my mind is constantly racing to find something brilliant to share. Now, I take a deep breath and remember that the most effective way to recognize and understand their needs is to be in a place of deep listening."

7. **T-iming:** Clients needed to know that there is a time and a place for vulnerability and confidence. Knowing which is half the battle.

Diversity on the Front Line: An Asset, Not a Liability

The essence of building a masterful Guerrilla team is to embrace the diversity of everyone on your team. Whether diversity comes in the form or cultural differences or in varied communication styles, when we embrace diversity rather than try to escape it, we likewise "embrace" a whole new aspect of Guerrilla leadership: sensitivity. *Sensitivity* just happens to be the common Guerrilla Marketing competency that ties these three exemplary leaders together.

Whether it's Elyse being sensitive to her staff dynamic, Pam being sensitive to her core customer's specific needs, or Greg recognizing that his current mood can have a profound effect on conference calls, each of these self-styled Guerrilla leaders knows that the best way to market themselves to their clients is to put their clients first.

Sensitivity is the vision to realize the dream, the courage to open yourself up to criticism, the passion to try something new, the commitment to powerful relationships, the willingness to listen and the ability to lead a team out of the position of strength and not the vulnerability of weakness. Isn't that what Guerrilla leadership is all about?

I'm going to end with a short exercise that I have my clients do. It will help you identify your strengths and those areas you need to work on. It will help you to see if you are ready to lead your team to the front lines. It's called the L.E.A.D Test, and it will help you to see if *you* are ready to lead *your* team to the front lines. Here it is:

- **Leverage:** Do you leverage every opportunity to build a focused and driven team? Guerrilla leaders make the most of every opportunity to build a results-based team.

- **Energize:** Marketing Guerrilla style requires stamina and endurance, both of which can fail if a strong leader is not there to energize his or her team.

- **Assess:** Regular and targeted assessment helps keep the Guerrilla leader alert to valuable progress—and potential danger zones.

- **Direct:** Check yourself often to make sure that your instructions are clear and direct. If *you* don't understand instructions after they've been issued, how will your team?

A good leader has the courage to make the tough calls. The front lines of marketing are always tough. So take the time to strengthen your skills as a strong leader, so that you, too, can build and lead a masterful Guerrilla Marketing team.

About Bea Fields

*Bea Fields is an Executive Coach and the Owner President of Bea Fields Companies, Inc. and Five Star Leader Coaching and Training, **www.FiveStarLeader.com**, a leadership coaching and training company which services over one thousand national and international clients with headquarters in Pinehurst, North Carolina. She is the author of* Millennial Leaders: Success Stories From Today's Most Brilliant Generation Y Leaders *and* Edge: A Leadership Story. *For more information, visit **www.BeaFields.com**.*

CHAPTER 29

THE GUERRILLA SALES FORCE

The Science of Hiring, Training, and Paying Salespeople on a Shoestring Budget

Todd Beeler

> *"Small opportunities are often the beginning of great enterprises."*
>
> ~Demosthenes

One of the more surprising things I learned from Jay Levinson early on in my career as a sales trainer and consultant was that you do *not* need money to make money. Guerrilla Marketing teaches that imagination makes up for a lack of financial capital. If this bold assertion is true, then lack of capital is no longer a constraint to business success.

Capital is based on the principle of leverage. Leverage is what happens anytime you make a small investment and get back a larger return and/or less risk. Ideas are a form of capital—intellectual capital. Since the upside is big, and the downside risk to create a thought is zero, that's excellent leverage. So if you can discover a practical way to apply one of your ideas, then people will exchange their money for your idea.

In addition to intellectual capital, human resources are another form of capital—talent capital. So if capital is anything that gives you leverage, and if leverage is about big upside and low downside, then hiring a team of commissioned salespeople is an effective way to create capital.

Hiring commissioned salespeople not only offers you a large potential return, it also keeps your financial risk at zero. This is possible because you are only paying for performance and results. One way to create leverage is through the process of duplication.

In this chapter I'll share with you how I used my hiring system to help one company shatter their sales records. I'll share how a guy I trained with a Fortune 500 company went on to close the largest sale of his sales career for over $15 million. You'll discover how I attracted a top sales gun with a business degree from Vanderbilt and an M.B.A. from University of Alabama while only offering a commission only sales position.

In addition, you will discover the three-step hiring system I've used that has enabled me to market for free and leverage myself. The first time I used this three-step system in June 1997, I made more money in a month than a brain surgeon. And I only "worked" five hours a week. My "work" consisted of giving out checks to my team of seven salespeople and going to the bank. I did this without ever paying a single salesperson a penny or spending an extra dime on marketing.

In the pages that follow, you may find that the process that I use to hire, train, and compensate a sales force is radically different from the typical way of doing things. The truth I want to embed into your brain is this basic Guerrilla Marketing tenet: you don't need money to make money if you have imagination.

I'm not the brightest light in the room. I pulled this off with no business background. I was actually a religious education major in grad school so I can't go so far as to say I didn't have a prayer, but the odds were not good. However, if I can execute this system, so can you. I'm not saying my system is the *only* system that will work. There are other ways to market for free. I am simply saying that this system I will share with you has been Guerrilla tested and verified. It's the highest upside, lowest downside system I was able to discover that allowed me to market for free. It's a capital generation system that maximizes leverage. I'll try to answer the questions you would ask and to give you examples of the system in action so you can duplicate it for yourself.

I will cover three steps for you in this chapter. They are Guerrilla hiring, Guerrilla training, and Guerrilla compensation.

Guerrilla Hiring

The first step is you need to develop a Guerrilla hiring system. Why do you need to hire a top performing Guerrilla sales team? Well, hypothetically speaking, if you could accurately duplicate yourself as many times as you desired, at no out of pocket cost, then would you agree you could create unlimited wealth? If so, then your first challenge is to figure out how to accurately duplicate yourself so you can get a larger return while reducing your risk.

As a launching point, you need to understand why it's so hard to accurately hire top performing salespeople. The reason is that most use low validity hiring methods. For example, if you base a hiring decision on an interview, you'll be wrong about 86 percent of the time because people exaggerate. People put on a public persona that masks their normal self. If you base your decision on the criteria of previous job experience, you'll be wrong 82 percent of the time because they might have been a low performer with experience. Checking references is unreliable 74 percent of the time because the companies you call on are afraid of lawsuits, so they guard the truth.

Most people are not aware of new methodologies that have been created and verified to double, triple and quadruple your hiring accuracy. If you can triple your hiring accuracy, you can triple the odds of finding a top sales performer. This will allow you to duplicate and leverage yourself with accuracy, which is what Guerrilla hiring is all about.

When I first started out in my own business hiring salespeople, I let anyone try sales since it was a commission only position. The ones who were good stuck around and closed deals. The ones who were not a good fit didn't produce. I call this the "sink or swim" philosophy of sales hiring. This resulted in a high turnover and I had to be constantly running classified ads to replace salespeople. The other problem was I experienced a large lost opportunity cost from having so many sub par salespeople on my team.

To calculate your lost opportunity cost, figure out the annual financial differential between a top performer and a bottom performer and multiply this by the number of salespeople you intend to hire. For example, if the differential is $900,000 and you intend to hire ten salespeople, then the lost opportunity cost is $9,000,000 per year or $45,000,000 over a five-year period. Once I considered my lost opportunity cost, I decided I had to find a much more accurate hiring system than "sink or swim." Here are the steps I've found to be the most predictive to double or triple your hiring accuracy.

First we create a benchmark from the top performers within your company or your industry. This gives us an objective standard of comparison for the people that you will eventually hire. Once we created this benchmark, we then use it to design an ad that will attract that kind of candidate.

To recruit those candidates, I run a classified ad in the largest local newspaper and online. I write the advertising copy based on research of top performers to add science to the advertising. I use benefits that appeal to them. I show them big income is feasible. I get the newspaper to bill for the ad, so I can pay them out my profits later. Remember, this ad is an example of what I use. You must contextualize your own ad to work for your business or industry.

I run an ad like this:

> ### Are You a Top Sales Gun?
>
> I made $_____this week. Average $_____per hour. Hiring 2 positions. 9-5 hours, casual dress, no travel. Are you a money motivated, resilient, persuasive achiever? If so, fax resume or proof to _____or e-mail to_____"

This step of writing and turning in a resume requires some effort on the part of the potential candidate. They have to type up a couple of pages and actually go to a fax machine or a computer. That weeds out some more of the wrong type of candidates.

If the resume looks like we might have someone that's money motivated, then we invite them in for an interview. I compile the best interview questions according to the benchmark we had compiled before we wrote the ad. For my business, and for the sake of an example, the benchmark is "money motivated." I might ask, "Can you share an example of a time when you were extremely money motivated?" We also ask three or four other questions from the "best practice" benchmark. We throw in a few questions from the worst performer benchmark to see if they excel at these red-flag areas. During the interview, our objective is to get to the truth, so we ask them to offer proof and third party verification for their claims. It costs nothing to verify claims, yet it does require imagination. Imagination, as always, substitutes for money again. Imagination gives us leverage. Leverage increases probability.

I then call their references as a verification process and ask the reference to verify what was said in the interview. For example, if in the interview Steve said he was the number one sales rep for three years straight, we might ask the reference: "So how did Steve compare sales wise to the other reps there. Was he in the bottom, middle or top tier?" Then I might follow that up with: "Did he ever finish as the number one sales rep, to your knowledge?"

After the reference check, if everything checks out as truth, I have the candidate complete our five online assessments to see if they are a custom fit for the position, compared to the sales benchmarks we previously created. These assessments allow us to look objectively at the prospective sales person's business talents, values, behaviors, personality, and sales skills. I also look to see if they are someone who is a fast learner by comparing to the fast learner benchmark. This will slash ramp-up time later. I want people who are wired to sell and who learn fast.

In one company where I used this system, every single person I ultimately advised for hire went on to become a top dollar producer. Remember, capital is about using leverage, not necessarily money. Hiring commissioned salespeople using a scientifically validated, high probability methodology, dramatically reduces the risk of missing out on big financial opportunities. At the same time, it increases your chances of hitting it big.

Guerrilla Sales Training

The second step in my plan is Guerrilla sales training. Training is important because you want to leverage and maximize the upside of the talent that you have discovered. Without training, you will experience a high turnover. When people are in a commission only job, they need to generate cash fast and succeed right away.

Guerrilla sales training is different from traditional sales training because you are usually limited to a smaller budget. You can't afford to bring in some big name sales trainer. So you have to find other effective ways to train salespeople, without spending a lot of money.

I strongly advise sales training—both initial and on-going—because repetition is the key to establishing your message in the minds of your salespeople. It takes repetition for salespeople to nail down door openers, presentation, and closes. New hires also need more confidence. A key to building confidence quickly is increasing their skill level. In the initial sales training, I start by sharing the best practice sales scripts in written form. I tell them to memorize these scripts. I do not allow them to sell until these scripts are memorized.

Guerrilla sales training also uses role playing, a lot of it. I ask questions like "What do you say if they say they want to think about it?" I drill the scripts into their brains by rehearsing them over and over until the salespeople deliver the lines as naturally as I do.

Then we send them out immediately with a top sales gun to simply observe and in order to get rid of their limiting beliefs. Once they see the top sales gun close a couple of sales, they are sold on the idea. Success now seems feasible. This is important. Nothing helps confidence like firsthand proof. This really cranks up their motivation. Success breeds success. There is no financial cost for this kind of hands-on, in-the-field sales training, but it does require an investment of imagination, energy, and time.

We do ongoing weekly sales training from that point on. Weekly sales training is a Guerrilla Marketing core tactic. Success in Guerrilla sales training is about quality not quantity. You can get better results with one superstar than training ten average salespeople. It's not about hiring tons of salespeople. It's about going deep with the maximum you can manage with excellence.

Additionally, I coach them in the areas where they need improvement. I use the "best practice" benchmark to guide me. This puts science into my sales training and really accelerates their ramp up time. It accurately identifies the causes of low or slow performance quickly.

Guerrilla sales training is also about understanding the psychology of how people make decisions. I see myself as a decision engineer. My goal is to sincerely help a client make a solid decision, with or without buying from me. There is a lot of research today on the subject of decision making that didn't exist ten years ago. Persuasion is becoming a science instead of an art, so as part of my weekly training, I take a scientifically valid persuasion principle and have my sales force practice that for one week.

For example, a scientifically validated persuasion principle I discovered is to help clients make a good decision by not presenting one-sided information. The more neutral and consultative you are perceived by the prospect, the more you attract them to your offer. I taught this to a sales pro who went from an absolute stalemate with his client to closing a deal. I taught my client to basically say:

> You know Mr. Prospect, my job is to help you make the decision that's right for you. I've done everything I can to help you here. If you feel it's not in your best interest to move forward, I'm 110 percent okay with walking away. In fact, I insist on doing what's best for you.

I told him if he used any of these strategies to manipulate a customer they would backfire. I told him his motives had to be 100 percent pure and sincere. He was there to sincerely care about the decision making process for his client. It sealed the deal for his new record of $15 million!

I was once doing some weekly sales training by phone with a top sales gun with a Fortune 500 company. The sales gun was close to losing a $15 million deal he had been working on for over a year. He needed to reduce the sales package by a million dollars or he would lose the deal. Even though that's far more money than most Guerrilla Marketers ever would use for advertising and sales, we still used Guerrilla Marketing tactics. We had an emergency meeting at a coffee shop, and I drew up a plan on a napkin. I used imagination to show him exactly how to find him the million dollars he needed to save the deal. We basically went to one of the prospect's vendors and we got them to invest the $1 million we needed to keep the project alive. We created a win-win situation where the vendor made money by getting exposure and publicity for their investment. Guerrilla Marketing saved the day because imagination matters more than money.

Since Guerrilla marketers are usually operating from a much smaller budget, we use low cost, high impact training tools such as audio training resources, large group training, one on one coaching, books, multi-media computer based learning, and shadowing.

Guerrilla sales training, executed with excellence, will usually increase your profits by 15 – 100 percent. Guerrilla sales training is effective because it increases the upside financial potential of your new hires. That's an effective use of leverage.

Guerrilla Sales Compensation

The third and final step of my system is to develop a Guerrilla sales compensation plan.

Remember, capital is about leverage. We use leverage by accurate duplication and multiplying human talent capital, using Guerrilla hiring. Leverage is about high upside. We increase upside through Guerrilla sales training. Leverage is also about low downside. We reduce your downside risk by using Guerrilla commission only compensation plans. The way you compensate your salespeople predicts the risk level of your enterprise. Obviously, if you can figure out a way to pay top salespeople by commission only, based on performance and results, then your out-of- pocket financial risk is zero. That's leverage!

The main constraint to the final step in my system is how to attract high quality salespeople without spending a dime out of pocket. This keeps your financial out-of-pocket risk at zero.

Commission-only pay means your salespeople are paid entirely by performance and results without any type of base income. You give them a percentage of the sale once the money clears. Commissions can range anywhere from 5 – 50 percent, depending on the size of the sale and sales volume. I find that generosity is a key to making a commission-only sales compensation work.

Another key is you need to pay out fast. For example, if a salesperson makes a sale on Monday, deposit the check on Monday and pay them as soon as the check clears. The reason being they do not have a salary, so they need cash fast.

My commission plans reward the heavy hitters with higher commissions. The small achievers get a lower commission. This is objective and fair. I prefer a sliding scale commission plan. I might pay out 20 percent for the first ten sales of the period, then 35 percent for the next ten, and then 50 percent for anything above twenty-one sales.

I also like to pay the top sales performer a little extra by letting the top performer train and manage the other salespeople for me. This frees up my time. So I usually gave my commission only sales manager a 50 percent commission on their own sales, and an override based on the performance of their team. I also base this on a sliding scale. For example, for fifty sales, they might get a 5 percent override; seventy-five sales, an 8 percent override; and one hundred sales, a 10 percent override.

For top sales guns, the beauty of this kind of compensation plan is they get paid fast, and they get paid for results. They also have no cap on their income or hourly average pay. That's what makes it so attractive.

Let me close out with a concrete example. I once attracted a stellar salesperson who had a business degree from Vanderbilt and an M.B.A. from the University of Alabama. He decided to move from Alabama to Charleston to work with me.

How did I attract such a high caliber sales professional? The generous pay plan and unlimited hourly potential attracted him. He also liked our flexible schedule, selling a product with a high perceived value, high demand, and low cost. He also was proud to sell a product for a high quality company.

It also helps if you give your salespeople an irresistible offer to sell. This keeps their conversion rates high, which keeps their motivation high. You want to create packages that range from a really low cost to a really high cost so you can have a high conversion rate for your salespeople.

Let me give you a few examples of how companies in different industries have created an irresistible low cost option. A golf course could sell a buy-eighteen-holes-get-eighteen-holes free card for $50. A hotel could sell a getaway weekend package during a slow season for $69. A hair salon could sell six visits for $60. A restaurant could sell ten buy-one-get-one-free dinners for $20. An automotive service center could sell six oil changes for $40. A consultant could sell a two-hour seminar or teleseminar for $49. A photographer could sell a package for $59, including the studio time and a few prints. A sports team could sell a package of games for $69. A movie theatre could sell a package of movie tickets for $49. A day spa could sell a relaxation package for $49. The possibilities are endless when you use your time, energy, and imagination.

What makes this low pricing possible—and attractive—is the back end lifetime value of a customer. If the lifetime value of an average automotive customer is worth $5000, doesn't it make sense to invest $20 worth of oil changes to initiate the relationship, earn trust, and lock out the competition?

So there you have it my friend, my three step system of marketing for free with your own commissioned Guerrilla sales team. Just remember, capital is about leverage, and you can create leverage by hiring others. Leverage is about high upside. You can raise your upside with sales training. Leverage is also about low downside. You can lower your downside with a commission only compensation plan. Hiring others on commission is an effective way to duplicate yourself and generate more capital without investing or risking any of your own money.

It doesn't *take* money, to *make* money. Lack of capital never should be a constraint again. In Guerrilla sales hiring, training, and compensation, you are only limited by your imagination. Imagine that.

About Todd Beeler

Todd Beeler started his own magazine publishing company and sold out three magazines full of advertisers by himself. In the last seven years, Todd has helped over two hundred clients increase their sales. He has been featured in magazines like Sales and Marketing Management, Incentive, *and* Personal Excellence. *Beeler is also the author of* The Seven Hidden Secrets to Motivation, *and his firm,* The Scientific Selling Group, *offers scientifically validated sales hiring & sales training services. To contact Todd, please call 1-800-925-8633, or visit **www.ScientificHiring.com** or **www.ScientificSalesTraining.com**.*

CHAPTER 30

DEAR CLIENT FROM HELL—"YOU'RE FIRED!"

Save Your Resources for the Clients You Want to Keep

David A. Scarborough

> *"We can reach our potential, but to do so, we must reach within ourselves. We must summon the strength, the will, and the faith to move forward—to be bold—to invest in our future."*
>
> ~John Hoeven

Not All Customers are Created Equal

Most small business owners have never fired a customer. They're focused on getting and keeping customers—not getting rid of them.

They practice the long-accepted principle that "the customer is always right," made famous by Stew Leonard who went one step further and etched the following two rules on granite outside of his business:

> **Rule #1**—The customer is always right.

> **Rule #2**—If the customer is ever wrong, reread Rule #1.

Based on these rules—which most of us still believe—it may feel counter intuitive and even ungrateful to think about firing anyone who is willing to pay you for your product or service.

Well, it's time to think again, because all customers are not created equal, and as Guerrilla Marketing mentor, Jay Conrad Levinson, says, "it's a jungle out there." Competition is stiffer than ever and if you're going to grow and sustain a successful business in today's marketplace, it's vital that you understand when to keep a customer and when to let one go.

Yet, every Guerrilla marketer knows that marketing is all about building and maintaining positive relationships with your employees, suppliers, community and customers. Although it may seem trite in this fast-paced world, the old "golden rule" still applies. Treat people the way you like to be treated—with kindness, respect, joy and trust. But it doesn't mean you have to accept business with folks who don't demonstrate those same behaviors.

I essentially agree with Stew Leonard. Customers *are* your business. If you don't have customers, you don't have a business. And client-focused businesses—ones that attend to the entire customer experience—are more successful than those which are not. So yes, it's essential that small business owners provide superior customer care and adopt a whatever-it-takes attitude for dealing with customers—*as long as those customers are cooperative and profitable*. If they are not, you need to let them go.

> *"Guerrillas know well that...20 percent of their customers help generate 80 percent of their profits. Not only are they able to identify the less productive 80 percent and the very effective 20 percent, but they have the insight to do something about it..."*
>
> ~Jay Conrad Levinson, *Mastering Guerrilla Marketing: 100 Profit-Producing Insights You Can Take to the Bank*, 1999

This guerrilla concept is illustrated perfectly using Pareto's 80/20 rule.

How the 80/20 Rule Can Help You

The Pareto Principle, commonly known as the 80/20 rule, is one of the most helpful tools in managing businesses *effectively*. It states that 20 percent (or the minority) of anything is vital and as much as 80 percent (or the majority) is trivial.

The formula is named after Italian economist, Vilfredo Paredo, who in 1906 noticed that 80 percent or Italy's income was generated by 20 percent of the population. It was articulated and applied in the late 1940's by business philosopher, Joseph M. Juran, who used it to make sense of sales data.

The concept was further explored by Richard Koch (author of "The 80/20 Principle: The Secret to Achieving More with Less"), who has written extensively on applying the principle in all areas of life.

In *Guerrilla Marketing*, Jay Levinson speculates that most businesses earn 80 percent of their profits from 20 percent of their customers. I couldn't agree more. And after many years of experience working with companies of all sizes, I know that it works both ways: 20 *percent of customers cause 80 percent of the problems*.

I learned this lesson the hard way. But thanks to my experiences, you don't have to.

Mrs. Snodgrass (not her real name)

My first experience with a "client from hell" occurred when I was twelve years old. I delivered sixty newspapers daily to folks in my neighborhood, the very street I lived on for fifteen years. Before allowing me to accept the job, my mother reminded me that I was responsible for ensuring that my neighbors were not disappointed (i.e. that they received their paper on time, every day) and that no matter what "the customer is always right." I agreed to these rules.

For the most part, it was fun. I enjoyed the money I earned (I was able to save enough money in three years to buy my first car), and I got to know some very nice and pleasant people.

Then I met "*her*"… Mrs. Snodgrass.

She insisted that I put her paper between the screen door and the main door of her house. I felt her request was reasonable even though her mail box was equipped with a newspaper rack. So I cheerfully complied with her wishes. And everything was fine as long as she was not home and her front door was closed. I hopped off my bike, walked up her driveway, opened the door and was on my way to the next house in no time.

However, problems arose when her main door was left open and her screen door was the only thing separating me from the inside of her house (and as luck would have it, she did this quite often on warmer days). As long as Mrs. Snodgrass was home (and located near the front door) this worked fine as well. However, it was a different case when she was in the back of the house or not at home. If I'd drop the newspaper exactly where she asked, her mean little dog, Sparky, would tear it to shreds in ten seconds flat.

To say the least, Mrs. Snodgrass was not happy and felt obligated to scold me every time this happened, but still insisted that I leave the paper inside her front door. This created *a no-win situation for me*. I even began knocking on the door before I left the paper. I figured this was a great way to give her fair warning that she better grab the paper before Sparky ate it. Sometimes this worked and sometimes it didn't.

Over time I decided that it was best to leave the paper in its rightful place on her mailbox hook when I was greeted at the door by her crazy dog. But that wasn't good enough for old Mrs. Snodgrass, who continue to scold me every time I saw her and rarely paid me on time.

What could I do? You guessed it—

I went home and complained to my mother, who replied, "The customer is always right."

I put up with Mrs. Snodgrass and her nasty little dog for three more years. If I had been smarter, I'd have asked her to find another paper boy.

So my first experience with the 80/20 rule began with Mrs. Snodgrass and a handful of others on my paper route—even though I didn't know it at the time.

The First Time is Always the Hardest

I will never forget the first time I fired a customer. At the time it was an extremely difficult and heart wrenching decision, but one that I'd make again today.

When I was a budding marketing consultant with few clients, I was understandably thrilled to accept a large retainer from George Smith (not his real name), the owner of a creative advertising company. George hired me to conduct an overall business assessment, that is, review, analyze and provide recommendations for improving and streamlining processes, marketing, systems, etc.

After a month-long "courting" process (several face-to-face meetings and dozens of e-mails and phone conversations) I signed a three-phase contract worth $7,500 to $10,0000—a lot of money at the time—and started to work.

Right from the beginning, George's behavior was troublesome. For instance, he:

- could neither give nor accept constructive feedback;
- regularly amended the project requirements and goals (which he could rarely articulate so I was never sure what he wanted me to do);
- called me unexpectedly and began most conversations with, "Do you have a minute?" then kept me on the phone discussing trivial matters for over an hour;
- continually questioned my expertise and voiced concern over the project's direction, only to call the next day to apologize and gush over my work; and
- frequently paid me late—and only after he quibbled about every charge.

Nonetheless, I thought I could figure out a way to make it work. First, I needed the business. Second, I knew I could help him—if he let me. Third, I believed that I could work with just about anyone and didn't want George to prove me wrong. But most importantly, I put up with him because in the back of my head I still believed that "the customer is always right."

I was wrong. One of the basic tenets of Guerrilla marketing—and one I heartily agree with—is that businesses should measure their success by profits, rather than by market share, revenues or sales. And even though he was paying me, he was an unprofitable and unpleasant client!

He wasted my time—my most precious asset—on senseless handholding, reworking, and cajoling. It got to the point where everyone in the office dreaded talking with George, and his rotten attitude made him the topic of many negative conversations, both inside and outside of work.

His behavior left me and my staff feeling stressed, frustrated, unappreciated, and confused. Moreover, because of his demands on our time we weren't able to devote as much attention to our other, nicer, more profitable clients, which finally made the cost of doing business with George unacceptable.

After a few more months, I fired George. It was the right decision. In no time, I replaced George with three smaller clients, ones who were pleasant, paid on time and appreciated the superior services my company provided.

More important, as a result of this experience, I redefined what I wanted in a customer and continue to use it as a model for getting (and keeping) new clients.

How Did I Fire George?

Carefully. By that point I was ready to "vent," but I understood that it was my responsibility to end our working relationship amicably. After all, this was not just a tough decision for me, but it was also going to be a very unpleasant experience for him. Though I knew it was time to move on, I wanted to be sensitive to his feelings and make certain that he didn't feel embarrassed, defensive or unimportant.

Additionally, I was careful to minimize any potential word-of-mouth damage that George could do to my new business by ensuring that he was treated with the utmost respect throughout the process.

So I did the following:

■ Sat him down and politely discussed our professional differences (e.g. working style, project goals, scope of work, etc.) only. Although I firmly stated that it was in both our best interests to cease our working relationship, I did not accuse, blame, intimidate or insult George.

■ Offered to finish up the work to a logical end point. Because the project was in three phases, I agreed to complete all of the first phase. This would make it easier for him to transition the work to another consultant. I also agreed to personally review the project with my successor and answer any questions they had concerning any of the work that I had accomplished.

■ Provided recommendations of companies that he might consider using to complete the work.

■ Sent him a pleasant, follow-up letter which summarized our discussion and reiterated my offer to complete phase one and help transition the work.

And although I was tempted to either "vent," keep him as a client but charge him twice as much as everyone else, or send him a terse form letter reminding him that I'm not his personal lackey, I was glad I resisted the urge. Techniques like these may make you feel better for the moment, but in the end they only make things worse—even when anger is justified.

What Was George's Reaction?

At first he was very apologetic. He even admitted that he "could be very difficult at times." He also thanked me for my time, patience, and expertise. However, after he had more time to think about it, he became understandably more offended, and the "old George" returned—but now his unreasonable demands fell on deaf ears. But he was not all that different from many clients who understand that they are "significant" in your business and choose to take advantage of the situation.

The Moral of the Story

If you offer something of real value, you do not have to offer it to every single person who is willing to pay you. If they do not behave in a manner that is acceptable to you, your employees, or your bottom line—*fire them.*

When is it Okay to Fire a Customer?

The simple answer is that it's okay to fire a customer whenever he or she behaves badly. And since past behavior is the best predictor of future behavior, do it sooner rather than later. Thankfully, it's only a small percentage of clients that cause the majority of the pain. And although there are a myriad of possible grounds—objective and subjective—it's up to you to decide what you'll tolerate and what you won't.

However, I think you should consider firing your customer if they are:

1. **Outrageously and routinely demanding:** Complain unnecessarily; change requirements mid-stream; use up precious time on frivolous matters and stress over minute details.

2. **Rude to you and/or your staff:** No one, not even a customer, should be allowed to insult your employees, use demeaning language, or belittle anyone in your business.

3. **Unresponsive or No-Shows:** This is particularly important for service providers who depend upon their clients to send critical information, timely feedback or review, or show up for scheduled appointments on time or at all.

    For example, I recently "fired" a new client we'll call Larry Jones (not his real name), the owner and president of a small, local telecommunications company, for this reason alone. Larry was not the typical "awful" customer. He was pleasant. He paid his bills (sometimes a little late, but not overly). He was able to give and receive constructive feedback in a positive way. He never called to complain about anything. In fact, he never called at all—not even when he promised to do so.

    As a matter of fact, Larry regularly postponed or canceled scheduled meetings and conference calls at the last minute. He'd "forgot" to return phone calls and e-mails until sometime after I'd left the fifth message, and he consistently failed to send me promised information. After dealing with this for several months, it became increasingly clear that Larry's behavior was not going to change and, therefore, I would not be able to provide him the help he needed and deserved. We parted ways amicably and he even vowed to call me again if and when he "got it together." I have yet to hear from him and I am sure it is one of the reasons his company is not as successful as it could be.

4. **Consistently Slow or Non-Payers:** These are the customers who plan on paying you late—for as long as they can get by with it—or deliberately ignore repeated invoices. They are not the folks who are experiencing a financial crisis (we advise you to continue to work with these people). It doesn't matter how much business someone does with you on paper, if you don't get paid or have to waste time and money badgering them.

5. **Unprofitable:** When the costs associated with serving a customer are more than the profits you receive, it's time to fire them. Additionally, if you're not spending enough time with important customers because of excessive handholding; rework and the like, you're likely to lose the valuable clients and get stuck with the clients from hell!

Can You Turn a Bad Customer into a Good One?

Sometimes. There are instances when a difficult customer may be behaving poorly because of something that happened in the past, usually a situation that was not satisfactorily resolved.

In this case, it may be possible to make things better and end up with a happy, profitable customer. If your client is receptive, ask them what you can do to "make things right." Then be prepared to listen with an open mind and look for ways to uncover a workable solution. You'd be surprised how much you can learn from less-than-happy clients and sometimes a problem customer turns around and become a valued one.

In any event it's a good idea to ask yourself some basic "what if" questions before firing a customer because you want to make sure that your customer is the one being difficult—not you. This is a very important distinction.

For example, if you have customers who are pleasant but don't always pay you on time ask yourself, "What if I could figure out a way to accept automatic credit card payments?"

Or if you're spending too much time on the phone answering questions ask yourself, "What if I add a "Frequently Asked Questions" or "Troubleshooting" page to my Web site to minimize call-ins?"

You may be surprised at what you'll come up with. For example, I recently had a client, Jane, who owned a small company that provided and maintained plants in office buildings. She complained about the amount of time she regularly wasted answering questions from unqualified prospects and low value customers who called her.

Jane also spent a great deal of time driving to sites and meeting with prospects, but felt it was necessary since they needed to see pictures of her work. The solution? My company developed an inexpensive, but impressive Web site, which contained a robust FAQ page, pricing information, pictures of plants and arrangements, etc. Jane referred certain callers directly to her site. They obtained the information they were seeking and she saved a lot of time and money.

However, if all this fails, it's time to move on.

Bottom Line—Use this principle as a reminder. Focus on the 20 percent of your customers (and tasks) that matter most. First, ask yourself how your best customers *behave*. For example, which ones pay on time, provide referrals, and are pleasant to work with? Then create a list based on your answers and use it to help identify your top clients, ones who behave responsibly, respectfully and professionally. If you have a customer database—whether on note cards or in your computer—this is a fairly simple exercise. If not, it's time to begin gathering as much information on your customers as possible.

Next, try to identify the other 20 percent, those customers that contribute 80 percent of the stress and problems, and devise a plan to make them better customers—or fire them.

Then begin each day with a commitment to focus on who (and what) is most important and refuse to let others sap your time and energy. Use it wisely, and don't just work smart, work smart on the right things.

You are responsible for getting and keeping profitable customers. It's the only way to grow and sustain a healthy business in this rough and tumble marketplace. That's why it vitally important to make a conscious choice about the type of behavior you will, and will not, tolerate.

So although I agree with Stew Leonard for the most part, I wish his rules etched in granite read:

Rule #1—Pleasant and profitable customers are always right.

Rule #2—If a pleasant and profitable customer is ever wrong, re-read Rule #1.

Rule #3—If a customer is neither pleasant nor profitable, fire them.

About David A. Scarborough

David A. Scarborough is a gifted business leader, writer, educator and speaker has had the opportunity to use his expertise in business, finance, economics and strategic marketing to help entrepreneurs grow and maintain healthy businesses. He draws upon his real-life experiences as a business and marketing professor; founder of two successful small businesses; and an independent strategic marketing consultant to aid companies, organizations, and non-profits both nationally and internationally. A former US Air Force aviator, David was recently named by Jay Conrad Levinson as one of the nation's top twenty-five Guerrilla Marketing Coaches—a hard-earned honor. Additionally, he and his wife, Mary, are authors of The Procrastinator's Guide to Marketing *(November, 2007, Entrepreneur Press, Irvine, CA). He continues to write marketing articles for many online publications and the company's own Web sites—www.StrategicMarketingAdvisors.com and www.TheProcrastinatorsGuideToMarketing.com.*

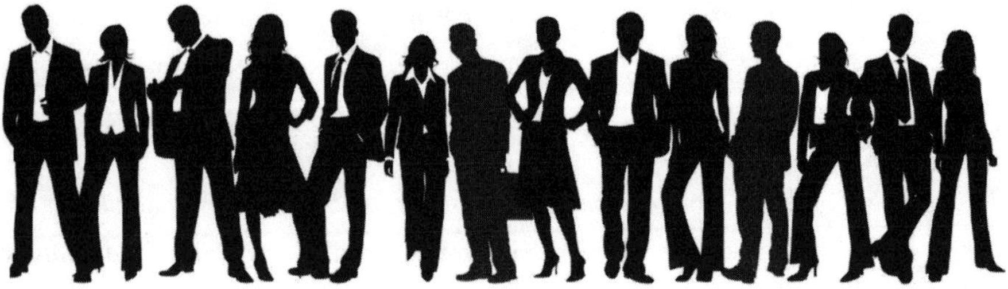

PART SEVEN
Guerrilla Marketing on the Internet

Every Guerrilla Marketer knows the Internet is no longer a luxury but a necessity. The Internet is the perfect Guerrilla Marketing tool because it levels the playing field, allowing the small business owner to have a huge business presence at minimal expense. And now with the addition of Web 2.0, there are countless ways for the Guerrilla Marketer to reach millions of hungry customers at the click of the mouse. This section will take you through the most effective ways to build a profit producing online business from generating web traffic to closing the sale. Tap into the global market place! Get on the Web and get moving.

→ CHAPTER 31

GUERRILLA MARKETING ON THE INTERNET
Powerful Guerrilla Tools to Create a Lifestyle of Financial Freedom

Mitch Meyerson

> *"You are a child of God; your playing small doesn't serve the world."*
> ~Marianne Williamson

It used to be true that anyone starting a business needed a big startup investment and waited years to see a profit. The Internet changed that. With Web sites people could launch e-commerce enterprises at a fraction of the cost of a brick and mortar store. Some Internet startups began with no up-front investment at all, just a few Web-savvy folks teaming up to sell services online.

Now that the Internet has grown to unimaginable proportions and almost everybody is selling something online, the Internet entrepreneur can't make it without an edge. No matter how talented they are, they must know the best cutting edge marketing strategies. Since most online entrepreneurs are starting shoestring operations, they must also know how to market *affordably*. In short, today's online entrepreneur needs Guerrilla Marketing.

E-Commerce Meets Guerrilla Marketing

Guerrilla Marketing is consistently more effective and affordable than traditional marketing. Here are just a few of the reasons why:

- Instead of being oriented to large corporations with limitless bank accounts, Guerrilla Marketing is geared to the small business and entrepreneur, the primary beneficiaries of the e-commerce boom.

- Instead of investing a lot of money in the marketing process, Guerrillas invest time, energy, imagination, and knowledge.

- Instead of considering other business owners "the enemy," Guerrilla marketing promotes cooperation for mutually supportive partnerships—an even easier strategy on the Internet.

- Instead of ignoring technology, Guerrilla Marketing encourages you to be "techno-cozy." This means launching a Web site, automating your follow-up with autoresponders, taking money online with merchant accounts and using Web 2.0 technology, as well as audio and video.

This book is built upon the idea that when you're learning a new set of principles, it's best to follow real-life examples. Because I was intentional in applying Guerrilla Marketing principles and the success secrets of the top online marketing success pros, my story makes a useful model to follow.

My initiation into e-commerce demonstrates how the capabilities of the Internet and the low-cost, high energy methods of Guerrilla Marketing can propel anyone with a good business concept to rapid success. I have found this to be true even for people who have never run a business before and who have no past experience in marketing. That was the situation I faced five years ago when I decided to leave my career as a psychotherapist to become a solo entrepreneur.

Up until 1999, I was a well-known and respected psychotherapist living and working in Chicago. I had a successful practice, several published psychology books, a nice home, a comfortable lifestyle, good friends, and a beautiful downtown office in a thriving metropolis. But after working in the same profession for seventeen years, I was burning out. And I found the northern Midwest winters, with their gray skies and bone chilling cold, downright depressing.

I wanted to change my life completely, to start something new and live someplace sunny and warm, fulfill my creative dreams, spend more time with friends—*to really live*! But the thought of *starting from scratch in a new marketplace* seemed overwhelming.

Looking for an answer, I started exploring possibilities on the Internet and noticed other counselors building online coaching and training businesses. I immediately saw the incredible opportunity this presented to me—to create a whole new career using my existing expertise but one that defied geographic boundaries. I could live anywhere in the world!

Using the principles outlined in this chapter, I was soon earning more than enough income online to leave Chicago and move to the sunny paradise of Scottsdale, Arizona, where I live today. Now I play tennis often, hike scenic mountain trails, swim in my waterfall pool, write, and produce the music I love, enjoy time with my closest friends, and run my thriving e-commerce business from the comfort of my home. I am happy to say I am truly living my dream.

I could never have accomplished this, however, without a clear vision, effective partnerships, and the ability to market successfully over the Internet.

Guerrilla Marketing Coach Certification

My first breakthrough came in when I partnered with the father of Guerrilla Marketing, Jay Conrad Levinson, to create the Guerrilla Marketing Coach Certification Program.

I knew that if I partnered with Levinson, I would not have to reinvent the wheel by creating new content and building a new brand. The Guerrilla Marketing series was (and still is) the best selling marketing series in history.

I explained to Levinson how he could geometrically grow his Guerrilla Marketing brand through a coaching certification program and he wouldn't have to do anything.

As I explain more thoroughly in chapter 1, he quickly became enrolled in a joint venture concept that would combine his marketing models with my coaching expertise to build an army of Guerrilla Marketing experts all over the world. Within a few short months, we were partners developing the Guerrilla Marketing Coach Certification Program, a twelve-week class with targeted curriculum and training sessions.

Making best use of the Internet and other technologies, the program incorporated teleconferencing, a Web-based learning environment, downloadable course materials, voice recordings of sessions, and Webinar capabilities. The web-friendly format of the course made it accessible in real time to hundreds of people all over the world. Because they're able to interact with one another of the Web, classmates can learn from each other, network, and form supportive relationships that extend far beyond the period of the course.

The web elements dramatically expanded the program's accessibility, effectiveness, and appeal, as compared with, for example, a set of pre-recorded CD's shipped out by mail.

Guerrillas Market to Existing Customers

My success did not come from one program alone. As soon as I began to see initial success, I applied another Guerrilla Marketing principle to leverage it: new offerings to existing customers.

Guerrilla Marketing says a company's largest base of prospects is its *existing customers*. In fact, Guerrillas invest 60 percent of their marketing efforts in new offerings to existing customers. So I asked myself, "what new offerings do my Guerrilla Marketing Coach Certification customers genuinely need and want?"

That question led me to another joint venture partner, Michael Port, with whom I created two new programs, The Product Factory and Traffic School. *The Product Factor*—Anyone who is marketing a business on the Web needs a digital product that's easy to download, and preferably, free.

Guerrilla Marketing teaches businesses to use a concept called, "the marketing funnel." The funnel is a metaphor for providing easy ways for people to enter your business (the top of the funnel) before you ask them to buy an expensive product (the bottom of the funnel). Think of it as a relationship; you don't meet someone and immediately ask them to marry you. So why would you introduce yourself to a prospect and immediately ask them to buy your most expensive product?

Guerrillas learn that giving away free offerings is the best way to engage people. Once they get great value from you for free, it builds their confidence, and over time, they will be more apt to buy products from you. While my Guerrilla Marketing coaching clients could instantly see the value in this, hardly anyone knew how to create the products they needed to give away and sell as part of their marketing plan.

So an obvious new offering to my coaching clients was a course on how to design, develop, and market their own digital products. The Product Factory walks people through a step-by-step process of conceptualizing, creating, and marketing products at every level of the marketing funnel.

The Product Factory was an instant success. Its graduates have created everything from their first free report to a twelve-week teleseminar with curriculum guides and CDs. The course proved to be a perfect product to offer to my existing customers, and it also attracted new ones who then wanted the Guerrilla Marketing Coaching program, too.

Again, I wasn't satisfied to stop with this success. I was determined to create *multiple streams of income*, to ensure that, if one product lost its steady stream of new customers, my income and lifestyle would not suffer.

So I asked myself, again, the Guerrilla question: "what else do my clients need?" *Traffic School* was the answer.

Anyone marketing a business on the Web also needs to know how to increase visitor traffic to their site. This was an area I had been studying intently since going live with my first Web site, and I had learned quite a bit.

My partner, Michael Port, was studying the same issues. Combining our knowledge with that of other experts in traffic generation, we created a new online course, Traffic School. This program teaches the basics of e-mail marketing, search engine optimization, autoresponders, blogs and e-zines, and other practices that drive traffic to a site. Like The Product Factory, there are regularly over one hundred students enrolled in Traffic School.

This course also appealed to newcomers, who were then interested in my other offerings. It drove sales of my online marketing books and another product that I saw as a perfect offering to my online marketing clients: Easy Web Automation.

Guerrilla Follow-up through Online Automation

To build a loyal customer base, a Guerrilla must build rapport and credibility and become a resource to their customers. The problem is, most people know this, but they get busy, distracted, and just don't want to manage the details. I was no exception.

When I created the Guerrilla Marketing Coach Certification program, one of my first marketing tactics was to make contact with the existing customers and prospects in the already sizeable Guerrilla Marketing mailing list. Of course, when these contacts responded, follow-up was required, and quite a lot of it. I soon realized that I could easily get buried in administration of a successful program and have no time for the creative and mentorship activities that excited me most about being an entrepreneur.

Knowing I didn't want to become the online equivalent of a paper pusher, I immediately went to work finding a web automation system. Fortunately, it has never been easier or more affordable for business owners to put their marketing and management on autopilot, by using Web-based software.

I soon discovered the system used by online marketing superstars like Alex Mandossian, Mark Victor Hansen, Marlon Sanders, and dozens of others: EasyWebAutomation.com. This easy, web-based program combines a database, a sequential autoresponder, a shopping cart, a merchant account, and an affiliate-management system, all in one.

I was amazed to find that with these tools all in one place I could automate almost every function of my online business, making it easier for everyone, including my customers.

Here are just a few of the things Web automation can do for your business:

- ■ Send e-mail promotions to your prospects.

- ■ Accept payments online.

- ■ Deliver products by e-mail or download.

- ■ Deliver a mini-course.

- ■ Track and measure marketing-campaign results.

- ■ Manage an affiliate program so others can sell your products on commission.

Web Automation Case Study: Superstars Course

A perfect case study of combining web automation with other Guerrilla Marketing principles is my "Online Marketing Superstars Mini-Course and Success Kit."

In February, 2004, I was writing a book that has since been published (and became an Amazon.com bestseller), *Success Secrets of the Online Marketing Superstars*. The content of the book was composed of chapters written from interviews I held with top online marketing experts.

After I had completed eight interviews, the Guerrilla Marketing principle of leveraging again came to mind: I could repurpose this content by putting it into sequence of e-mails packaged as a mini-course. I could give it away for free to build my mailing list and start generating buzz for the book.

I delivered the mini-course with a sequential autoresponder. My automation software tracked the e-mail addresses of those who requested the course and automatically sent them the lessons at the precise date and time I defined. Once I created the course and defined the settings in Easy Web Automation, I didn't have to do another thing. The system did it for me. Moreover, I built an e-mail list of sixteen thousand people within six months.

But the real success of Easy Web Automation is yet another Guerrilla Marketing mandate: sell things that you believe in so that you can be authentic and passionate in marketing them. I was completely sold on the value of Easy Web Automation to my own business and the businesses of my clients. So it was a natural product to add to my offerings.

To get an idea of how well web automation can save you from "admin overload," and why this product was a great fit with my offerings, visit www.EasyWebAutomation.com, and take a test drive.

Guerrilla Partnerships on the Web: Affiliate Programs

Online marketing offers one of the best and most powerful ways to develop fusion-marketing partnerships—the affiliate program. An online business with an affiliate program recruits individuals, entrepreneurs, and e-commerce sites to sell their products on commission. Anyone can sell such products through their own Web site, e-mail lists, blogs, and so forth.

Becoming an Affiliate

To start earning income through affiliate programs, follow these guidelines:

- Promote products that you have tried and liked.

- Go online and look for products that your customers and targeted prospects are already buying.

- Choose companies that commit to paying commissions and incentives quickly and that allow you to continue earning commissions on recurring monthly fees (such as subscription and membership renewals).

- Look for programs that provide marketing tools and other resources (e.g.banner ads, articles, promotional e-mails, etc.).

Using Affiliates to Sell Your Products

You can also set up your own affiliate program so others can market your products and services for you. You'll first need to set up processes for managing the program. Once you choose and purchase your affiliate management system you'll be ready to recruit, pay and reward your affiliates. Here are three simple steps for getting this accomplished.

Step One: Define Your Program

Decide how much you will pay people for making sales of your product or service. Your affiliate program must be appealing to prospective affiliates and competitive with others in the marketplace. Therefore, you should offer them no less than what I advised affiliates to look for in the preceding section on becoming an affiliate.

Step Two: Recruit Affiliates

You'll need a process for recruiting new affiliates. Here are some suggestions:

- Place an affiliate program sign-up link in a prominent location on your Web site.

- Invite, via e-mail, current business contacts to become affiliates.

- Promote your affiliate program through your e-zine, teleseminars, joint venture arrangements, etc.

Step 3: Reward Affiliates

When affiliates make sales of your products or services, pay them promptly and consistently. Consider hosting competitions with prizes for the top sellers. Finally, take good care of your "super affiliates"—people who consistently sell your products at a higher than average volume—or they'll go elsewhere.

Remember, Guerrilla Marketing experts know how to market with time, energy, and imagination instead of large budgets, and this makes them ideal candidates to establish or join an affiliate program. You can find simple and affordable ways to automate your affiliate program at: www.OnlineMarketingSuperstore.com.

Living My Dreams

I decided on the Guerrilla Marketing brand as my first venture partnership, I had no way of knowing that it would propel me—and so many of my coaching clients—to a life of financial freedom. But my success wasn't by luck or chance—far from it. It was by systematically applying Guerrilla Marketing, as well as my psychology instincts and creative passions, to strategic partnerships and quality programs.

To me, the ultimate Guerrilla outcome is that, through my programs, everyone wins. As I created multiple streams of income on the Internet and automated it to minimize my workweek, I simultaneously created a system to teach others how to repeat my success. And I did it all using time, energy, and imagination instead of limitless budgets.

In true Guerrilla form, I'll continue to ask myself what else my clients need. And I'll find creative, new ways to place the amazing entrepreneurial power of Guerrilla Marketing and the Internet into the hands of the next wave of Guerrilla Marketers on the front lines.

About Mitch Meyerson

Mitch Meyerson is a coach, consultant and speaker. He is author of six personal and business development books published in twenty-four languages, and he has been a featured expert on the Oprah Winfrey *show. To find more about his online programs and his upcoming books on online marketing, visit* **www.MitchMeyerson.com**.

CHAPTER 32

GUERRILLA MEMBERSHIPS
The Power of Internet Membership Programs

Travis Greenlee

> *"People rarely succeed unless they have fun in what they are doing."*
> ~Dale Carnegie

Imagine building a revenue stream that dumps cash into your bank account month after month, year after year while reducing your work load. What could you do with that kind of money? Provide financial security for your family, work fewer hours and play a bigger game? Take twelve weeks of vacation a year? The possibilities are endless.

When it comes to creating massive wealth, Guerrilla Marketers need to know about an insider secret in Internet Marketing. It rests in the power, simplicity and incredible leverage found within membership programs, or, as they are referred to in Internet marketing terms: membership sites.

The Power of a Membership Site

Essentially, a membership site is when anyone pays to access information you publish in a password protected area on your site. You can offer exclusive articles, information, or even a service (like software, games, e-books, or music). People are willing to pay for online content. In fact, the "Online Publishers Association" revealed that pay-for content is emerging as a hot revenue model. And while they are relatively new, with less than 9 percent of online users currently paying for online content. This means the market is wide open for the savvy entrepreneur.

Did you know that among all the existing Internet Business Models online, membership sites are often perceived to be of higher value as compared to other kinds of viable business models? In fact, paying for content in the year 2007 was more than five times what it was in 2006. That's a whopping 500 percent growth! Those who capture the market first in their niche will have the obvious advantage. And since the whole world is your marketplace, anyone can play!

You can take your hobby, specialized knowledge, or profession and turn it into an incredibly profitable membership site almost overnight. You can make mounds of residual income from your membership site by charging a periodical fee (i.e. monthly, annually) for your members to subscribe to your membership service.

You can easily prove your credibility and expertise to your members through creative use of membership sites. With your reputation built among your members, you can instill a positive influence over your members when it comes to sharing an expert opinion, referring an affiliate product, or even buying more from you! Joint Venture proposals and exclusive business opportunities will come flooding your way, so you can have the luxury of picking and choosing who to work with, since other marketers now value your influence and marketing power.

Common membership programs can range from a simple fan club to an online learning environment, including a private forum where members can meet, interact, and mastermind. Using the power of the Internet, membership programs provide a friendly and accessible forum to hundreds if not thousands of people all over the world.

For example:

- **Local or "hometown" memberships:** Groups with a common interest get together. They may never meet, but they *can* come together because of the Internet. You can set up membership sites for Harley Davidson Motorcycle owners, for example, or for people who own those cute little Pug dogs, or Texas Hold'em Poker players, just to name a few.

- **Business Member community:** members connect with one another and "talk shop." These membership sites help interested business owners, much like you, get tried and true information that can shorten the learning curve for what works and what doesn't saving time and money.

- **Get information, motivation, and inspiration—fast!** Find mentors and form a brain trust of peers and advisors, creating your own inner circle or think tank. Network and form supportive relationships that extend far beyond the reaches of geographic boundaries, like home-based business owners from all over the world.

Membership fees

Think about having three hundred members pay you $47 a month. Now think about that over the course of a year. Or, what about hand-picking fifty of those three hundred members and allow them to become "platinum level" members and pay you $250 a month. Let's do the math:

Members	Fee	Monthly	Annually
250	$47	$11,750	$141,000 USD
50 Platinum	$250	$12,500	$150,000 USD
Total		$24,250	$291,000 USD

Looks like creating a membership or subscription Web site is a real no brainer—right? I thought so!

Getting Started

A membership site is a Web site that only allows private members to access the resources, strategies, tools and secrets inside. Most of these sites charge a fee (usually monthly) to access the materials. Membership sites often offer premium information that you can't find elsewhere, providing each member with exactly what they need in terms of coaching, education, and support.

Following Guerrilla Marketing principals and the success secrets of the top online marketing professionals, it is critical that you create a business plan for your site and do the research up front to determine if this strategy will be a viable profit center for your business and how you'll integrate it into your current business model.

A vital piece of advice: Don't go it alone! This is no time to be the Lone Ranger. Find a coach or membership site expert that will take you by the hand through design, development, implementation, and ongoing management.

Finding the right niche and proper planning is the key to your overall success. Having a clear and concise plan will save you hours of time, tons of money, and lots of head aches.

Preparing to Launch Your Program

Some tips to keep in mind, as you prepare to launch your own membership program are:

- Pick a niche market with which you have some experience and credibility. Your audience is paying for your expertise and insight. Talk to and survey members of your target market to evaluate their enthusiasm, excitement and specific needs. You may learn that they'd prefer your content delivered via many mediums such as video, audio, or newsletters in the mail.

- Determine the size of your market:

- How competitive is it?

- How does your pricing compare?

- How will your prospects find you?

- What will be their incentive for joining?

- What sets you apart and makes you different from others offering a similar product or service?

- Is the information you're providing readily available offline? If it is, people may not be willing to pay a monthly or yearly membership fee to access the information.

Don't think of a membership subscription Web site as a "get rich quick" effort. Depending on how much content you already have, it will take some time for you to develop and launch your site. However, unlike writing a course or book, which requires long hours of intensive research, outlining, writing, editing (and banging your head against your monitor every now and then) membership programs don't require long, drawn-out material.

Automation

One of the most common ways to automate your marketing efforts in today's ultra competitive and noise polluted world is to take advantage of the most recent advancements in technology to leverage and simplify your program.

For instance, in our mastermind coaching club, www.MasterBusiness BuildingClub.com, we use auto-responder programs to distribute content to our members in predefined sequences allowing us to communicate more simply and effectively. We use our online shopping cart system to accept payments automatically, deliver products by e-mail or download, track and measure marketing campaign results, manage affiliate programs, and much more.

Guerrilla Marketers understand how critical it is to maintain ongoing rapport using interactive communication systems to build credibility and constant value for their members. The system we use to automate the entire process is: www.PracticeBuilderCarts.com. As an Internet marketing and business development expert, I simply love the comprehensive tools and resources provided within this system.

The Sales Page

Setting up a membership site, like anything else that you're selling, requires a pitch, and every good pitch needs good copy. Guerrilla Marketers understand the importance of great copy in all aspects of your launch and the sales page for your membership site is no exception. There is nothing worse than spending all your time and effort doing a great launch just to have your sales page let you down. Good sales copy is part of a successful launch process and should not be neglected—every piece of the puzzle augments the other—so don't neglect your copy. Good copy will increase your conversion rate dramatically. It's as simple as that, so be sure to spend some quality time getting it right.

The Launch

During pre-launch and launch, Guerrilla Marketers use the marketing channels and relationships they have established to build buzz about the membership program they are about to release. Two elements play a crucial part of the launch process: affiliate partners and a low- or no-cost, high-perceived value.

An affiliate partner program is a powerful resource used by Guerrilla Marketers to generate massive traffic and high quality prospects to their membership sites. Affiliates are partners who use their influence and preeminence to reinforce the value of your product or service with people they know and care about. In Chapter 31, in this section on Guerrilla Marketing on the Internet, you can learn how to set up and manage this valuable resource.

Low or no cost, high perceived value is derived from sharing a sample of the product, training materials and content found within your membership site. Guerrilla Marketing teaches this critical concept as part of "The Marketing Funnel." Introduced in the previous chapter on Internet marketing, this concept is a powerful marketing tool geared toward providing an easy way for your potential members to experience your program before making the commitment to becoming a paying member. Typically, the more you deliver in low or no cost, high perceived value, the more inclined your prospects will be to join your membership program.

In terms of providing free, high perceived value, video training has certainly become the tool of choice for recent online product launches. With the explosive growth of online video- YouTube, GoogleVideo, and others, using programs like Camtasia and Articulate Presenter makes video production and distribution very simple. By simply grabbing a video camera like www.flipvideo.com and sharing your most exciting information about your program, you will instantly connect with your best prospects and begin to build long term, quality relationships.

The possibilities to build your membership program using video are literally endless. In our www.MasterBusinessBuildingClub.com we use video to share testimonials and case studies, provide "insider" sample tours of our private members area, view training videos, and so much more. We've even developed a system that allows our members to download training videos directly into their iPods to take on the road with them. How cool is that?

Attrition

Attrition is simply the fancy word for people leaving your program. Attrition is going to happen, but if you think your attrition rate is too high, check your assumptions as to why this is and get feedback from your members. This is one of the best ways to get a feel for what might be the cause of attrition with your membership. When you know what is causing it, you can then decide the best way to combat it. Test different responses until you settle on an acceptable attrition rate (what is acceptable is up to you, but obviously your profit margin plays a big part in that decision).

A common cause for attrition is a need to filter members. Sometimes due to the nature of the product or service you offer and the way you market it, you attract a large quantity of people who are not quite the right target market, so you can never truly satisfy them no matter what you change. However, if you also hit a lot of members who absolutely love what you provide, it becomes a matter of slowly filtering until you isolate only the perfect customers for what you offer and accept that a large chunk of people will quit your program.

Moving Forward

Keeping members interested and involved means keeping your members! If they are involved in your forum and visiting your site regularly, they are more likely to continue to subscribe. A newsletter, RSS feeds, downloads, and a schedule of upcoming events can all help you hold onto members. Those members, in turn, are more likely to refer their friends.

Savvy small business owners, entrepreneurs, and service professionals have caught on and use membership programs to leverage their time, energy, and expertise while creating an extremely lucrative profit center for their business. They are learning that a major secret to success is to offer products and services on a continual basis to your valued customers keeping them happy and hungry for more.

So in true Guerrilla form, you must continue to ask yourself: what else do your clients need and find creative? In order to apply the truly amazing entrepreneurial power of Guerrilla Marketing to your business, you need to constantly be asking yourself what else do your clients need and find creative. Membership sites can provide so much service and value to your clients while giving so much back to you. That's truly a win-win situation.

About Travis Greenlee

Travis Greenlee is one of the most respected and sought after Internet marketing and business development consultants in the industry. He specializes in teaching small business owners, entrepreneurs, and service professionals to leverage the power of technology to automate, simplify, and rapidly increase their bottom line. To learn more about building a fully automated, highly successful business visit: ***www.MasterBusinessBuildingClub.com****.*

CHAPTER 33

GUERRILLA MARKETING 2.0 ON THE WEB

The New Rules of Internet Promotion

Bob Baker

> *"Innovation distinguishes between a leader and a follower."*
>
> ~Dale Carnegie

More than a billion people around the planet now have Internet access. That's a lot of people and a lot of opportunities at your fingertips. It can also be bewildering, as the number of new Web sites and the variety of online tools continue to grow at dizzying rates. Just when you get a handle on how to promote yourself effectively with existing web-based tools, something new comes along to cloud your vision and fill up your to-do list.

What's a guerrilla marketer to do? Don't despair. In this chapter, I'll give you a crash course on the most important things you need to know about marketing your product, your service, and yourself on the Internet today.

Grabbing the New Economy by the Tail

The first thing I recommend you do is read Chris Anderson's book, *The Long Tail: Why the Future of Business Is Selling Less of More*. It's a real eye-opener, because in it he writes at length about the changing face of commerce in the Internet age. Anderson devotes a lot of space in the book to examining the entertainment industries, but these principles apply to anyone in any field—especially those with a true guerrilla attitude.

Here's a summary of the Long Tail concept with my own spin on it: for decades, we lived in a scarcity economy. We got introduced to new music, books and films via retail outlets, radio, TV and print publications. But all of these avenues of exposure had physical limitations. There was only so much shelf space, air time and editorial pages to fill. So to appeal to the widest audience and turn a profit, only those things that were determined to be the most popular were stocked or covered.

This lead to a lopsided cultural mentality: A person, product or service was either a big hit or a giant dud. There was little ground in between the two extremes of popularity. You were either part of the system—or an outsider.

Then came online retailers such as Amazon and Netflix, which were not constrained by the physical space limitations of traditional sellers. For example, the average Borders bookstore carries about one hundred thousand titles, while Amazon offers nearly four million books. The average Blockbuster store carries about three thousand DVDs, while Netflix offers more than sixty thousand. The average Wal-Mart carries about forty-five hundred music CDs, while the online music subscription service Rhapsody offers more than one-and-one-half million individual song selections.

And guess what? About 25 percent of the total revenues on Amazon and Netflix come from products not available in retail stores. On Rhapsody, that figure is about 40 percent. Yes, that means from titles outside the "hit list." Anderson's overwhelming research concludes that, when given unlimited choice (along with the ability to filter through the choices), people will stray from hits and big brand names and spend a good chunk of change on non-mainstream products.

I may be using books, movies and music as examples here, but the same concept applies to everything from handbags and laundry detergent to dry cleaners and accounting services.

Good News for Guerrilla Marketers—and Bad News

This new trend is a great thing for creative marketers and small business people like you. Unfortunately, the old scarcity business model is so ingrained in our culture, it has lead to many unfounded beliefs that continue to this day, such as:

- If it isn't a hit, it's a miss.

- The only true success is mass success.

- Low-selling = low-quality.

- If it were good, it would be more popular.

Luckily, a growing number of creative entrepreneurs are figuring out ways to make the most of this new "abundance economy," where practically everything is available to the public, where the cream rises to the top based on what consumers actually want, and where you can make an impact (and a living) without ever ranking on the *New York Times* Bestseller list or the *Fortune* 500.

So what kind of world do you want to live in? One of scarcity, hits and *misses*? Or one of abundance, hits and *niches*? As a true guerrilla, the choice is ultimately up to you.

The Age of the Empowered Consumer

Another big change the Internet has brought involves the evolution of the tech-savvy, modern consumer. This is crucial to your future success, so read carefully.

Old-school Business Model

Back in the day, corporations would determine who the ideal audience was for a given product or service. Then they would hunt down those specific types of customers via targeted radio stations, magazines, TV shows, retail outlets, etc.

As I mentioned earlier, consumers had limited ways of gaining access to new products in the marketplace, so they relied on commercial, programmed media sources to filter new things to them. Sure, some adventurous individuals made the extra effort to dig for specialized stuff via alternative sources such as mail order catalogs, fringe magazines, word of mouth, etc. But most people weren't willing to work that hard to discover new things.

So consumers were mostly prey—reactive to the efforts major corporations made to track them down and feed them the latest music, books, shampoo, deodorant, and more. That's where the term "target marketing" comes from. You aim your marketing message at your prey and fire away.

New-School Business Landscape

Today consumers are in control. They rely less and less on programmed, corporate-sponsored media sources and are finding it easier than ever to discover new things on their own. Using an iPod, MySpace, satellite radio, Internet downloads, podcasts, TiVo and more, members of the digital generation are determining what they want to hear, see, do and use, and just as important *how* and *when* they hear, see, do and use them.

The Hunted Become the Hunters

Consumers who in the past were primarily hunted down by big business have now become proactive hunters, empowered to seek out the products and services that are best suited for them. This shift has thrown the creation, promotion and distribution of practically everything into a tailspin. And that's one of the biggest lessons we all need to learn from this. For years I've preached about "self-empowerment" and how entrepreneurs should take their careers into their own hands. But what needs to be equally stressed is the huge movement toward "consumer empowerment."

Buyers today don't respond very well to being "marketed to" in the traditional ways. However, they are more passionate than ever about discovering new things that interest them. It's just that now a growing number of people prefer to discover things on their own, through the recommendation of a friend, from a trusted blogger or podcaster, or on Web sites like MySpace and YouTube.

As a self-empowered guerrilla marketer, what should you do in this environment? You should still understand who your ideal customer is and actively seek them out. Simultaneously, you need to put yourself in the best position to be "discovered" by a curious consumer searching for the very type of service you offer the world.

Key Lesson: The best way to promote yourself online in today's environment is to think outside the box of your own personal Web site. Yes, you want to use your own domain name as a home base to which you steer potential buyers. In addition, it's vitally important that you leave traces of yourself all over the Internet so your prospects can find you.

That's why you need to establish a small presence in all the places where your target customers congregate online. Get set up on MySpace and YouTube. Publish a blog, a podcast and video content. Post your own online press releases that get picked up by news site feeds. In short, give people an easy way to find you online and a reason to talk about you once they do.

Why Consumers Need Filters

In the old scarcity economy model, the items that got stocked in stores and covered in the press were determined by what Chris Anderson calls "pre-filters." They include corporate product development people, retail store managers, radio station program directors, TV show producers, magazine editors, etc.

Actually, these pre-filters are still very much a force today but, as I'll show in a moment, their power is dwindling. So it's this small elite group that decides what is worthy of entering the corporate pipeline. Their decisions are made in two ways:

- They produce, stock, broadcast and cover more of what has already proven itself popular, giving the general public more of what it seems to want.

- Of the new products that come out every month, the pre-filters predict what they think will be popular (in addition to giving prime retail placement to companies and distributors that pay for it).

Again, this system led to the black and white "hit or miss" mentality of the past several decades. The good news is that the Internet and digital technologies have created an open economy where everything and everybody have equal access to the marketplace. The only problem is, the online world is flooded with products and noise of all kinds. It would be easy for consumers to become overwhelmed and confused by all the choices.

That's where "post-filters" come in. Consumers who search online for things they need don't have to wade through everything to find the gems. They simply use some new tools and trusted sources to help them sort through it all.

Here are just some of the post-filters that consumers use today to find new stuff to spend their money on:

- **Friends**: Personal recommendations from familiar people will always be the leading way that consumers discover new music, restaurants, clothing, service providers, and more.

- **Customer reviews**: Being able to read what other people think of a given book on Amazon.com or an appliance on Epinions.com influences a lot of purchase decisions.

- **Popularity lists**: They come in all shapes and sizes online: top sellers, most discussed, highest rated, most downloaded, etc.

- **Blogs and podcasts**: The new niche tastemakers are bloggers and podcasters who cater to narrow audiences.

- **Genre-specific resources**: From AllHipHop.com and HarryPotter Fans.com to HotAirBallooning.com and CheapBowlingBalls.com, people gather where their main interests are addressed.

- **Search**: When in doubt, users "Google" their favorite keywords and see what comes up.

Your job as a guerrilla marketer is to tap into these sources. To make the best use of post-filters, do the following things:

- Encourage your current customers to share your Web site address or your free tip-filled e-book with their friends—and make it easy to do so.

- When a customer sends you a glowing e-mail about your product, ask them to post their comments as a review on Amazon or Epinions or on their blog, if they publish one.

- Ask your entire mailing list to go to a certain site on the same day and vote you to the top of one of the popularity charts.

- Search for the terms your customers use to find products or services like yours, then try to gain exposure through the top sites you find.

These are just some of the new rules of Internet music marketing, but they're the most important ones. Focus on them and you will see more results, more customers, and more money.

MySpace, YouTube and the Social Media Revolution

Is your head spinning with thoughts of MySpace, YouTube, Technorati, Del.icio.us, Digg and all these new "social media" and "Web 2.0" Web sites? Well, relax. Because, believe it or not, all of these new Internet tools aren't so mysterious after all.

When it comes to technological advances, you must remember one thing: Your focus should *not* be on the tools and gadgets themselves. Your attention must stay on what's powering all of these electronic and digital systems. No, it's not electricity. What's really running the show is—people. That's right. Plain old human beings.

So wrapping your head around "social media" all boils down to understanding people. Human beings are social creatures, always have been. For generations, people have gathered in groups: The tribe, the town square, the corner bar, the family reunion, the gang at work, the sports team, the church picnic, you name it.

What's Really Going on Under the Hood?

Humans have a primal need to be around and communicate with other people—especially with people who share their outlook, interests and values. It's easy to get bogged down with ever-changing tech tools and file formats, but when you look under the hood, you'll see something that never changes: human nature at work.

Insight: Think of our basic need to communicate as a body of water. It flows when and where it can. Blogs, podcasts and video streams are simply the latest tools that allow people to express themselves and make connections with others. Ideas flow regardless, but technology gives people more powerful options to deliver their messages to other humans.

Tagging: A Way to Sort Through the Noise

There are more people surfing the Web and more stuff available to read, hear and see than ever before. As you know, it's a crowded, noisy Internet. So how do people find the things that are most relevant to them? Of course, the post-filters discussed earlier and search sites like Google are some of the most common ways that consumers discover things. But a growing method people are using to filter through the clutter is something called "tagging."

If you've ever used Web sites like Flickr, YouTube or Del.icio.us, you may already be familiar with tagging. It takes place when someone posts a new photo, video or favorite link on one of these sites and then gives it a descriptive "tag," one or more words that describe what it is. For instance, if you publish a picture on Flickr taken during your trip to the Grand Canyon, you might give it tags such as "Grand Canyon, Arizona, vacation, hiking."

The important thing about tags on most of these social media sites is this: You aren't the only one who can see and use your tags. Anyone who visits Flickr can search the entire site for photos tagged "Grand Canyon" or "hiking." And you can quickly find out who else is posting Grand Canyon photos too. This allows you to find other people with similar interests and for them to find you. It's online interaction on the most personal level.

Key lesson: The best way to use tagging to promote yourself is to think about the words your prospects use most when searching for stuff online. You can load up your tags with references to what you offer, such as "car repair, auto repair, oil change, tune up." Or descriptions based on how your product might be used or how it makes people feel, such as "lose weight, increase energy, feel great."

I'll cover some of the individual tagging sites later in this chapter. But for now, just be aware of this potent method to reach your ideal customers online.

The Giants of Social Media

As I've mentioned, so many new Web sites and technologies are popping up on the Internet, it's hard to keep up with them. Many new sites and services arrive in a flash with great fanfare—and then dissolve quickly or die a slow death. (Remember the heyday of the original Napster and Pets.com?) But a few of them stick around for the long haul.

In recent years, two sites in particular have made undeniable seismic (and seemingly permanent) splashes both online and off. Even if you've never been near a computer, you've certainly heard of MySpace and YouTube. There's no ignoring them. With many millions of users and visitors—not to mention buzz and media attention out the wazoo—MySpace and YouTube are the undisputed kings of the Web 2.0 world, a new stage of Internet evolution where community and interactivity rule.

Key thing to note: Most of the content on these sites is user-generated. Think about it. Every profile on MySpace and every video on YouTube is created and/or uploaded by users. In earlier days, a Web site had to bulk up on news, books, music or some other kind of owner-created content to attract web traffic. But now, whether you're talking about eBay, CraigsList, Flickr or Match.com, what draws people in is all the other people posting their stuff on these sites.

With all of this interacting going on, shouldn't you be tapping into the flow? Of course. Here's a rundown of the major social media Web sites you should consider using to reach more customers and market yourself better:

MySpace.com

Meet the undisputed heavyweight champ of social networking sites. By the time you read this, MySpace could have five hundred gazillion registered users—who knows? But one thing is for sure: As of this writing, it is the most traveled online destination where creativity and expression reign supreme. Don't kid yourself and think that only teenagers and rock bands use this site. As its popularity has grown, the age of the average MySpace user is now about (according to stat-tracking company ComScore), with more than 40 percent of the site's two-hundred-million-plus users in the thirty-five to fifty-four age range. That's not kid stuff.

Here's how it works: It's as if each MySpace user has his or her own private club of special friends who share similar interests. Once you've been approved as someone's official friend, you get access to their entire network of friends. And each of those friends has a network of friends. So when it comes to social "business networking," if you can get a few excited people talking about you, word can spread to thousands fast.

Three ways to use MySpace effectively:

- **Sign up for a MySpace Music account, even if you aren't a musician.** An artist account gives you special features that a regular account simply doesn't, such as a streaming audio player, an event calendar, a blog, and more. A music page gives you more bells and whistles to use to market yourself guerrilla-style. So when you register for a MySpace account, go to the Music section and click on Artist Signup. Plus, you just might develop a following of groupies who will treat you like a rock star!

- **Don't make people dizzy with bad design.** One of the great things about MySpace is the freedom the site gives users to manipulate the layout of their profile pages. The big drawback is that many people simply don't have good design skills. That explains why you see so many horrid profile pages on MySpace that are bloated with heavy graphics, multimedia, and contrasting colors that make reading the text nearly impossible. Don't do this! Err on the side of simplicity.

■ **Be prepared to put in the time**. To make the most of MySpace, you can't just throw up a profile page, let it sit, and expect it to work miracles. It's called "social networking," which means you have to be *social* and *network* with other people. Therefore, allot time every day (or at least a few times a week) to responding to comments, messages and friend requests. Be proactive and seek out users who have interests that are in alignment with the product or service you offer. Send them friend requests and messages. Also, update your profile regularly, upload and embed video clips, and check out other MySpace areas such as Groups, Forums, etc.

Here are a few other popular social networking sites to consider: LinkedIn.com, Facebook.com, Friendster.com, Ning.com, Bebo.com, Topix.com and Xanga.com.

YouTube.com

At first, the Internet was primarily a text-based medium. Then high-speed access and the MP3 and Flash formats made audio commonplace online. It was only a matter of time before video caught up. There are now an endless number of video sites across the Web. But the granddaddy of them all is YouTube.com, which at last count was serving up some one hundred million videos a day to its users.

Here's how it works: Once you register for a free YouTube account, you can upload video clips of ten minutes or less in a variety of formats. The site then converts them to a streaming format that you and your customers can view on the YouTube site itself or embedded into your own Web site. There's a lot of competition for attention on the site, but many videos rise to the top and are seen by millions of people.

Here are three ways to make the most of YouTube:

■ **Don't let a small budget stop you**. If you're sweating because you think a promotional video has to be a big-budget extravaganza, splash some cold water on your face right now. In this new era, it's more about the idea behind the visuals than it is the production quality. Granted, it helps to have a nice camera and editing software (and the chops to use them tastefully). But many people have received widespread exposure using only a $50 web cam on their home computer.

- **Think outside the format box.** On YouTube and other similar sites, videos come in many different forms. It can be as simple as a single-camera shot of you speaking in your living room or on a stage, or as complex as a documentary or traditional music video. Record interviews with your best customers or shoot footage of you in action. Product demonstrations, commercial parodies, addressing a heartfelt issue related to your business identity—it's all fair game, as long as you're using video to share some part of yourself with your prospects and customers.

- **Develop your YouTube profile page.** Like MySpace and other sites, YouTube allows you to design a profile page that contains links to all of your videos, a short bio, and a link to your personal Web site. Also, people can subscribe to your "channel" and get updates whenever you post new video content. You want to encourage this connection. And while you're at it, subscribe to and leave comments on other YouTubers' profile pages, which will cause your name to appear on their pages.

Other video sites to consider: Google Video, Joost.com, Revver.com, DailyMotion.com, Jumpcut.com, Stickam.com. Here are seven more Web 2.0 sites you should know about and consider using as part of your Guerrilla Marketing arsenal:

Technorati.com

This site tracks and organizes what's being talked about on millions of blogs across the Web. It also sorts through other forms of user-generated content (including photos, videos, voting, etc.), which it refers to as "citizen media." Technorati is the place to go to discover the most popular social media sites, tags and topics.

How to use it: Search Technorati to find the blogs that are covering your industry and businesses similar to yours. Then contact the individual bloggers and start a relationship with them. If you publish a blog of your own, be sure to sign up for a free Technorati account and register your blog. Doing so will help other people find you easier.

Del.icio.us

This online destination is the premier site for "social bookmarking." It's designed to be a one-stop site to store links to your favorite articles, blogs, music, reviews, and more, and you can access them from any computer on the Web. You organize bookmarks on Del.icio.us using descriptive tags (mentioned earlier).

How to use it: As you do with Technorati, you can search Del.icio.us by topic and tags. If you offer cooking advice that appeals to fans of Rachel Ray, for example, you could search the site for all bookmarks tagged "Rachel Ray." This could uncover a lot of new promotion sources. Also, if you start your own Del.icio.us account and store your bookmarks there, other surfers may find you based on the tags you use for your own links.

Flickr.com

When it comes to places that store and share still photos on the Web, Flickr is king of the heap. Millions of people post and tag their images on this mega site. From animals and architecture to water and weddings, you'll find it here. Now owned by Yahoo, Flickr has free and paid accounts with different feature levels.

How to use it: The primary way to use Flickr is to show yourself in action. Your product or service should speak for itself, but offering visual images that your customers and supporters can enjoy adds another layer of credibility to your career. Post photos of you with your customers, in the office, and on the road. Capture the interesting things you encounter along your journeys and share them with others.

Digg.com

Digg describes itself as "a user-driven social content Web site." What does that mean? The site's "about us" page explains: "Everything on Digg is submitted by our community (that would be you). After you submit content, other people read your submission and Digg what they like best." Digg in this context means vote. If your submission receives enough favorable "diggs," it may be promoted to the front page for millions of visitors to see.

How to use it: Digg has three categories: news, videos and podcasts. If you have created or were featured in an interesting article, video or podcast, register with Digg and submit a link to and description of the item. Then ask your friends and customers to "digg" it. The more diggs you get, the higher your item rises on Digg's pages, which means more people will find out about you.

Twitter.com

This is a social media site that allows users to send short, 140-character messages to mobile phones or instant message applications. According to the site, Twitter exists to help its users answer that probing question, "What are you doing?" Users then share their bite-size messages with whomever signs up to receive them.

How to use it: Most people do indeed use Twitter to let people know what they're doing—*everything* they're doing! Common messages report such meaningful activities as "Stopping to get gas and buy a pack of cigs" or "It's raining outside and I'm bored." These are unproductive time-wasters. On the other hand, one restaurant in Buffalo, NY, twitters its Daily Special to everyone who subscribes to its feed. Now that's useful. Mashable.com sends a headline and link for each of its new blog posts. That's smart. A financial advisor could send a money-making tip of the week. If you're going to use a site like Twitter, you may as well use it to your Guerrilla Marketing advantage.

SecondLife.com

Millions of people have been flocking to this virtual reality playground. Second Life is "a 3-D online digital world imagined, created and owned by its residents." Each user creates an avatar, which represents his or her persona in the virtual world. Once created, your avatar can visit dance clubs, casinos, shopping malls, vampire castles, movie theaters, and more. You can even spend and make money (called Linden Dollars) and buy and sell real estate.

How to use it: Second Life operates very much like the real world, with people offering goods and services in the virtual fantasyland. You can open a nightclub, sell hand-crafted jewelry, become a graphic artist or publicist or put on live music concerts and charge admission, sell merchandise for Linden Dollars (which can be exchanged for very real money), and much more.

CraigsList.com

This bare-bones site has become the free classified ad supermarket of the world. Founded by Craig Newmark in 1995 as a job-posting site in San Francisco, CraigsList now serves up ads and forums in 450 cities worldwide.

How to use it: You can use CraigsList for a number of purposes. There are well-read "For Sale" and "Services" sections where you can post announcements of what you have to offer. Promote your live events in the Events area. If you need a new sales rep, post an ad in the Jobs section. All for free!

*****

As you can see, along with Internet growth and technological advances come opportunities. As an open-minded guerrilla marketer, it's your job to examine all of the current tools available online (along with new ones that keep popping up) and figure out the best ways to use them to promote yourself to the world.

About Bob Baker

Bob Baker is a widely hailed music marketing expert, author, and musician dedicated to showing creative people of all kinds how to get exposure, connect with fans, and increase their incomes. He is the author of Guerrilla Music Marketing Handbook, *a book that has become the "Bible" of music marketing, so much so that it made a cameo appearance in the major motion picture* The School of Rock, *starring Jack Black. He has published several other successful books, including* MySpace Music Marketing, Unleash the Artist Within, *and* Branding Yourself Online. *Find out more about Bob at www.theBuzzFactor.com or at **www.Bob-Baker.com**.*

CHAPTER 34

GUERRILLA TRAFFIC

A Dozen Fun & Free Ways to Get More Web Traffic Now

Dearl Miller

> *"You must look within for value but must look beyond for perspective."*
> ~Lord Chesterfield

I've spent the last ten years researching and developing hundreds of innovative and unique ways to drive more traffic to your Web site and then learning how to turn all those visitors into happy, satisfied, profitable customers. I've tested, tracked and tweaked every possible web traffic tactic imaginable. And from all that time I can tell you one thing: free and low-cost "Guerrilla" traffic tactics are my favorite.

Guerrilla Traffic is all about innovation and creativity. It's finding better, faster, lower-cost ways to do the exact thing everyone else said was impossible. It's using your smaller size and cleaver wit to out think and out maneuver even the biggest competition.

And most of all, it's about having *f-u-n*!

I could sit here and list off 250 free or low-cost traffic tactics. And then I could easily give you another hundred innovative web marketing techniques. *But* that's not Guerrilla. Guerrilla is smart. Guerrilla is fast. Guerrilla is action.

So what you're getting here is the best-of-the-best. A dozen fun and free tactics you can apply directly to your site today and get significant, measurable, immediate results.

That's Guerrilla. Guerrilla Traffic.

But First

Before you start using *any* traffic generation tactic, there's one thing you must do first. You *must* know what keywords to use.

Keywords are the words, phrases, and sayings that people use when they want to *buy* your product or service. There are a lot of words you can use to describe what you sell. But there are only a handful of words that customers use when they want to buy now.

To be a Guerrilla is to know the difference between the words that just draw traffic and the words that draw visitors who are ready, able, and willing to purchase your product.

To find the best keywords for my product or service, I always do two things:

- Step One: I compile a high-quality list of popular keywords on my topic.

- Step Two: I determine which keywords attract the visitors who actually make a purchase.

If you are new to marketing online then I cannot emphasize enough the importance of compiling a massive list of "popular" keywords, and pairing them down using real test results. The number one mistake new web marketers make is not knowing which keywords customers *actually use*. We are always surprised to discover that the words we use to explain our product are rarely the same words other people use to describe it. And furthermore, the words we are sure will convert the best often don't convert at all.

Bottom Line: If you want people to find you. you must know the words *they* are using.

To create your own list of popular keywords, simply use one of the free online keyword research tools. I use WordTracker.com (free trial) and KeywordSecret.com ($1 trial). I also recommend using the keyword tools provided by Google and Yahoo (just search for "External Keyword Tool" on Google, or go to http://Inventory.Overture.com).

The next step is to figure out which words are profitable and which ones are not. This is done by driving traffic to your site using the all words on your list, and then using a free tracking tool like GoogleAnalytics.com to reveal exactly which ones generated sales.

But there's a better way. Guerrillas are fast, Guerrillas are nimble, and Guerrillas know exactly where to invest their money in order to get the greatest bang-for-the-buck. This is one of those places.

The best and fastest way to find out which words are studs and which words are duds is to use Pay-Per-Click advertising, such as Google AdWords. Depending on your budget and experience, a good AdWords campaign can sort through all your keywords and determine the profit producing terms in just a matter of days. But no matter how you do it, discovering the best keywords for your product or service could possibly be the best investment (of both time and money) you could ever make.

"Big-Box" businesses use the words their marketing departments come up with. They dictate to the public what things should be called and how things should be said. Guerrilla Marketers know better; we focus on the words our customers are already using.

Once you know the right keywords, then you are ready to start having fun.

Guerrilla Traffic 101: Fun and Free Marketing for Beginners

Hard-core web marketing is about Search Engine Optimization, Pay-Per-Click and Affiliate Programs. Yes, those are all essential pieces of every professional online marketers repertoire, but not all traffic methods are that difficult and expensive. In fact, sometimes Web site promotion can be downright *fun*!

Here are my eight favorite innovative and unique, free or low-cost ways to drive a flood of highly targeted traffic to your Web site very, very quickly. These are the tactics you can use to create a massive amount of traffic, even if you're starting from scratch, have absolutely no budget, and hate everything about marketing.

1. **Blogging**: These are sites set up for you to talk about issues. You post your thoughts on a blog site hourly, daily, weekly, however often you want. They are an excellent way to build community on the Internet because you invite people to your blog to hear what you have to say. Hardcore marketers strip all the fun out of blogging by auto-building all their massive "blog farms." For the rest of us, we can generate just as much traffic while doing something we love by becoming a legitimate member of the Blogosphere.

   Getting started with blogging is extremely easy. Most web hosting companies provide free blogging tools. (If yours doesn't, check out GoDaddy.com or get a free blog from Blogger.com.) All it takes to get traffic immediately is to start writing your own blog posts and interacting with other bloggers in your niche by commenting on theirs.

   You can get even more traffic by submitting your blog to sites like Technorati.com and using automatic blog submissions services such as pingomatic.com or pingoat.com.

   Blogging is one of those tactics that, once you start, you'll discover a whole new world, a world full of high-quality visitors, interested in your niche wanting a solution to the exact problem your product or service solves. The key to effective blogging is to not oversell. Instead simply provide information, interact with prospects and customers, and help them to see that you actually do have the solution they need. When doing this, not only will you drive a flood of traffic to your site, you'll also learn a whole series of invaluable lessons about your niche and new opportunities in your marketplace.

   I could easily write a hundred pages on how to create traffic with blogging. But the bottom line is, just jump in and start doing it today. When it comes to driving highly targeted people to your Web site, nothing compares to posting, commenting, and trackbacks—all simple, fun, and extremely powerful web marketing tactics.

2. **Social Networking**: Another area that pure profiteers suck all the life out of is MySpace, YouTube and the other social networking sites. The purpose of these of sites is to connect with other people, from all across the globe, who are interested in the exact same things you are. Each site has its own unique features, but they're all about sharing, communicating, and interacting with like-minded people no matter where they are.

    Guerrilla Marketers seize any and every opportunity to communicate with a group of people already interested in their niche. They are the perfect prospects for our products and services, and our mission is to find as many creative and innovative ways to communicate the value of our product or service to them as possible. Social Networking sites make this extremely easy by providing a wide assortment of tools designed to help find, communicate, and interact with other members.

    Now some marketers try to "beat-the-system" by using tools that automatically communicate with hundreds or even thousands of other users. Those tactics inevitably backfire. Using tools to help you communicate with other members is good, but having a "bot" program randomly leave pre-written messages for other people is essentially just spam.

    This is too great of a marketing opportunity to waste. Forget all the automated tools; they suck all the fun out of what could be the highlight of your day anyways. Instead just dive in, create your profile, join groups and start building your own massive online friend list.

    By following this strategy you'll have a great time building a large, responsive network, which will generate a serious amount of traffic to your site very, very quickly.

3. **Social Bookmarking:** In almost every case, the key to creating free or low-cost traffic is creating articles, audio and video files, or other content that people interested in your product or service would find exceptionally valuable. But if content is the foundation of good web marketing, then distribution is what gets people's attention.

For sites on a tight budget, social bookmarking is one of the absolute best ways to reach-out and draw high-quality visitors to your site. Just create something truly great to share, then bookmark it using popular social bookmarking sites on the Web like digg.com or del.icio.us.

If fellow members of community like it, they'll bookmark it too. Content with a lot of bookmarks will quickly gain a huge amount of in-bound links, generate a lot of click through traffic, and will rank at the top of the search results on these very popular sites.

In fact, when looking for information, a growing number of people are skipping Google entirely and are now going straight to social sites to perform their searches. Since the search results from Social Bookmarking sites are based on peoples' vote, the quality of the results are much better than anything a machine-based algorithm—the way Google does it—could ever produce.

There is also a networking aspect to social bookmarking sites. You can see everything another user bookmarked. As a result, legions of avid bookmarkers will often follow a hand full of star bookmarkers who are know for always finding the best info online about a particular topic. These "opinion leaders" have the power to literally swamp any site they bookmark with a flood of high-quality traffic. One of your goals as a social bookmarker should be to identify and befriend the star bookmarkers in your niche. And then, ultimately, become one yourself.

Other ways to create even more traffic using Social Bookmarking is to tap into the lists of your current clients and encourage them to bookmark your content. For example, you can post bookmarking links on every webpage or blog post you make. You can encourage your readers to join and bookmark your content if they like it. You can even ask your e-mail list members and MySpace friends to help you out and "digg" it together. If you can coordinate a large number of bookmarks at the same time, you might even make it on to a social networking site's "popular" page, which could yield as many as seventy thousand to one hundred thousand brand new visitors in just one day.

4. **Bonuses and Integration Marketing Tactics**: If another site already has the visitors you want, then find creative ways to get access to it through them. Provide the site with a free bonus to give customers after making a purchase. Write up an extra tip or lesson to include in their auto-responder series. Do a special free teleseminar for their list.

   Another particularly effective technique is inviting an expert with a large list to do an interview for your site. They will naturally want to share the interview (which contains a creative offer for your product) with their list as well. But there's one thing to remember about bonuses: contributing bonuses to paid products is significantly more effective than submitting bonuses to free giveaways. Avoid all those free JV (joint venture) giveaway sites. Yes you'll get people onto your list, but the quality of the traffic is very, very poor. In most cases, giveaway traffic is just a big waste of your time.

5. **Craigslist**: Online classified ad sites like Craigslist.org are one of the biggest untapped sources of high-quality web traffic. They are free, simple to use, and can literally overwhelm your server with traffic. There is quite a bit of trial-and-error involved with writing a good, traffic-pulling classified ad. But there are literally hundreds of free or very low-cost classified ad sites just like Craigslist.org. So once you've gotten your copy down (and it's proven to drive clicks that convert) then just roll it out across the web and sit back, relax, and watch the traffic come flooding it.

6. **Online Market Places:** Most people search the web for information, but people who visit online market places like Amazon.com or eBay are looking to buy. These are the type of people you want to visit your site. Each online market place has their own unique rules and regulations, but in almost every case they are the prefect place to find good prospects for your product or service. So no matter whether you prefer writing reviews or running $1 auctions, whenever you find a large group of buyers in one place, it pays to join the fun.

   Don't overlook the power of this tactic. I've had clients who were running $100,000-a- month Web sites decide to close up shop and focus entirely on auctions and other online market places. Why? Simply because they could make more money, in less time, with less work by going to where the buyers already are. It's the online equivalent of opening up a physical store in a popular shopping mall or high-traffic shopping center.

7. **Comparison Shopping Sites:** A close relative of Online Market Places (and another perfect place to find people who are ready to buy) is comparison shopping sites like Google Base (which use to be called Froogle.com) and BizRate.com. Some are free, others use a pay-per-click pricing model, but all are a great source of targeted web traffic. And don't think that comparison-shopping is about the lowest price. Yes, the money matters, but much more than a consideration of cost goes into the buyer's final decision.

8. **TrafficSwarm, InstantBuzz, and other ways to create traffic doing things you already do anyway:** A Web marketer's life is a busy life. Sites to optimize, links to build, auto-responder messages to write; it's all very time consuming. That's why you must always be looking for ways to create traffic that doesn't cost you any time.

   Time is your most valuable asset, so even if you can't afford to pay for traffic, there are still many ways to promote your site without spending all your time on it. For example, by using InstantBuzz.com you can earn free advertising credits just for visiting your favorite Web sites. And Ad Exchanges like TrafficSwarm.com give free credits when someone leaves your site. Make the most of your resources, always be on the look out for ways to create traffic that doesn't cost either time or money.

Advanced Guerrilla Traffic: For More Fun and Free Traffic Tactics

The first eight Guerrilla traffic tactics are fun and free ways to drive traffic for beginners. But if you're a seasoned web marketer, then here are four more advanced free and low cost ways to drive traffic to your site very, very quickly...

9. **Buy or Partner with sites that already have a lot of traffic**: Does a dead site (a site that is no longer up and running) have a top ten ranking on Google for your most important keyword? Then buy it. In most cases it's cheaper than paying for Google AdWords and a lot easier than trying to beat them by optimizing your own site. You will be shocked at how simple and inexpensive this really is.

    If you can't afford the asking price (or the current owner just won't sell) then partner with them. Simply show the profitless owner how effortlessly they can make a ton of money promoting your products and services on their site. Ideally you want them to join your affiliate program (so you only pay a portion of the sales they actually generate). But if they are resistant, and you are confident in the quality of their traffic, then offer to pay for some ad space. Once you can show exactly how much extra profit they will make as an affiliate, they will jump at the chance to be part of your program.

    Buying or partnering with sites that have the traffic you want could be the single most effective way to create a huge amount of traffic, extremely quickly—and it works in any niche. Most people don't realize that, while top marketers dabble in new-age tactics, at the end of the day, most of their time is spent building marketing partnerships. All of the big, million-dollar-Web-marketing events were and are driven by partnerships with huge, highly targeted e-mail list owners. Believe it or not, that is still the biggest traffic tactic of all.

10. **Mobile Marketing**: Mobile Marketing is the next big thing, and right now it is literally ripe with opportunities for Guerrilla Marketers to seize upon. There are more than 243.4 Million mobile subscribers in the US today (that's 81 percent of the entire population) who send one billion text messages per day—but it seems like no one has figured out how to tap into this massive marketing opportunity yet.

Right now is for Mobile Marketing what 1998 was for the web marketing. It's wide-open for innovative, creative thinkers to make discoveries and blaze new trials. But you don't have to be the next Lewis & Clark to make Mobile Marketing work. By simply offering a mobile-ready version of your Web site and taking advantage of mobile services like Text2Buy, you can open up a whole new world of marketing opportunities.

From SMS Ads (Systems Management Server Ads) to Mobile SEO (Search Engine Optimization) and everything in between, now is the time to leap into this exciting field—before your competition does.

11. **Start Multi-Lingual Marketing**: Though English is a second language for many, an increasing number of web users prefer to communicate online in their own native dialect. In fact, ten of the top twenty-five sites on the web are non-English. There is a whole host of software tools and services designed specifically to properly translate your site, create appropriate imagery and design for non-English speaking visitors, help with foreign-language SEO and guide you to all the other multi-lingual marketing opportunities.

Don't make the mistake of focusing on just Spanish speaking web users. They are a great place to start, but China's growing middle class (137 million Web users) makes them a prime target for your digitally delivered products or services too.

12. **Build an e-mail list** *and* **mail to it at least two to three times a week**: Finally, here is a tactic so fun and so powerful that if you use only one marketing tactic this year, make this one it. Do everything you can to funnel every Web site visitor on to your e-mail list. Sending regular e-mails to your list with links to high-quality content on your site is by far the quickest, easiest, cheapest way to create a massive amount of high-quality web traffic, and if you do it regularly you'll actually enjoy it too!

   The greatest source of traffic is repeat visits. Building your own in-house mailing list is quickest, easiest, most effective way to encourage visitors to come back again and again.

   Yes, building and bonding with your list is something that takes time, but if you want to create your own source of high-quality traffic that you can tap into on-demand, then make time to re-ignite your list building. Or, if you already have a large list, spend time recreating your bond, communicating more often, and better monetizing this asset.

   And don't forget about your customer list. Most marketers are completely negligent about following up with past buyers. That list could be your most valuable possession.

So that's my Dozen Fun and Free Ways to Get More Web Traffic Now:

1. Become a blogger.

2. Build a social network.

3. Encourage bookmarking.

4. Provide bonuses for other people's products and services.

5. Tap into power of CraigsList.

6. Set-up shop in bustling online marketplaces.

7. Get into the comparison shopping searching engines.

8. Spend your time wisely by using sites like TrafficSwarm and InstantBuzz.

9. Buy or partner with sites that already have traffic, ranking or large e-mail lists.

10. Leap into the world of Mobile Marketing.

11. Start speaking the Language of multi-lingual marketing.

12. And finally, build your own in-house e-mail list and create traffic on demand.

By using these twelve ways to promote your site not only will you have more traffic and increased profits, you'll enjoy yourself too! But always remember, no matter which web promotion methods you use, the best way to create traffic is to play by the rules, use tools the way they were intended, and focus on creating high-quality content.

Guerrilla Traffic Bonus Tip

Here's a super-hot bonus traffic tip for you: use Google's Website Optimizer Tool. It's one thing to get visitors to your site. It's a completely different thing to convert all those browsers into to customers. You can have all the traffic in the word, but that doesn't matter if you can't get any of them to buy.

There are many things you can do to optimize and improve your sales process, but it all starts with a firm commitment to testing and tracking your results. Google's Website Optimizer is an extremely to use tool that allows you to make various changes to your site and see exactly how those changes affected sales.

Consider this: One small change to your site has the potential to double or even triple your sales, from exactly the same amount of traffic you already have. That's zero extra money spent on ads, zero extra time spent on traffic, and double or triple your profit. To improve your sales process you should test different headlines, try various price points, experiment with different images and layouts, and even consider completely rewriting all your copy using an entirely different sales pitch.

But the real question is: will these changes actually increase or decrease sales? The only way to find out for sure is to test it and see. The free and easy way to track the results is to use Google's Website Optimizer Tool.

I hope you enjoyed learning my Dozen Fun and Free Ways to Create More Traffic Now. And I'm always on the look out for innovative new traffic tactics to try. So if you have and idea to share, check out http://Trafficology.com/tips. I have a contest running, and you could be a $100 winner.

About Dearl Miller

Dearl Miller is creator of the online traffic company, Trafficology. *He has spent the past ten years helping small businesses, entrepreneurs, and non-profit organizations use the Internet to compete with and triumph over even their biggest competition. Dearl specializes in using "The Science of Web Traffic" to transform money losing sites into million dollar profit centers. He was featured in* Success Secrets of The Online Marketing Superstars. *For more information, visit* **www.OnlineTrafficNow.com**.

CHAPTER 35

GUERRILLA CONVERSION

Take Your Online Leads Off-line and Sky-Rocket Your Profits

Matt Bacak

*"Whatsoever thy hand findeth to do,
do it with all thy might."*
~Ecclesiastes 9:10

A Guerrilla Marketer is many things, but above all, he or she is innovative. A Guerrilla Marketer is very able to look at what other people have done that works, and then model that to fit his or her own business. You take what works and make it happen for you. It's almost intuitive, really.

I'm what's called an Internet marketer. What that means is that I use the Internet as my main marketing tool to sell my products and services. I happen to be one of the best because I'm a firm believer in the old adage, "success leaves clues." Early on in my business ventures, I had the opportunity to meet and talk with a billionaire. I wanted to know what he did to get to that point, and this is what he told me: I needed to have a plan, a short, simple plan for my business. In the course of our conversation, this guy asked me to write my marketing plan on a napkin. He gave me one of those little cocktail napkins and I started to unfold it. I needed a lot of room to show him how my business was laid out. He stopped me quickly and said, no, I needed to be able to put it all on the folded-up napkin. This man truly understood the importance of Guerrilla simplicity.

At that point, I couldn't do it, but as I honed my marketing skills, as I found out what worked and what didn't, I developed a plan that can really fit on that folded cocktail napkin, no problem, because it consists of three steps. In true Guerrilla form, I focused my marketing efforts, and these three simple steps have generated millions—yes, that's right, millions of dollars—and these three simple steps can be modeled to build any business you want! Offline or online, in your basement or in a traditional brick and mortar, these three steps can help you harness to huge marketing power of the Internet so that you, too, can start earning the kind of income that you desire.

The Napkin Marketing Plan

I'm going to shoot straight with you. What I do isn't rocket science. I used to promote other people. I built a hugely successful business that way, actually, but I finally figured out that the really big money was in teaching others to do what I do. I make it simple. I like simple, actually. I've helped a lot of people build their business, and, no surprise, the number one thing that I find each and every one of my clients face is fear—that some old gnawing fear. But it's not a fear of failure. No, it's a fear of *success*. Odd, huh?! So one of my favorite sayings is: "do what you fear and the money will follow." And it is so much easier (like a hundred thousand times easier) to face your fears when you have a simple plan.

And my simple plan, what I can now put on that cocktail napkin is this:

Squeeze page ➔ Free CD ➔ Phone

If you're saying, *that's it* (with perhaps a little bit of skepticism), I understand. But really, *that's it*. That's the way that I make millions of dollars. Every marketer knows that you have to have a list of prospects. In some industries, they call it a "book," in Internet marketing, it's your list, but whatever you call it, it's all the same thing—a database of names of people who are interested in your services. The two previous chapters in this section give you tons of ideas on how to drive traffic to your Web site and thus create your lists so I won't go into the details on how to do that—what I want to show you is how you go about getting those people into your Web site and buying from you.

Part One: The PowerSqueeze Page

It's one thing to get a person to your Web site; it's another problem altogether to get that person to do something once they're there. You basically want anyone who comes to your Web site to do two things: give you their contact information and get them to buy something.

You cannot market anything if you don't have the 'anyone' to market to. In order to sell, you have to have prospects.

In the olden days, before Internet marketing, smart people came up with all sorts of clever ways to get the names and contact information for people who might be interested in their products. These are the "qualified leads" that all marketers seek. The only other way to find prospects was to cold call, and I've met very few people who really like to go this route—it really is the route of last resort.

In my book, *The Ultimate Lead Generation Plan*, I talk about the three different sites that a person needs to set up to run a successful Internet Marketing business. The first type of Web site is what people typically think of as a Web site. What that type of Web site really is, is what I call your branding site. This is the site that *brands* a person. It gives you a business identity. The branding site allows a viewer to learn more about you and what you do. It typically offers a series of pages such as "about us," "products" and any other special information you want your potential clients to know about. If you want an example, visit my branding site: http://www.PowerfulPromoter.com.

Now the second type of site is called the Power Squeeze site. There's also only one outcome that you're looking for and that's to powerfully squeeze information out of the people who are visiting your Web site.

The *whole purpose* of this single webpage is to capture people's name and e-mail address. That's all you need for you to be able to market to that person over and over and over. There's only two ways for you to lose that person's contact information—if you stop selling products or if that person "unsubscribes" from your list. (He or she clicks on a link that will take their e-mail address off of your list.)

This is powerful stuff. The idea and even the name squeeze page has been around since the first fearless marketers tried out that new fangled WorldWideWeb tool back in the late 1980s. I trademarked the name Power Squeeze because I'm the "Powerful Promoter" and it's my twist on the idea of the Squeeze page.

Now, let me repeat this: your Power Squeeze site is the site that is dedicated to getting contact information from people. It isn't the site that your repeat clients will visit. That site is your branding site, and your branding site will always have a different domain name than your Power Squeeze page. My branding site is www.PowerfulPromoter.com. The main squeeze page for my company is www.PromotingTips.com. If I tried to sell from my branding site, I wouldn't sell much because it is an information site, not a selling site. From a sales perspective, realize that a confused mind never buys. Well, when a prospect goes to a branding site and there are tons of little different things to click on, the prospect is going to click away and he or she is never going to reach the outcome that you want them to reach. That's why you want to have specific Web sites for specific purposes.

How to Set Up a PowerSqueeze Site

The PowerSqueeze page actually follows a very specific format. And to make your Power Squeeze page really powerful, you need to have really great copy. Crap copy will get your nowhere fast. There are also two basic types of copy: content copy and the actual sales copy, the copy that makes an offer to the potential customer to buy your product. The Power Squeeze page is basically sales copy but with a twist. You're not getting them to buy something; you're getting them to give you something.

Now, there's some squeeze pages that have practically no copy on them. They give a little bit of information and then there's a place where the prospective customer or client puts in their name and e-mail. Because of these sites, some argue that people are getting smarter about this particular Internet marketing technique. I don't just put a little copy on my Power Squeeze site. I make my standard squeeze page a bit longer—but not too long. I make it one page, and I use it to start educating my clients about what they need and how I can help them and the "squeeze"—the actual place where they give their name and e-mail—is made as an offer.

I'm going to take you through the basic set up of a Power Squeeze page to give you an idea of what an effective squeeze page can do.

The Power Squeeze page starts with a great headline. The headline has one purpose and one purpose only: to get the prospect's undivided attention. What you want your readers to say when they see your headline is, "Wow, I have to get more information," so they keep reading. What they come to next is the sub-headline.

This works much the same as the main headline. It keeps the reader interested and wanting to know more. There's also a bit of content in this headline. In mine, I talk about what I know everyone has—an e-mail account— and because mentioning that will get heads nodding, they'll keep reading.

Now that you have them nodding their head, you get into the meat of the letter. It starts like a letter: "dear friend," and then it goes on to give actual, useful information, stuff that they could use in their business immediately or some benefits to using this product. Benefits, by the way are key in any sales letter. When you think in terms of benefits, you stay "you" centered instead of "me" centered. Your potential clients don't care about you so much as they care about what you can do for them.

Then, as part of the Power Squeeze, I actually offer them something free in return for their information. It's all about exchange, and exchange is important. Have you ever given something, your time or even your thoughts, but you didn't get anything back in return? The people who are looking at your site are giving you something very valuable—their information! So you give them something valuable in return. I give my new potential client a free newsletter when they sign up on my Power Squeeze page. It's something that I do as part of my business and with a smart autoresponder (a piece of software that allows you to automate your e-mail responses to everyone who signs in). It takes no time at all to send out a newsletter to hundreds, thousands, and even hundreds of thousands of people. And a newsletter is a powerful marketing tool, so it's win-win. You get their contact information and thus build your list, and you give them valuable information that they can use in their business, or life, right away.

Once you have them so excited about what they can get from this free newsletter, I give them the close. Once you've captured someone's interest, you must give them something to do. People will follow an action command, and so I tell them exactly what I want them to do: "Just type your First Name and Primary Email Address" and then I tell them, specifically, "then click the "<<Click Here for FREE Signup>>" button below.

Then, I add another command "Do it now!" because you want people to sign up before they have second thoughts—and those second thoughts usually come within seconds of them making the decision to do what you have asked them.

I don't end with the close, however. I make sure that they feel safe. Because of all the hype about identity theft and privacy, I *always* include a "secure and confidential" piece at the bottom of all of my web pages, including the Power Squeeze page. What I put in this section mirrors the concern that people would have at that particular site. On actual sales sites, I put a picture of a lock and text that tells my clients that their credit card information is secure. On the Power Squeeze page, I let my new prospects know that I respect their e-mail privacy.

So that's how you set up a Power Squeeze page.

Now, because this idea has been around for awhile, I know what some of you are thinking: "I don't want to use a squeeze page because it's going to turn people off. They know that they're going to get barraged with e-mails and so won't sign up."

I have one thing to say: that's hog wash. That's not playing to win. That's being scared about marketing, and that is definitely not a hallmark of a Guerrilla Marketer. You have to be an aggressive marketer. You have to be willing to do what has been proven to work, and the squeeze page gets the information that you need. And remember, these people want your information. If you have something that will legitimately help them, make their lives better, easier, or more pleasant, they want what you've got to sell. I think it's un-American not to sell a product that people want. So let them give you their information!

And here's the interesting thing. If you put a Power Squeeze site in front of one of your sales letter pages, you will find what we have tested over and over—*your conversion rate does not change*. (The conversion rate is how many times you can convert a person looking at your site to actually buying from your site.) What this means is that the people who are going to your sales site by way of your squeeze page aren't upset about the process at all. They're still buying!!

The only thing that is changing with a Power Squeeze page is that you are capturing more people's information, so now you have the ability to market to people more and more.

This has been a huge success with all my companies. I do it consistently and I see results. You will see results too!

Part Two: The Free CD and Sales Letter

In the first edition of my first book, *The Ultimate Lead Generation Plan*, I list the three types of Web sites that I used at the time. I say 'at the time' because while I still use all three, I wouldn't list them in the order that I do there, which is: branding site, sales letter site, and Power Squeeze site. In the three years that I spent perfecting my plan, it became crystal clear that the sales letter comes after the Power Squeeze page.

Why? Simple. Once you've captured your prospective client's information, you want to sell them something. But you don't want to look at this person as simply a number in your sale's statistic. You want to begin to develop a relationship with that person. Remember, that's what makes Internet marketing so powerful and so much fun. It isn't just about I the prospect, close the prospect, and move on. All good sales people know that generally people buy from you because they like you. This takes on a whole new meaning on the Internet. With all the new technology available—the Web 2.0 stuff like YouTube and

MySpace—you are able to start having conversations with people from all over the world. People want to know what you're all about. But while the Internet has made ours a global community, it hasn't changed the need for the good old-fashioned sales letter, a letter tells people about you and your product. It is tried, tested, and if you look at the Internet as the new form of direct mail advertising, then the sales letter is true for that venue as well.

So this second step in my plan has two parts to it: having a sellable product—for me that is a free CD for which the customer pays shipping and handling—and fronting that product with a sales letter. Now this is where your marketing efforts have to become intuitive. A free CD works for me because it contains information about a product that I want to sell and it gives me a way to give people some very useful tips on how to market themselves better on the Internet. For some companies, a free video works better and for others, it might be a free book. Whatever the product, it's always free plus shipping and handling.

If you're thinking that that sounds like a sales pitch, it is. The free CD that I offer is actually a recording of a teleseminar that I've held on that particular product, and at the end of the teleseminar, I'm making a pitch to my audience to buy one of my more expensive products that will give them more information on how to market themselves better on the Internet. And something amazing happens when you have someone pay for a free CD.

The Free CD Qualifies Your Leads

After a person has signed up on your Power Squeeze page, I land them on a page that is dedicated solely to selling them a Free CD. I offer them a free CD and then I have them pay a minimal shipping and handling fee: $4.77. Research has found over and over that dollar figures ending in seven have the biggest draw. Hence, the $4.77.

Why do I need to sell them something that is free? Because, getting a person to pay $4.77 for shipping a free CD qualifies your leads. These people are going to be a lot better prospects than the people who get on your list directly from a squeeze page They want your product! The better quality people are going to come from this free CD.

I know this because I've tested it...and tested it. And what I've found is really interesting: If we take a person's contact information from just the squeeze page and we contact them in any way, say to invite them to a free tele-seminar, I have found that only about 1 – 5 percent of these people are present at the teleseminar. However, when I send e-mails for that same free telesem-inar to the CD buyers, I have seen up to 80 percent of the people that bought a CD get on that tele-call. If I send out an offer to a list that I got just from a squeeze page, then I get 1 – 5 percent buying. If I send an offer to a list that I created selling a free CD, then I consistently get a 25 – 28 percent conver-sion, and I've gotten as high as 80 percent of the people I e-mailed off of my free CD list to buy a product or listen to a teleseminar.

Let's put that into real figures. From just one of my lead generating programs, I get about 1346 people a month signing up through a squeeze page to a free CD. Now if you take 25 percent of 1346, that's 336 buyers. When I take my leads straight from the Power Squeeze page, I consistently get a 1 – 5 percent conversion which results in anywhere from thirteen to sixty-seven people. That's a significant difference, and I don't know about you, but I would much rather have 336 buyers over sixty-seven any day!

Any salesperson knows that the qualified leads are the best ones, and the Free CD is the best way I know how to qualify my leads. And I have a hard and fast rule: one product, one squeeze page with its follow-up sales letter page. That's the winning combination!

Part Three: The Phone

Now this is when you as the Guerrilla Marketer really get to shine. One of our most important weapons as marketers is to develop and maintain relation-ships with our clients. A Guerrilla Marketer is also looking for cheap ways to market their products. I've combined both weapons into one, an old fash-ioned one, to be sure, but a powerful one nonetheless. Once we have a person opting into the free CD offer, we don't sit around. We jump on the phone because that's where the real money is!

Now don't get me wrong. I make money selling different products on the Internet, but, they're mostly small ticket items like the $4.77 for shipping and handling for all the free CDs I send out. You can't make a million dollars off of $4.77 sales. Well you can, but there's a much easier way....

You get on the phone because that's the best way to sell your big ticket items—your home study courses, your seminars/workshops or one-on-one coaching programs.

People are very willing to give you their credit card for the small stuff. They want to talk to a real person if they're going to give your $500 or $1,000 or even $5,000 of their money.

If you're groaning inside saying I could spend all day on the phone with these prospective leads, relax. There's two ways to sell on the phone: one-to-one and one-to-many.

One-to-one phone selling is the traditional way to sell, and some traditions are worth keeping. I use one-to-one phone selling as a way to sell my top ticket items like the $5,500 Big Boy/Big Girl boot camp that I offer. Internet marketing is great stuff, but don't think that you're getting out of any actual selling to do it. The ability to sell, and sell well, is what makes you a millionaire. And part of selling well is giving the client or customer what they need to help them better their businesses or their lives.

The one-to-many phone selling option is simply a teleseminar—a seminar on the telephone with people calling in on a conference line and then you talk to them for an hour or so. Sometimes, you can even have a question and answer session afterwards. I don't know who actually invented it; I don't think anyone does. What I do know is that it is a brilliant marketing tool that was made possible by the ability to teleconference. *All* the big Internet marketers use teleseminars to sell their products and have done so since Internet marketing was invented.

Why are they so popular? Simple. They're a great way to get a bunch of people on the phone at one time from all different parts of the country or even the world. These are all people who want to be there. How do I know this? I always have people sign up for my teleseminars on, you guessed it, a Power

Squeeze page. This is a captive audience. Now, some people charge for tele-seminars, but I either do mine for $1 or for free. They take one to two hours to do, and it's an amazing way to teach people about your product—why it benefits them, what value it has to their life, that kind of thing—so that they get hyped up to buy it.

Teleseminars are actually a central component to my business. And make no mistake; the teleseminar is one of the main reasons why my napkin sized marketing plan works well for both online and off-line businesses. And just in case you didn't get that: any business can do a teleseminar! If you're a brick and mortar, look at what kind of information your customers need and want, put together a seminar that delivers that information, invite everyone on your list to come, and watch what happens.

*****

So there you have it, the essence of my napkin sized business plan. It is simple so it keeps me focused; it prompts me to action because I know that I will have qualified leads that are willing to buy my products, both Guerrilla essentials. With my plan, I build strong relationships with my clients so they buy from me again and again, and above all, I know that with this plan, I can win. I hope that you can win with it to!

About Matt Bacak

Matt Bacak, The Powerful Promoter and Entrepreneur Magazine eBiz radio show host, became a number one best-selling author with his first book The Ultimate Lead Generation Plan *in just a few short hours using the secret power of leads and big lists. He has helped thousands of people learn to harness the power of the Internet and is not only a sought-after Internet marketer, he has coached some of the top Internet marketers on the planet with his system. Please visit* **www.PromotingTips.com** *to learn more about Matt.*

EPILOGUE

Now that thirty-five world-class Guerrilla Marketing Coaches have shared their strategies with you, it's time for you to act! As you know by now, the hallmark of Guerrilla Marketing is using your time, energy, imagination, and knowledge instead of your marketing dollars. You've been presented with the best-of-the-best ways to launch your Guerrilla attack. In true Guerrilla form, you now need to choose the weapons and tactics that best suit your strengths and most actively engages your marketplace.

Guerrillas know that marketing is not an event but a process. A successful Guerrilla Marketer also knows that they need a commitment to action over time and accountability to their plan—the hallmark of Guerrilla Marketing Coaching—to get the job done. For any Guerrilla Marketer, the true test is "not can I launch an attack," but "can I sustain one?" and that requires, focus, persistence, and consistency. In Guerrilla Marketing on the Front Lines, we've given you the tools. It's now up to you to take what you've learned in this book and apply it to your own business.

To your profits! Jay Levinson and Mitch Meyerson

For more information on Guerrilla Marketing Coaching, visit www.GMarketingCoach.com

For more information on Guerrilla Marketing, visit www.GMarketing.com

RESOURCES AND CONTINUING ONLINE TRAINING

Become or Find a Certified Guerrilla Marketing Coach

www.GMarketingCoach.com

*   *   *

More Resources in Guerrilla Marketing

www.Gmarketing.com

*   *   *

Online Marketing Training and Resources

www.MasteringOnlineMarketing.com

JOIN THE GUERRILLA MARKETING ASSOCIATION

A Unique Interactive Small Business Marketing Support System to Help You Succeed

If you are not already a member of our association, you're missing out on a treasury of Guerrilla Marketing action steps to grow your profits. Check it out below.

Let hundreds of experts grow your business for free! GMA members gain instant access to:

- Weekly teleclasses with the world's leading business experts

- Monthly live calls with Jay Conrad Levinson, the Father of Guerrilla Marketing

- Video Interviews with marketing gurus who reveal secrets of growing your profits

- A Coaching Forum Board where you can ask and get all of your tough business questions answered

- Hundreds of reports that teach you how to leave your competitors in the dust

- Vast library of tele-conferences with over 200 famous authors and speakers, available 24 hours per day at the click of a mouse

- Discounts on many Guerrilla Marketing Products

- Reduced tuition on Guerrilla Marketing Business University Courses

- Invitation to attend the Annual Guerrilla Marketing Conferences

Let our Association help your business grow and prosper.

To join and sample one month as our Guest, go to: www.GuerrillaMarketingAssociation.com

GET YOUR FREE GIFT!

As Promised On The Front Cover...

Get Your **FREE Guerrilla Marketing Jumpstart Kit** Today
containing loads of resources to build your business
even if you are on shoestring budget!

Download Your Guerrilla Business Building Manual right now at:

www.GMarketingFrontLines.com

*   *   *

Automate Your Online Business Today

- ■ Take Money Online 24/7

- ■ Build Your Mailing List

- ■ Put Your Business On Autopilot

Get 30 Days Free Right Now:
www.EasyWebAutomation.com

ABOUT THE AUTHORS

About Jay Conrad Levinson

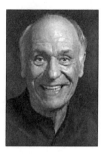

Jay Conrad Levinson is the author of the best-selling marketing series in history, "Guerrilla Marketing," plus 57 other business books. His books have sold 20 million copies worldwide. And his guerrilla concepts have influenced marketing so much that his books appear in 52 languages and are required reading in MBA programs worldwide.

Jay taught guerrilla marketing for 10 years at the extension division of the University of California in Berkeley. He was a practitioner of it in the United States—as Senior VP at J. Walter Thompson, and in Europe, as Creative Director of Leo Burnett Advertising.

A winner of first prizes in all the media, he has been part of the creative teams that made household names of many of the most famous brands in history: The Marlboro Man, The Pillsbury Doughboy, Charlie the Tuna, Morris the Cat, Allstate's Good Hands, United's Friendly Skies, and the Sears Diehard Battery.

Jay is the Chairman of Guerrilla Marketing International. His Guerrilla Marketing is series of books, workshops, CDs, videos, a CD-ROM, a radio show, a University, a series of podcasts, an Internet landmark, and The Guerrilla Marketing Association—a support system for small business.

Guerrilla Marketing has revolutionized marketing because it is a way for business owners to spend less, get more, and achieve substantial profits. To transform you into a marketing guerrilla, there is no better person than The Father of Guerrilla Marketing—Jay Conrad Levinson.

JayView@aol.com ■ 415-453-2162 ■ www.GMarketing.com

About Mitch Meyerson

Mitch Meyerson is a visionary, speaker, consultant and author of eight books in 24 languages. Over the last 25 years, he has coached and trained students worldwide to break through barriers and create the personal and professional lives they desire.

His books include: *Success Secrets of The Online Marketing Superstars, Mastering Online Marketing, Guerrilla Marketing On The Front Lines, Guerrilla Marketing On The Internet, World Class Speaking, Six Keys To Creating The Life You Desire, When Is Enough Enough?* and *When Parents Love Too Much.* He has been the featured expert on the Oprah Winfrey show.

Since 1999, Mitch founded four groundbreaking Internet-based programs: "The Guerrilla Marketing Coach Certification Program," which has certified over 280 Guerrilla Marketing Coaches worldwide, "The 90 Day Product Factory," "The Online Traffic School" and the "Master Business Building Club," a state of the art web 2.0 community. In these leading-edge online environments, he trains business owners worldwide in his online innovative marketing strategies.

Mitch is also a dynamic speaker and an accomplished jazz guitarist and composer who delivers content rich presentations punctuated with live music. He can be reached at:

www.MitchMeyerson.com